LEGISLATIVE POLITICS U.S.A.

INTRODUCTORY READERS IN AMERICAN POLITICS

LEGISLATIVE POLITICS U.S.A.

Readings Selected and Edited

by THEODORE J. LOWI *The University of Chicago*

Second Edition

LITTLE, BROWN AND COMPANY
Boston • *Toronto*

Contents

v

IV. EXECUTIVE AND CONGRESS

V. CONGRESS AS AN INSTRUMENT OF GOVERNMENT

A. THE FORMULATION OF POLICY

B. INQUIRY AS AN INSTRUMENT OF GOVERNMENT

VI. THE MEANING OF THE MODERN ASSEMBLY

EDITOR'S INTRODUCTION

Representation and Decision

In all forms of collective life there is at least one simple division of labor—leaders and followers. Most people accept the fact until it is called to their attention.

The first problem of popular government is to recognize the inevitability of leadership and power, not to deny it: to establish some fair and regular pattern for the selection of leaders and, further, to secure a minimum of control over leaders once they are granted a position of authority over others. "Representation" is such an attempt. Theories of representation are made for the purpose of *legitimizing* leadership. Obeisance to the proper rituals converts "leaders" into "representatives"; popular election converts "power" into "authority." Where doctrines of representation are accepted, there is a much higher probability that followers will do the bidding of representatives than that of leaders.

Constitutionally, the representation formula works a limitation on governmental power, along with other constitutional formulas such as Separation of Powers and Federalism. Our form of representation requires not only the periodic election of office-holders; it also requires that the law-making body be drawn from every geographical area of the country.[1] Thus we attempt to limit our legislators by making them electorally dependent *and* by placing in the assembly a very heterogeneous collection of leaders, giving our system several hundred "checks and balances."

[1] The "geographical constituency" is not the only method of representation, and it is not universally accepted as the best. Professor Friedrich discusses alternatives and their consequences in his essay.

There is also an ideological dimension to the concept, which is not always sufficiently appreciated. Acceptance of the doctrine of representative government directs the representative to act "in a representative way." His role requires that he seek the perceived and even the unperceived needs of his constituency. Since the Supreme Court handed down *Baker v. Carr* much has been made of the problem of apportionment, for *Baker v. Carr* and succeeding decisions require much greater effort to achieve a closer approximation of equality in the numbers of people each legislator represents. But even under conditions of near perfection in the mechanics of representation a truly representative government could still be unattainable. Mechanical accountability to an electorate is a necessary but, in itself, insufficient condition for representative government. Without a widely shared acceptance of representation as a "good thing" regardless of the price, the whole structure becomes a sham.

A successful system of representation, therefore, requires a special kind of leader. This man is generally outgoing and casual in personality, good in small gatherings but generally poor and bumbling in large ones.[2] Besides his belief in the goodness of the role of representative, his ideology tends to be vague and basically methodological. He is a man of many interests but rarely does he seriously rationalize those interests in terms of grandiose concepts. If he does, he is never quite too serious to refuse to submit interests or grandiose concepts to mediation. To him any interest can win or lose so long as existing institutions and ways of doing things are preserved. In the United States this type of leader is the creature of the process of nomination and election that has developed around him over two centuries. Leadership selection in the United States is more open, uncontrolled, and unpredictable than anywhere else in the world. There are many problems with such a system, the most important being that national party responsibility is next to impossible to achieve. But it does insure the selection of the type required by our mixed and decentralized legislatures. No matter what formal basis of representation is used, and no matter how consistently the criteria of unit size are enforced, the resulting units of representation will always be composed of too many diverse elements to allow for clean

---

[2] Former Speaker Joseph Martin, whose public image was one of colossal clumsiness, is more typical of the true representative than was his Massachusetts colleague, John F. Kennedy.

lines of authority and accountability. Uncertainty as to the size of his own local following and the amount of support for those who would unseat him renders the representative vulnerable to a far wider range of interests than those he himself might choose if he were totally a free agent. Uncertainty in the chamber itself as to where the opposition to his interests might come from simply reinforces his sense of the essential ambiguity of political life. As he and others like him begin to believe in this system and the amoral manner in which it deals with interests, then they begin to make the system work. Whatever the Supreme Court says after *Baker v. Carr*, their original position on apportionment, which was reversed by *Baker v. Carr*, will always be the inescapable truth: that representative government is *a political question*.[3] Many districts are going to change as a result of the reapportionment cases, but the essential problem of Congress and of representative government will remain.

That problem is the inconsistency between *representation* and *government* or, synonymously, participation and decision. The inconsistency of the two basic norms is the determining characteristic of the institution. The interplay between the two types of forces, of representation *versus* decision, is the integrating theme of this volume. Achieving a balance between these two forces is the basic problem of all authoritative institutions—American and non-American, democratic and non-democratic—for even an autocrat cannot depart too far or too long from the prevailing values of his subjects. The autocrat, feeling the pressures for representation, typically creates the myth of *virtual* representation—that he *is* the people or the vanguard of the people. But of course the significance lies in where the balance is struck. With the autocrat the reality is the overwhelming stress put on efficiency and decision. The problem of successful limited government is to balance the two forces without getting a maximum of either.

A healthy fear and hatred of autocracy and irresponsibility in the United States, as well as all Western democracies, led to a strong preference for government by representation, government that would

[3] *Colegrove v. Green*, 328 U.S. 549 (1946). Professor of Political Science Colegrove sought to prevent the conducting of the 1946 Illinois election until the state obeyed the laws of Illinois and the requirements of the Constitution and eliminated the inequities among congressional districts. The Supreme Court simply refused to review on grounds that it lacked jurisdiction over "political questions." All *Baker v. Carr* did was to reverse Colegrove and to redefine apportionment as within judicial scope.

be both limited and popularly based. But government can all too easily be made *too* representative; we can react too strongly to fear of irresponsible, unlimited government. In the immortal words of James Thurber, "You might just as well fall flat on your face as lean over too far backwards." A *perfectly representative* government would be virtually incapable of making a decision! The reformer's schemes of proportional or occupational representation, recall, or referendum are schemes that could, if employed meticulously, make the legislature an almost perfect replica of the society; but how would the members of such a legislature face the problem of agreement? If a majority vote is required, and a *two-thirds* majority must be ready for many controversial matters (in order to close debate and bring the question to a vote, as in our Senate), we can easily see that perfect representation would result in complete stalemate. It cannot be emphasized too strongly or too often that you can surround government with innumerable restraints, but not to the extent of taking away its capacity to act. The answer to autocracy is not a completely popular government. Every degree of representativeness is likely to be paid for in inefficiency.

The problem of achieving a proper balance between these two forces is best seen in Congress; thus Congress becomes our focal point for studying the process of representative government. Beyond its intrinsic importance for study as an instrument of government, Congress serves as an excellent laboratory for the study of politics and the political process. The political process begins when many people perceive that they have some sense of distress or injustice in common. Through many successive stages of organization, which may take years, these common interests become legislative problems. Congress and legislation are, therefore, located at a very late and very mature stage of social life. However, Congress can only be understood in terms of all that went into making up its agenda and all the forces that militate for and against Congress' action on any specific item on its agenda. Factors such as the committee and subcommittee system, the opposition or minority party, most of the parliamentary rules (dull and dry in themselves but politically potent—no rule is neutral!), seniority, floor debate, interest groups and regional blocs are almost constantly working for delay, for the fullest possible deliberation of one interest or another. Against those the (usually weaker) forces of the President and his immediate following in the executive branch, the President's party in

Congress, the Speaker and other congressional officers, "gag rules" in the House, are supposedly at work molding the variety of interests into policy. (Of course, expediting decisions is not a synonym for "progress." A decision can amount to "turning the clock back.") To complicate matters further, the contribution of any one of these factors or participants to the legislative process depends upon the issue in question. For example, a committee chairman who strongly favors a piece of legislation becomes a strong force for result rather than "deliberation." The fight in January and February of 1961 to enlarge the Rules Committee was a struggle to convert that powerful committee from an instrument of delay into a lever of expedition. And the Congressman least involved in an issue usually supports its quick settlement in order to get on with business he deems most important. Thus, the process of representative government can be characterized abstractly in simple terms, but in practice it is very complex. Each factor must be assessed carefully. The intelligent, sophisticated student of Congress is one who does not take any participant at face value but tries instead to assess each participant's *functional* value within the total context of which the participant is only one small part.

The chapters in Parts II, III, and IV were chosen to guide the student in this effort. Each Chapter analyzes and assesses one or more of the most important participants, structures and procedures. The fact situations in many of these are now dated, but that hardly matters if the analyses capture timeless elements and relationships. No one, for example, has ever captured the essence of committee government better than Professor Woodrow Wilson (published in 1885). After reading Wilson, the student ought to be equipped to handle recent situations for himself. Professor Shuman's case study of the 1957 Civil Rights Act is another good example. Two civil rights Acts have been passed since then, and neither involved so elaborately the rules and strategies of the House and Senate. But Shuman's article is good not because it tells all about civil rights legislation, but because it reveals so dramatically the reality of the rules and the potency as well as the existence of the formal institution. "The First Richard Nixon" was chosen not so much because it was about a former Republican leader, but because it presents such an excellent picture of the way in which constituencies really do influence representatives—more by the choice among alternatives in the *nominating* process, a kind of "type-casting," than by any mysterious processes influence. As the saying goes, it is more often the "influence in" than the "influence on" that explains the M. C. Professor Dexter shows why interest influence tends to be diffuse. Professor Ripley captures what little there is of a party institution in Congress and how and why it works. And so on.

It is difficult to determine just where the balance between representation and government has been struck in the United States, and it must shift from one period to the next. But it is certain that Congress has always shared in the real powers of government and therefore in the responsibility for making decisions. And Congress is the sort of representative institution it is, precisely because it is a real governing body. The responsibility and need for making decisions converts an otherwise somber debating society into a *power arena.* Congressional life becomes something quite separate and distinct from, albeit influenced by, constituencies. The constant attempt to put issues on the agenda for serious consideration and to reach agreement on them requires organization, skill, and compromise. In a collective decision-making body like Congress, agreement *equals* power. Every participant in the "legislative struggle" is seeking at least enough agreement or power either to enact a law or to prevent one from being enacted. Only a body without important decisions to make can afford the highest degree of representation, and only in such a body can the members afford to be perfectly straightforward and perfectly equal. Our representative institutions can afford neither. But the consequences of this, sometimes ludicrous, more often mystifying, are all too easily denounced. A representative system not only depends upon partisanship, compromise, manipulation; it could hardly work without them. This is why it will always be true that in a real governing legislature "the socialist deputy," as the saying goes, "is more deputy than socialist." Edmund Burke in his "Speech to the Electors of Bristol" (his constituency) is not only arguing what ought to be the legislator's role, but in great part also what it almost necessarily must be. Professor Dexter later on in the volume provides reasons why the representative *can* as well as *must* behave as a legislator as well as a delegate.

The precise location of the balance between representation and government, as well as the very role of the legislative assembly in it, is further complicated by modern problems and new requirements. The twentieth century is an "executive-centered" era. We achieve productivity and abundance through specialization, but specialization leads to *interdependence*. Few men are now autonomous; all the rest are part of a very common destiny because each depends on others as well as himself for sustenance. The farmer lives by market patterns set by anonymous others. Laborer and manager alike have become part of a product over which they have no personal control, to which they contribute in only a minuscule way, in which they can take only the remotest pride. Informal ties such as family, community, and traditional values are weakening. An increasing number of class and intergroup relations must therefore be regularized by deliberate and formal procedures—*administered* social relations. Not all of these administered relationships are governmental—for example, trade associations and other interest groups, labor unions, civic groups, and "red feather" ("family service" and the like) agencies—but an increasing number *are* governmental.

And this means that legislators have less and less time and less and less "slack" in the system within which to play at their deadly serious game of bargaining with unpredictable compromise as the result. With government's more frequent direct involvement in crises, representation can lead to stalemate only at the risk of becoming illegitimate. Twentieth-century America is not a happy time or place for government by representative assembly. The technical complexities of modern life that require "administered" social relations also require expert administration and continuity in administration. Statutes become less and less self-executing. The legislature must delegate to the administrative agency a larger and larger role in legislation, which is done by leaving the administrator an increasingly large scope for making his own decisions and writing his own rules for the conduct of citizens. In delegating discretion, Congress is also delegating conflict, and the management and settlement of conflict comprise the essence of Congress.

The growing burden of public management coupled with America's sudden exposure to the uncontrollable outside world have made us an executive-centered government. Congress' response to this undeniable fact comprises the real history of representative government in America in the twentieth century.

Out of all this, the President has emerged as the most important legislator, the most important force for decision in our scheme of representative government. In the past, only "strong" Presidents have taken the initiative and set the agenda of Congress (in a "program"). Nowadays, this initiative is the norm; it is virtually thrust upon every President. (See Professor Neustadt's observations in "Planning the President's Program.") So often is this the case that the relations between the two branches have in large part been *reversed*, with the President proposing (in budget, State of the Union, and special messages) draft legislation and the like, and Congress exercising the powers of amendment and veto.

But the President, with his advantageous position and vast resources, does not *legislate*. His powers, like congressional statutes, are not self-executing. The President has become the most important but not the only participant in the legislative process. Modern problems may have shifted the centers of power, but laws must still be made in Congress. Thus the struggle is not materially different from the struggle of earlier days. In the age-old way, *a majority must be created for every issue*, and every participant plays some role in the creation or the obstruction of that majority. The difference from earlier times lies in the need to bring each struggle sooner to a close. We may, then, be witnessing a decline of representation without a decline in representative government.

Thus, there is no longer any controversy over the fact that relations between President and Congress have been profoundly altered in the past generation or two. But this is not to say that the power of Congress has declined. As an instrument of national government Congress is more powerful than ever. Congress' power over domestic economic affairs was set anew in 1937 with a single Supreme Court decision (*NLRB v. Jones and Laughlin Steel Corporation*) that has needed little enhancement since that time. By 1964 interstate commerce powers were found adequate for getting at local discriminatory practices that had heretofore existed behind a wall of protective Federalism.

In the field of foreign affairs, always considered executive business *par excellence*, congressional power has also vastly increased. The charge that the executive has 'usurped" the power of Congress by use of executive agreements rather than treaties[4] has been much too strongly emphasized. Because we are a world leader, most of our international affairs involve money, or troops which involve

---

[4] Executive agreements have all the force and effect of treaties but do not require approval by two-thirds vote of the Senate.

money. And money involves Congress—not only the Senate but now the House of Representatives—in foreign policy as never before. The degree of congressional participation in foreign policy decisions depends, of course, on the nature of the decision. A quickly developing crisis might require an executive action with congressional approval only after the fact. But more often than not, some congressional leaders become involved in even the most urgent cases, as shown in "The Day We Didn't Go to War." On the longer range, more elaborately considered policies, Congress is intimately involved. Marshall Plan, NATO, and the other bulwarks of our international involvements were as much congressional as executive. The problem of enactment is about the same here as in the domestic field; presidential initiative is simply more frequent and presidential power is more telling. However, when a sufficient number of congressional leaders feel strongly enough on an issue, Congress can grab the initiative. Our Spanish policies, for instance, were shaped almost entirely by congressional influence.[5]

Thus, it is not toward decline of the governing power of Congress that we must look for the meaning of the influence of twentieth-century developments on the assembly. Rather, as the relation of Congress to the executive suggests, it is the very nature of the problem itself that has changed: The power of Congress, still immense, manifests itself in new ways. Legislation remains the most important power of Congress, and without it Congress would

[5] Between 1946 and 1950, the Administration was adamantly against close relations with Spain, particularly opposed to economic aid and military alliance. Due to the efforts of leaders such as Senators McCarran, McKellar, Taft, and Brewster and Congressmen O'Konski, Multer, and Richards, our position shifted in 1951, and by 1953 we had a treaty with Spain which included millions in economic aid and several air bases. The following is an example of the congressional technique:

Senator McCarran (in Hearings before the Subcommittee of the Senate Appropriations Committee for State Department Appropriations, 1949): Mr. Secretary (Dean Acheson), during the course of these hearings there will come up in this bill the matter of diplomatic items. I should like to ask you why it is that this country refuses to recognize Spain. . . . Let me say to you, Mr. Secretary, that so far as I am personally concerned as chairman of this subcommittee, I am not in favor of your policy with reference to Spain and until that policy is changed I am going to examine your appropriations with a fine-tooth comb.

(For the full story see Theodore J. Lowi, "Bases in Spain," in Harold Stein, editor, *American Civil Military Decisions,* Twentieth Century Fund, University of Alabama Press, 1963.)

possess no power at all. But even the problem of legislation has changed as part of the new forms of congressional power. In brief, the major problem and major focus of Congress is no longer simply that of prescribing the behavior of citizens but more often that of *affecting the behavior of administrators*. This is the constitutional implication of "executive-centered" government.

This aspect of the problem facing Congress is often dignified in the political rhetoric as the achievement of a "responsible bureaucracy," and indeed this would be the ideal outcome. But the workaday problem is one of power, electoral power versus the power of organ· ization and specialization. Until the twentieth century there was no power in the West (where violence was not involved) to match electoral power. Wealth, status, monarchy fell before it. Now, however, it faces a sturdier foe in the esoteric authority of *expertise*. Almost every statute passes through the hands and the discretion of the full-time, expert administrator. As never before Congress faces the truth—that its laws are not self-executing. With the President, although too often at cross purposes with the President, Congress is concerned with the job of *reducing the discretion of the administrator*, if it is to enjoy its status as creator of law and not merely the enunciator of a pious, platitudinous public will.

The process of influencing administrative behavior begins with the statute, substantive, and appropriations enactments; nothing, including presidential orders, influences administrative decision like a statute, *if said statute is a clear expression*. But that is only a beginning even when the statute is unambiguous, which is almost never. In an executive-centered world it is not only the administrator but also Congress whose job is continuous. Thus more than ever before congressional government is government by committee and subcommittee. Most of the important legislative decisions are still made in committees as in the days of Woodrow Wilson's "Imperious Authority of the Standing Committees." Now these committees are almost exclusive agents of continuing congressional supervision ("oversight") and clarification of law. Hence, the new forms of congressional power.

In Section V, there are two groups of readings, "The Formulation of Policy" and "Inquiry as an Instrument of Government." This way there is some insurance that the student will learn to appreciate the new forms as basic to the system. As already stressed, the latter would not exist without the former, but to say that the one is more fundamental than the other is the same as asserting man's importance over woman because of the nature of Eve's birth. Inquiry includes hearings and investigations; the peculiarly bland term "legislative oversight" is current usage for these procedures. If I dwell on inquiry at some length in the remaining paragraphs of the introduction, it is because its importance is most likely among all subjects to be over-looked. Inquiry is not a new device. It is as old as Congress itself, having developed along with the committee system. The growing importance of hearings and investigations stems from the increasing need of Congress to grant discretion, therefore to delegate its in-trinsic powers of legislation. What Congress gives away in chunks it tries to take back in bits.

Hearings are used for a variety of purposes. The manifest purpose in all cases is that of collecting information from administrators, non-governmental experts, and interest-group leaders for the draft-ing and revision of proposed legislation. As such, hearings are intimately connected with the process of representation, a crudely systematic means of taking the largest possible number of views into account. But hearings are also used effectively as a strategy for building support or opposition in the legislative struggle. The chair-man of a committee or subcommittee has the power to pick his witnesses, the order of their appearance, the amount of time to be devoted to the issue and most of the key questions. This includes the power to avoid witnesses if publicity is expected to bring adverse reactions (note Representative May's strategy in "A Law Is Passed—The Atomic Energy Act of 1946").

Most significantly, hearings are a lever for influencing the adminis-trator. The Standing Committees are organized along departmental lines (e.g., Committee on Foreign Relations, Committee on Agri-culture, Labor and Education), and the vital subcommittees of the House and Senate Appropriations Committees are organized in the same manner.[6] The occasion of a hearing can be a time of trepidation for the bureaucrats; no hearings are taken lightly. Many of these committee chairmen are old-timers who consider the bureaucrats either birds of passage (which is *true* of the top political appointees!) or their own servants. These old men get to know departmental

[6] Appropriations Subcommittee hearings are singled out for special treatment in Macmahon's "Congressional Oversight of Administration: The Power of the Purse." Although this essay is almost twenty years old, it still stands as the best on the subject.

business as well as any bureaucrat, and when one of them threatens to examine appropriations "with a fine-tooth comb" you can be sure that it is not an idle promise. These hearings can be effective even if no new laws are passed, and often it is understood that no important new legislation is even contemplated. Every administrator called as a witness can expect to defend last year's activities and to receive some instructions on expected practice for next year.[7] The hearings in general build up a record of "legislative intent," before *and* after the fact, that has great bearing on administrative conduct even if it does not, as is often hoped, influence the judiciary very much when their turn comes to interpret a statute.

The second tool of "oversight" is the investigation. Roughly the same as the hearings in outward appearance, the investigation covers a problem area (which can be co-extensive with one department or can include more or less than a department) rather than a specific piece of proposed legislation. For this reason, the investigation can be a more potent device, but it is also more slipshod in that it usually covers so much territory. Investigation has become a discredited technique in the estimation of many because of abuses of witnesses. But there is an important distinction to be made between investigation of the executive branch and investigation (*à la* grand jury) of the past and present conduct of private citizens. It is only in the latter case that constitutional problems of procedural due process arise. (See Professor Hacker's *Dialogue*.)

Through hearings and investigations Congress carries the process of representation over into the bureaucracy. And it may well be that

[7] Of course, the administrators have their means of reprisal. Senator McCarran (Dem., Nevada) did not always get his way: In 1948, Congress—in effect, McCarran's Subcommittee on State, Commerce, and Judiciary Appropriations—reduced Commerce's appropriations for field offices in a fierce effort to effect budget reductions. In the 1949 hearings, here was the result:

> *Senator McCarran:* I notice the [Commerce] Secretary's statement this morning makes reference to the elimination of four field offices. That arrests my attention because he makes mention of the elimination of those four field offices in the West. Would you kindly tell me, if you know, what offices are to be eliminated?
> *Secretary Sawyer:* The basis of elimination is the volume of business done, and the ones indicated . . . are Reno, Cheyenne, Albuquerque and Phoenix. . . .
> *Senator McCarran:* You cannot do that to Reno, Mr. Secretary.
> *Secretary Sawyer:* After all, you are the doctor . . .
> *Mr. Gladieux* (Sawyer's Executive Assistant):
> . . . But under the House reductions this is the only alternative we have, to eliminate those particular offices. (From Hearings before the Subcommittee of the Committee on Appropriations, U.S. Senate, on H.R. 4016, 1949, p. 7.)

the most abiding role of Congress in the years to come will be its *service as a place where the needs of the bureaucracy are continually being balanced against the prevailing special interests in the community.* We call this our insurance against an irresponsible administrative government, but it is not quite so simple. We pay the price in decentralized and inefficient administration. Congress reaches down into the departments creating split loyalties between the President and the Committees. Thus Congress builds into the executive its own problem of representation versus decision, creating many barriers to effective Presidential co-ordination. The continuing relations between Congress and the executive tend to create a kind of triangular trading pattern involving a Standing Committee or Appropriations Subcommittee (or both), an executive agency, and one or more agency clientele groups. The situation in my "How the Farmers Get What They Want" is suggestive of possible consequences. In many of the agriculture agencies it is very difficult to find just where "public" ends and "private" begins. It is representation carried to its outer limits in a pattern not unlike European corporatism. Here is a problem of balance that must be solved in every generation and for every area of policy. Continuous congressional committee participation short-circuits Presidential responsibility and can lead to a fascistic pattern of economic privilege. But, on the other hand, how centralized and independent and efficient a bureaucracy can we afford?[8]

These problems can only be raised; they cannot be solved. Every area of governmental activity challenges Congress in its own peculiar way. The balance between administrative autonomy and political control must be adjusted accordingly. In older, well-established activities Congress might, for instance, slacken its reins. In new and unplotted areas, where every administrative decision may be a "hard case," a precedent, closer congressional-administrative relations might follow.

In sum, the representative assembly performs a number of functions vital to the democratic political order. The making of laws is its manifest or constitutional function and is the most important if only because without it no other functions would follow. But legislation is not the only function of the assembly; if legislation *were* the

---

[8] Ironically, the sins associated with "bureaucracy" in its pejorative sense, such as inefficiency, waste, overlapping, duplication, etc., result from not enough bureaucratization! The perfect bureaucracy would have none of these.

only function, the assembly could hardly justify its existence. A totally bureaucratic organization, for instance, would be a much more efficient instrument and would probably be more rational and fair, however these ambiguous terms might be defined. It is the subsidiary, extraconstitutional or "latent" functions of the assembly that make it an indispensable feature of government.

The most important subsidiary or "latent" function of the representative assembly is—through its powers of policy, appropriation, inquiry, and supervision—that of balancing adminstrative needs against organized community desires. This extension of the representative principle into the bureaucracy may, so I have argued, prove to be its most abiding function as its legislative power atrophies into general, even if significant, policy expressions.

Finally, there are several equally significant functions that are not so directly involved in statutes or administrative control as such but are part of the legislative struggle itself. Exact assessment of these functions is impossible but their importance cannot be doubted. These will be briefly summarized:[9]

(1) *Communications.* The exposed deliberations of the assembly enlarge the area of conflict and widen public awareness of problems and proposed solutions. Woodrow Wilson offers suggestions for improving this function.

(2) *Legitimacy.* The ritual of formulating public policy among 535 participants and hundreds of influential outsiders tends to reaffirm faith in democratic procedures. Modern civilizations never entirely eliminate the more primitive instincts, including the need for ritual. By acting out the social struggle before the world, Congress is the grandest of all stages for the political passion play. Furthermore, to commit the powerful to this *method* of settling conflicts tends also to commit them to the *outcomes,* even in adversity.[10] And, to be Machiavellian, with so many participants it is possible for dissatisfied groups to blame individual members *without losing faith in the institution itself.* Majority rule, said Toqueville, "made obedience very easy; it enabled the subject to complain of the law without ceasing to love and honor the lawgiver."

(3) *Power.* "Representation stabilizes the power structure by providing a mean between the extremes of concentration and dispersion

---

[9] I have relied heavily upon Harold Lasswell and Abraham Kaplan, *Power and Society.* (Yale University Press, New Haven, 1950, pp. 161-169.)

[10] See Professor Friedrich's interesting notion of "recurrent integration."

of power."[11] The one is intolerable, the other is impractical. There may be more powerful men in the country than ordinary Congressmen, but they must eventually go to Congress to build greater support if their demands are to be made legitimate claims. Again to be Machiavellian, the size of the assembly makes it easier for the individual Congressman to hide his pursuit of the public interest when such pursuit conflicts with constituency interests.

Here then are some fragments and intimations of the total context of representative government. It is the responsible citizen's task to study and evaluate the inner workings of the system for himself. I have, in Section VI, offered two somber but reflective interpretations of representative government today. I have deliberately juxtaposed differing views in hopes that the student might become crosspressured sufficiently to undertake his own inquiry.

The materials in this anthology offer, I feel, an excellent basis for such an undertaking. They have been arranged in an order consistent with the theme set out above, that of representation *versus* government, and it was my aim in this introduction to give continuity and inter-relation to the essays.

A good story can, of course, be the source of several morals. Many of the articles included here can, therefore, be used for purposes other than those for which they have been categorized. Perhaps it would be useful to offer a few suggestions for alternative uses. With each section is listed the various readings from other sections appropriate to the subject:

Section	Related Chapters
I.	Chapters 7, 8, 12, 18, and 19 all get into the problems and/or consequences of representation.
II.	Chapters 6, 9, 13, 14, 15, and 16 provide some aspects of structure and procedure neglected in Chapters 3-6 as well as providing a variety of stage settings for the many factors Chapters 3-6 do identify.
III.	Chapters 5, 6, 11, and 13 all add significantly to the party dimension. Chapter 5 contains one of the best uses of "roll call analysis" to be found anywhere.
IV.	Chapters 9, 13, 14, 15, 16, 17, 18, and 19 can hardly be

[11] Lasswell and Kaplan, *op. cit.,* p. 166.

approached without a rich appreciation of executive roles in legislation.

V.   Chapters 4, 10, and 12 are good here because each is a policy-making case or has a policy-making focus.

VI.   All of the previous Chapters should be used in evidence and evulation.

Every reader and every teacher will discover gaps and weaknesses in subject-matter coverage. This is inevitable and unavoidable in anthologies and is likely to be especially evident here. This is the price I was willing to pay for a short and inexpensive volume with substantial pieces rather than fragments. For many purposes, including armchair study and introductory American Government courses, this anthology ought to be more than sufficient. For further work in the field, particularly for use in advanced courses in the legislative process, this volume is best used as supplementary reading—as a filler source—in conjunction with the *Congressional Quarterly* and any basic textbook on Congress.

I am grateful to the authors and publishers of the works included herein for granting their permissions. The words and ideas from here to the end remain those of the original authors, although I am alone responsible for all harm done in editing and in the creation of their setting.

ACKNOWLEDGEMENTS

The editor, like the author, always carries to press a considerable burden of indebtedness to others. While my greatest debt is to the original authors and their publishers, there are others who have an important share in this volume. The hardy professionals on the staff of Little, Brown head the list, particularly Donald R. Hammonds whose advice was invaluable and whose carrot-and-stick strategies were brilliant. I would also like to thank Professors Murray Levin, Donald Matthews, Richard Fenno, Fred Greenstein, Raymond E. Wolfinger, James David Barber, Nelson W. Polsby, Robert L. Peabody, and John Schaar for their many helpful criticisms and suggestions at various stages of preparation. Miss Anna Lane of the Cornell School of Industrial and Labor Relations is deserving of special mention not only because of her extraordinary stenographic talents but also because of her uncommon patience with my crude editorial markings. I am also deeply obliged to my sister Bettie for the sacrifice of many holiday hours. Finally, there were my students in Government 318 at Cornell, to whom I gratefully dedicate this little volume.

T. J. L.

REPRESENTATIVE GOVERNMENT: THE NATURE AND SCOPE OF LEGISLATIVE POWER

1   *The Dual Nature of Representation*
CARL FRIEDRICH

Historically speaking, representative assemblies developed in most European countries in the course of the later Middle Ages as an important part of the medieval constitutional order. Very often the three "estates" were composed of nobility, clergy, and the merchants of the cities (the burgesses.) But the greatest variations existed in this respect. The most important of these assemblies is undoubtedly the English Parliament, where the higher nobility were joined with the higher clergy in the "Lords Spiritual and Temporal," while the knights together with the burgesses constituted the Commons. Thus the more important groups in the community—nowadays often referred to as "classes"—were represented and called together by the king through his "minister" for the purpose of securing their consent to extraordinary taxes or levies. This was necessary because the undeveloped state of central administrative systems and the absence of effective means of coercion . . . rendered the collection of such levies impossible without local co-operation. Quite naturally, these representatives when gathered together undertook to bargain for their consent to such grants of money; they presented complaints and petitions, which the crown had to heed in order to secure what it wanted. These, then, were not national representatives but agents of local powers acting under special instructions or mandates. This was true, however, only as long as they acted separately. When the king and the two houses of Parliament acted together, after having

From Carl J. Friedrich, *Constitutional Government and Democracy,* revised edition, (excerpts from Chapters XIV-XVI), Ginn and Company, Boston, 1950.

settled their differences and reached a compromise, they were taken to *represent* the whole body politic. More particularly, they were supposed to represent the entire body politic of the realm of England when acting as a high court, which was taken to be their most solemn function down to the seventeenth century. Historically, then, one cannot draw a hard and fast line between agents with definite instructions or mandates and representatives empowered to attend to a general task. An elected body may and usually will be both a set of agents from different interests, and a representative group determining the common interest. Therefore, . . . [with] Burke, a parliament is both: a deliberative assembly from *one* nation, with *one* interest, that of the whole, and a congress of ambassadors from different and hostile interests. . . .

How can we explain the fact that legislation came to be considered the peculiar province of representative, popularly elected bodies, when in fact medieval representatives had little or no concern with legislation? Because ever since the sixteenth century, legislation was believed to be the most striking manifestation of political and governmental power. Legislation entailed the making of rules binding upon the whole community. Bodin maintained that this power was the peculiar characteristic of a state. As we have seen before, the medieval notion of law as eternal custom, as something already there and merely to be discovered by learned men, was giving way to a realization that laws are man-made, that they are essentially decisions as to what ought to be rather than as to what is. The shift, of course, was merely one in view and emphasis. The High Court of Parliament had changed the law in the process of finding it, and so had the other courts of the realm. But the great Coke, before his identification with Parliament, insisted at times upon the "higher law" as a standard and criterion by which to evaluate parliamentary enactments. . . . He saw it as fixed and immutable, the peculiar and precious heritage of every Englishman, an embodiment of the principles upon which his life was built. This relation of general rules to religious, moral, and other principles was the other pillar upon which men's preoccupation with laws and legislation as a manifestation of governmental power rested. That human beings cannot be forced in matters of principle is the underlying idea. A specific act of government may be justified in terms of a specific emergency, but no general rule ever can be so justified. This leads to the important if elementary consideration that the making of a rule presupposes that there is a series of events which have certain aspects in common. In other words, there must be a "normal" situation. This means that time is available for deliberation to determine what had best be done regarding such a situation. Representative, deliberative bodies require time, obviously, and therefore legislation seems to be peculiarly fitted for such bodies. Some writers on the Continent have thereby been led into linking parliamentary deliberation to the romantic passion for everlasting conversation, a generalization which is as glittering as it is uninformed. For parliamentary deliberation is entirely focused upon and organized with a view toward action, the enactment of a general rule. The history and practice of parliamentary procedure proves this beyond doubt. But the enactment of such a general rule requires careful co-ordination of conflicting viewpoints. Really effective compromises must be reached. Such compromises are justified, because any considerable group of people in a given community possesses the capacity effectively to resist the enforcement of certain rules which they do not, or which they cannot, approve.

To put the foregoing analysis into a very abstract formula, one might say: the community requires recurrent integration. The failure to perceive this fact underlies the totalitarian contempt for elected representatives as valuable guides in the enactment of permanent legislation. The totalitarian emphasis upon the desirability of unity in a community does not solve the problems which arise from the diversity of actual interests. They assert that only a single leader, or a small elite, can achieve effective integration. They assert that when the conflict of norms in a given community becomes insoluble, when therefore the several groups have no common ground upon which to reach an effective compromise, the arbitrary superimposition of one possible solution is the only alternative to civil war or complete dissolution. Communists and Fascists both maintain that such was the case in recent times, and they both proceeded to impose their particular norms. Once one grants their premise—and one has to when *their* factions grow to any considerable size—he cannot escape from their conclusion. But this is so not because there is a disagreement on fundamentals, for such we have had all the time. It is so because these particular groups have adopted organized violence as a method of party warfare. Constitutionalism and democracy, if they are true to themselves, will outlaw such methods of party strife as private uniforms, police, and the rest. This outlawing was done in the British *Public Order Act* of 1936 . . . and also in a number of American states. Federal legislation may be desirable. If this is done, there is no need for denying the rights of citizenship, such as our civil liberties, to people whose views are antidemocratic. The provisions exempting Germans with certain antidemocratic views from the protection of the basic human rights of the new German Basic Law . . . appear much too broad from this standpoint; "abuse" of these rights "to attack the free, democratic basic order" seems much too vague a criterion for so dangerous a limitation on rights which the first article had declared to be "inviolable and inalienable." Compromise is, therefore, essential in making general rules; through argument and discussion the area of agreement is determined in the representative legislature. . . .

The underlying idea of all the various systems [of proportional representation] is to secure a representative assembly reflecting with more or less mathematical exactness the various divisions in the electorate. Why should such divisions be reflected? They should be "represented"! The voice of minorities should be heard! Justice requires that no votes be lost. . . . A man of the eminence of John Stuart Mill extolled the virtues of the scheme in his *Considerations on Representative Government* and called it one of "the very greatest improvements yet made in the theory and practice of government." Yet proportional representation shifts the basic meaning of representation. An important part of representation . . . is to represent the citizenry as a whole, not just the divisions among them. Representation means the exercise of the people's influence through a smaller number acting in their behalf. Proportional representation, on the other hand, looks upon the divisions in the electorate as the only entities to be represented; in the last analysis it looks upon the individual as the representable element or unit. . . .

. . . [L]et us assume for a moment that representation through a person elected by the majority of your fellow townsmen is "unjust" to some minority, and that this can be remedied by giving this minority a chance of combining with others constituting a similar minority elsewhere. If there were only one such minority, it would simply mean that there would be more men in parliament to criticize than before. This would mean less action, rather than different action. If there were many such minorities, so that no group any longer had a majority, it would mean complete inaction over long periods. In either case, is it not a question of competing claims? Why should the problem of what is just to a minority be given precedence over what is just to the majority? Admittedly the majority wants action. Such action is, through Proportional Representation, or P.R., being delayed or altogether prevented. What is the justice of that? It would appear that Mill, in his concern over the minority, had neglected the majority. Problems of justice are problems of adjustment between conflicting claims. The election of representatives therefore always involves the paring down of *some* claims; justice can only be achieved if these claims are equitably adjusted. Presumably the majority's claims are weightier than those of any minority. Representation is a broad thing; representatives are elected so that many may participate indirectly in the essential tasks. The majority participates through acting, the minority through discussion and criticism. If the majority fails to be represented adequately, because its representatives are unable to act, the injustice is just as great, or greater, than if the minority fails to be represented adequately, because its representatives cannot talk as much as they would like to. It is not a question of justice, then, but of more adequate representation of minorities. This may or may not be a desirable thing. But it should be considered on its merits. . . .

Unquestionably, Bagehot put his finger upon the central objection from a governmental standpoint. . . . In terms of the accepted focal interests of political science, it is more important that a majority system of elections oblige the voter to *decide* between two or more alternatives than that the constituency be compulsory.° The need of a decision is paramount when the representative body has over and above everything else the function of constituting either the executive or the government which is to hold office as long as the representative body is willing to support it. As everyone knows, such a system of parliamentary government makes the executive dependent upon and responsible to a majority in the representative assembly. For, if the assembly becomes divided into so many factions that there cannot be found a stable majority for the executive's support, all governmental activity becomes paralyzed. It is appalling to read with care the astounding documentation which Dr. Hermens has assembled to show how in country after country precisely this paralysis crept in. Eventually the people lost hope that effective action would

---

° *I.e.*, to Bagehot, the simplifying of alternatives in the single-member geographical constituency of Britain and the United States outweighed the sacrifice of the unrepresented minorities—those who consistently voted for the losers.—Ed.

ever be produced, and "parliamentarism" became a by-word for inefficiency and inaction. England resisted the lure of proportionalism. Sticking to their traditions, most Englishmen, including the Labour party, rejected P.R., recognizing it as the most important function of the English Parliament to support the government. For a long time this function was obscured by the doctrine of a separation of powers, particularly since such a separation prevailed in the United States. Parliament was looked upon as a legislative assembly. But while the legislative function is quite important, it is not *as* important as the maintenance and functioning of the government itself. The influence of the whole electorate upon this executive management must become focalized into a few clear alternatives. For, as Lowell has so clearly shown, large numbers of people cannot decide between any but two or three very simple alternatives.

But what if the elected representatives do not have this function of constituting the executive? It is, after all, by no means a foregone conclusion that the function of the representative assembly should be a decision as to who shall govern. Not only in the United States, but in Switzerland and in prewar Germany, the main function of the representative assembly was legislation. Such legislation, particularly modern economic and social legislation, touches the everyday interests of all citizens, and the divisions of interest between them are fairly persistent. It cannot, for example, reasonably be expected that the employer and capitalist would be persuaded to hand all profits over to his workers, nor can we hope that the workers will readily yield to those who expect them to be satisfied with the joy of work, and be content with long hours at starvation wages. Legislation touching these and many similar issues between the various groups in the community must be framed as an acceptable compromise in which all relevant views are voiced with a vigor approximately comparable to their actual strength in the community. A representative assembly, then, whose primary function is the framing of such legislation, would greatly benefit from a well-thought-out system which would bring into it the various groups in the community in rough proportion at least to their strength. But there must still be an effective majority ready to support a fairly coherent policy. The difficulties in the way of achieving that purpose are great under the American presidential system even without any multiplication of parties such as proportionalism envisages and engenders.

. . . [T]he prevalent English and American opinion against proportional representation is practically sound. There are special conditions which might mitigate this conclusion. But the proportional representation enthusiasts, who would argue from the relative success of proportionalism in some small countries that we should try it in Great Britain and the United States, goes wrong. Although in the United States the constitutional order is based upon a separation-of-powers scheme, the President as chief executive must be elected by a simple plurality. While this might act as a deterrent to the development of minor parties, certain religious, class, and race cleaves might, in the course of time, emerge and plague us by their intransigeant attitude. The appeal of P.R. lies in the promise it holds out for breaking up corrupt machines. There can be no question that P.R. starts out by doing this quite effectively. But after the machine politicians have caught their breath, they are quite skillful in "taking over" proportional representation. Since proportional representation in the long run strengthens, rather than weakens party, that is, machine, control, the bosses return with another rampart added to their fortress. As Newton D. Baker put it in a communication to the *Cleveland Plain Dealer* on July 25, 1935: "We have groups of all sorts and kinds, formed around religious, racial, language, social and other contentious distinctions. Proportional representation invites these groups to seek to harden and intensify their differences by bringing them into political action where they are irrelevant, if not disturbing. A wise election system would invite them to forget these distracting prejudices." . . .

Parliaments until recently have been the institutional core of modern representative government. At present the executive, particularly when representing a majority party, is forging ahead and is tending to become the heart of representation. . . . [All] elected bodies have in common representative and deliberative functions which, though related, are quite distinct, and hence should be considered separately. The Fascist Grand Council also had representative functions; in letting itself be bellowed at by Mussolini it represented the Italian people as perfectly as the Nazi Reichstag represented the German people, but its deliberative functions were nil.

Traditionally, legislation is considered the peculiar province of representative assemblies. . . . Representative assemblies are in fact referred to as *the* legislature, although it is always at once conceded that these assemblies do not have exclusive control over legislation nor are they concerned only with legislation. Nevertheless, legislation is traditionally looked upon as their primary function. Such a view is formal rather than political. Politically speaking, the function of making laws is nowadays at least as much carried on by the central bureaucracy, which drafts all important bills in England, France, and other European countries, and to an increasing extent in the United States. The political function of representative assemblies today is not so much the initiation of legislation as the carrying on of popular education and propaganda and the integration and co-ordination of conflicting interests and viewpoints. The representative must be a master in the art of compromise. Parliaments and parliamentarians appear as integrating agencies through which the policy of the government and the claims of the various interest groups are expounded to the larger public with a view to discovering a suitable balance. There can be little doubt that this educational function is highly significant. The average citizen, that is, you and I, needs to have the pros and cons of pending proposals dramatized for him. The clash of argument in representative groups helps this greatly. The drama of the filibustering senator, though often arousing indignation, helps the citizen to appreciate the implications and significance of new legislation. The consequences of the lack of such contact between the government and the citizen are very apparent in totalitarian regimes. A great many measures of the government, which may be intrinsically necessary, meet with sullen indifference if not with hostility from the people merely because they are not understood. Occasional rhetorical outbursts on the part of a few leaders are not sufficient.

Integration is not, however, automatic but highly dependent upon the structure of thought and outlook, feeling and interest, of the electorate. Hence the pious formula that representatives are not bound by mandate, that they are subject only to their conscience and are supposed to serve the common weal, which is repeated in so many European constitutions, while significant as a norm, may lead to differentiating as well as to integrating results. As in mathematics, so in politics, differential and integral functions are interrelated. . . .

. . . [R]epresentation and responsibility are closely linked. Representatives of the people are intended to be responsible to those whom they represent; in turn such responsible conduct enhances the representative quality. In fact, it is not too much to say that systems of representation developed out of the need of insuring constitutional responsibility. More especially elections, by permitting a recurrent review of the actions of representatives at regular intervals, are supposed to be the most rational method of establishing responsible government. This review brought about the development of parties . . . they both differentiate and integrate. While trying to integrate as many voters as possible, they succeed in integrating perhaps half of them, the other half being integrated by a competing group of leaders. Such polarization of the electorate into two focal differentiations is characteristic of the majority system of representation, while the proportional system, as we have seen, produces multiple differentiation. . . .

2   *Speech to the Electors of Bristol*
EDMUND BURKE

I am sorry I cannot conclude without saying a word on a topic touched upon by my worthy colleague. I wish that topic had been passed by at a time when I have so little leisure to discuss it. But since he has thought proper to throw it out, I owe you a clear explanation of my poor sentiments on that subject.

He tells you that 'the topic of instructions has occasioned much altercation and uneasiness in this city'; and he expresses himself (if I understand him rightly) in favour of the coercive authority of such instructions.

Certainly, Gentlemen, it ought to be the happiness and glory of a representative to live in the strictest union, the closest correspondence, and the most unreserved communication with his constituents. Their wishes ought to have great weight with him; their opinions high respect; their business unremitted attention. It is his duty to sacrifice his repose, his pleasure, his satisfactions, to theirs—and above all, ever, and in all cases, to prefer their interest to his own.

But his unbiased opinion, his mature judgment, his enlightened conscience, he ought not to sacrifice to you, to any man, or to any set

From *Selected Prose of Edmund Burke*, Sir Philip Magnus ed., pp. 39-41.

of men living. These he does not derive from your pleasure—no, nor from the law and the Constitution. They are a trust from Providence, for the abuse of which he is deeply answerable. Your representative owes you, not his industry only, but his judgment; and he betrays, instead of serving you, if he sacrifices it to your opinion.

My worthy colleague says, his will ought to be subservient to yours. If that be all, the thing is innocent. If government were a matter of will upon any side, yours, without question, ought to be superior. But government and legislation are matters of reason and judgment, and not of inclination; and what sort of reason is that in which the determination precedes the discussion, in which one set of men deliberate and another decide, and where those who form the conclusion are perhaps three hundred miles distant from those who hear the arguments?

To deliver an opinion is the right of all men; that of constituents is a weighty and respectable opinion, which a representative ought always to rejoice to consider. But *authoritative* instructions, *mandates* issued, which the member is bound blindly and implicitly to obey, to vote, and to argue for, though contrary to the clearest convictions of his judgment and conscience—these are things utterly unknown to the laws of this land, and which arise from a fundamental mistake of the whole order and tenor of our Constitution.

Parliament is not a *congress* of ambassadors from different and hostile interests, which interests each must maintain, as an agent and advocate, against other agents and advocates; Parliament is a *deliberative* assembly of *one* nation, with *one* interest—that of the whole —where not local purposes, not local prejudices, ought to guide, but the general good, resulting from the general reason of the whole. You choose a member, indeed; but when you have chosen him, he is not a member of Bristol, but he is a member of Parliament. If the local constituent should have an interest, or should form an hasty opinion evidently opposite to the real good of the rest to the community, the member for that place ought to be as far as any other from any endeavour to give it effect, I beg pardon for saying so much on this subject; I have been unwillingly drawn into it; but I shall ever use a respectable frankness of communication with you. Your faithful friend, your devoted servant, I shall be to the end of my life: a flatterer you do not wish for. On this point of instructions, however, I think it scarcely possible we ever can have any sort of difference. Perhaps I may give you too much, rather than too little trouble.

THE ORGANIZATION AND WORKINGS OF THE AMERICAN CONGRESS

3   *The Imperious Authority of the*
            Standing Committees
            WOODROW WILSON

The leaders of the House are the chairmen of the principal
Standing Committees. Indeed, to be exactly accurate, the House has
as many leaders as there are subjects of legislation; for there are as
many Standing Committees as there are leading classes of legislation,
and in the consideration of every topic of business the House is
guided by a special leader in the person of the chairman of the Standing Committee, charged with the superintendence of measures of the
particular class to which the topic belongs. It is this multiplicity of
leaders, this many-headed leadership, which makes the organization
of the House too complex to afford uninformed people and unskilled
observers any easy clue to its methods of rule. For the chairmen of
the Standing Committees do not constitute a cooperative body like a
ministry. They do not consult and concur in the adoption of homogeneous and mutually helpful measures; there is no thought of acting
in concert. Each Committee goes its own way at its own pace. It ıs
impossible to discover any unity or method in the disconnected and
therefore unsystematic, confused, and desultory action of the House,
or any common purpose in the measures which its Committees from
time to time recommend.

And it is not only to the unanalytic thought of the common observer who looks at the House from the outside that its doings seem
helter-skelter, and without comprehensible rule; it is not at once

From Woodrow Wilson, *Congressional Government* (pp. 58-81), Meridian
edition.

easy to understand them when they are scrutinized in their daily headway through open session by one who is inside the House. The newly-elected member, entering its doors for the first time, and with no more knowledge of its rules and customs than the more intelligent of his constituents possess, always experiences great difficulty in adjusting his preconceived ideas of congressional life to the strange and unlooked-for conditions by which he finds himself surrounded after he has been sworn in and has become a part of the great legislative machine. Indeed there are generally many things connected with his career in Washington to disgust and dispirit, if not to aggrieve, the new member. In the first place, his local reputation does not follow him to the federal capital. Possibly the members from his own State know him, and receive him into full fellowship; but no one else knows him, except as an adherent of this or that party, or as a newcomer from this or that State. He finds his station insignificant, and his identity indistinct. But this social humiliation which he experiences in circles in which to be a congressman does not of itself confer distinction, because it is only to be one among many, is probably not to be compared with the chagrin and disappointment which come in company with the inevitable discovery that he is equally without weight or title to consideration in the House itself. No man, when chosen to the membership of a body possessing great powers and exalted prerogatives, likes to find his activity repressed, and himself suppressed, by imperative rules and precedents which seem to have been framed for the deliberate purpose of making usefulness unattainable by individual members. Yet such the new member finds the rules and precedents of the House to be. It matters not to him, because it is not apparent on the face of things, that those rules and precedents have grown, not out of set purpose to curtail the privileges of new members as such, but out of the plain necessities of business; it remains the fact that he suffers under their curb, and it is not until "custom hath made it in him a property of easiness" that he submits to them with anything like good grace. . . .

Often the new member goes to Washington as the representative of a particular line of policy, having been elected, it may be, as an advocate of free trade, or as a champion of protection; and it is naturally his first care upon entering on his duties to seek immediate opportunity for the expression of his views and immediate means of giving them definite shape and thrusting them upon the attention of Congress. His disappointment is, therefore, very keen when he finds both opportunity and means denied him. He can introduce his bill; but that is all he can do, and he must do that at a particular time and in a particular manner. This he is likely to learn through rude experience, if he be not cautious to inquire beforehand the details of practice. He is likely to make a rash start, upon the supposition that Congress observes the ordinary rules of parliamentary practice to which he has become accustomed in the debating clubs familiar to his youth, and in the mass-meetings known to his later experience. His bill is doubtless ready for presentation early in the session, and some day, taking advantage of a pause in the proceedings, when there seems to be no business before the House, he rises to read it and move its adoption. But he finds getting the floor an arduous and precarious undertaking. There are certain to be others who want it as well as he; and his indignation is stirred by the fact that the Speaker does not so much as turn towards him, though he must have heard his call, but recognizes some one else readily and as a matter of course. If he be obstreperous and persistent in his cries of "Mr. Speaker," he may get that great functionary's attention for a moment,—only to be told, however, that he is out of order, and that his bill can be introduced at that stage only by unanimous consent: immediately there are mechanically-uttered but emphatic exclamations of objection, and he is forced to sit down confused and disgusted. He has, without knowing it, obtruded himself in the way of the "regular order of business," and been run over in consequence, without being quite clear as to how the accident occurred. . . .

. . . [I]f he supposes, as he naturally will, that after his bill has been sent up to be read by the clerk he may say a few words in its behalf, and in that belief sets out upon his long-considered remarks, he will be knocked down by the rules as surely as he was on the first occasion when he gained the floor for a brief moment. The rap of Mr. Speaker's gavel is sharp, immediate, and peremptory. He is curtly informed that no debate is in order; the bill can only be referred to the appropriate Committee.

This is, indeed, disheartening; it is his first lesson in committee government, and the master's rod smarts; but the sooner he learns the prerogatives and powers of the Standing Committees the sooner will he penetrate the mysteries of the rules and avoid the pain of further contact with their thorny side. The privileges of the Standing Committees are the beginning and the end of the rules. Both the House of Representatives and the Senate conduct their business by what may figuratively, but not inaccurately, be called an odd device of *disintegration*. The House virtually both deliberates and legislates in small sections. Time would fail it to discuss all the bills brought in, for they every session number thousands; and it is to be doubted whether, even if time allowed, the ordinary processes of debate and amendment would suffice to sift the chaff from the wheat in the bushels of bills every week piled upon the clerk's desk. Accordingly, no futile attempt is made to do anything of the kind. The work is parceled out, most of it to the forty-seven* Standing Committees which constitute the regular organization of the House, some of it to select committees appointed for special and temporary purposes. Each of the almost numberless bills that come pouring in on Mondays is "read a first and second time,"—simply perfunctorily read, that is, by its title, by the clerk, and passed by silent assent through its first formal courses, for the purpose of bringing it to the proper stage for commitment,—and referred without debate to the appropriate Standing Committee. Practically, no bill escapes commitment—save, of course, bills introduced by committees and a few which may now and then be crowded through under a suspension of the rules, granted by a two-thirds vote—though the exact disposition to be made of a bill is not always determined easily and as a matter of course. Besides the great Committee of Ways and Means and the equally great Committee on Appropriations, there are Standing Committees on Banking and Currency . . . on the Judiciary, . . . on Agriculture, . . . and on a score of other branches of legislative concern; but careful and differential as is the topical division of the subjects of legislation which is represented in the titles of these Committees, it is not always evident to which Committee each particular bill should go. Many bills affect subjects which may be regarded as lying as properly within the jurisdiction of one as of another of the Committees; for no hard and fast lines separate the various classes of business which the Committees are commissioned to take in charge. Their jurisdictions overlap at many points, and it must frequently happen that bills are ready which cover just this common ground. Over the commitment of such bills sharp and interesting skirmishes often take place. There is active competition for them, the ordinary, quiet routine of matter-of-course reference being interrupted by rival motions seeking to give very different directions to the disposition to be made of them. . . .

* At present twenty, with several additional *ad hoc* committees.—Ed.

The fate of bills committeed is generally not uncertain. As a rule, a bill committeed is a bill doomed. When it goes from the clerk's desk to a committee-room it crosses a parliamentary bridge of sighs to dim dungeons of silence whence it will never return. The means and time of its death are unknown, but its friends never see it again. Of course no Standing Committee is privileged to take upon itself the full powers of the House it represents, and formally and decisively reject a bill referred to it; its disapproval, if it disapproves, must be reported to the House in the form of a recommendation that the bill "do not pass." But it is easy, and therefore common, to let the session pass without making any report at all upon bills deemed objectionable or unimportant, and to substitute for reports upon them a few bills of the Committee's own drafting; so that thousands of bills expire with the expiration of each Congress, not having been rejected, but having been simply neglected. There was not time to report upon them.

Of course it goes without saying that the practical effect of this Committee organization of the House is to consign to each of the Standing Committees the entire direction of legislation upon those subjects which properly come to its consideration. As to those subjects it is entitled to the initiative, and all legislative action with regard to them is under its overruling guidance. It gives shape and course to the determinations of the House. In one respect, however, its initiative is limited. Even a Standing Committee cannot report a bill whose subject matter has not been referred to it by the House, "by the rules or otherwise," it cannot volunteer advice on questions upon which its advice has not been asked. But this is not a serious, not even an operative, limitation upon its functions of suggestion and leadership for it is a very simple matter to get referred to it any subject it wishes to introduce to the attention of the House. Its chairman, or one of its leading members, frames a bill covering the point upon which the Committee wishes to suggest legislations; bring it in, in his capacity as a private member, on Monday, when the call of States is made; has it referred to his Committee; and thus secures an opportunity for the making of the desired report.

It is by this imperious authority of the Standing Committees that the new member is stayed and thwarted whenever he seeks to take an active part in the business of the House. Turn which way he may, some privilege of the Committees stands in his path. The rules are so framed as to put all business under their management; and one of the discoveries which the new member is sure to make, albeit after many trying experiences and sobering adventures and as his first session draws towards its close, is, that under their sway freedom of debate finds no place of allowance, and that his long-delayed speech must remain unspoken. For even a long congressional session is too short to afford time for a full consideration of all the reports of . . . [all the] Committees, and debate upon them must be rigidly cut short, if not altogether excluded, if any considerable part of the necessary business is to be gotten through with before adjournment. There are some subjects to which the House must always give prompt attention; . . . therefore the Committee of Ways and Means and the Committee on Appropriations are clothed with extraordinary privileges; and revenue and supply bills may be reported, and will ordinarily be considered, at any time. . . . The rest must take their turns in fixed order as they are called on the by Speaker, contenting themselves with such crumbs of time as fall from the tables of the four Committees of highest prerogative. . . .

. . . The House is conscious that time presses. It knows that, hurry as it may, it will hardly get through with one eighth of the business laid out for the session, and that to pause for lengthy debate is to allow the arrears to accumulate. Besides, most of the members are individually anxious to expedite action on every pending measure, because each member of the House is a member of one or more of the Standing Committees, and is quite naturally desirous that the bills prepared by his Committees, and in which he is, of course, specially interested by reason of the particular attention which he has been compelled to give them, should reach a hearing and a vote as soon as possible. It must, therefore, invariably happen that the Committee holding the floor at any particular time is the Committee whose proposals the majority wish to dispose of as summarily as circumstances will allow, in order that the rest of the [other] unprivileged Committees to which the majority belong may gain the earlier and the fairer chance of a hearing. A reporting Committee, besides, is generally as glad to be pushed as the majority are to push it. It probably has several bills matured, and wishes to see them disposed of before its brief hours of opportunity are passed and gone. . . .

These are the customs which baffle and perplex and astound the new member. In these precedents and usages, when at length he comes to understand them, the novice spies out the explanation of the fact, once so confounding and seemingly inexplicable, that when he leaped to his feet to claim the floor other members who rose after him were coolly and unfeelingly preferred before him by the Speaker. Of course it is plain enough now that Mr. Speaker knew beforehand to whom the representative of the reporting Committee had agreed to yield the floor; and it was no use for any one else to cry out for recognition. Whoever wished to speak should, if pssible, have made some arrangement with the Committee before the business came to a hearing, and should have taken care to notify Mr. Speaker that he was to be granted the floor for a few moments.

Unquestionably this, besides being a very interesting, is a very novel and significant method of restricting debate and expediting legislative action,—a method of very serious import, and obviously fraught with far-reaching constitutional effects. The practices of debate which prevail in its legislative assembly are manifestly of the utmost importance to a self-governing people; for that legislation which is not thoroughly discussed by the legislating body is practically done in a corner. It is impossible for Congress itself to do wisely what it does so hurriedly; and the constituencies cannot understand what Congress does not itself stop to consider. . . .

. . . [T]he debates of Congress cannot, under our present system, have that serious purpose of search into the merits of policies and that definite and determinate party—or, if you will, partisan—aim without which they can never be effective for the instruction of public opinion, or the cleansing of political action. The chief of these reasons, because the parent of all the rest, is that there are in Congress no authoritative leaders who are the recognized spokesman of their parties. Power is nowhere concentrated; it is rather deliberately and of set policy scattered amongst many small chiefs. It is divided up, as it were, into forty-seven seigniories, in each of which a Standing Committee is the court-baron and its chairman lord-proprietor. These petty barons, some of them not a little powerful, but none of them within reach of the full powers of rule, may at will exercise an almost despotic sway within their own shires, and may sometimes threaten to convulse even the realm itself; but both their mutual jealousies and their brief and restricted opportunities forbid their combining and each is very far from the office of common leader.

I know that to some this scheme of distributed power and disintegrated rule seems a very excellent device whereby we are enable to escape a dangerous "one-man power" and an untoward concentration of functions; and it is very easy to see and appreciate the considerations which make this view of committee government so popular. It is based upon a very proper and salutary fear of *irresponsible* power; and those who most resolutely maintain it always fight from the position that all leadership in legislation is hard to restrain in proportion to its size and to the strength of its prerogatives, and that to divide it is to make it manageable. They aver, besides, that the less a man has to do—that is to say, the more he is confined to single departments and to definite details—the more intelligent and thorough will his work be. They like the Committees, therefore, just because they are many and weak, being quite willing to abide their being despotic within their narrow spheres.

It seems evident, however, when the question is looked at from another standpoint, that, as a matter of fact and experience, the more power is divided the more irresponsible it becomes. . . .

In a word, the national parties do not act in Congress under the restraint of a sense of immediate responsibility. Responsibility is spread thin; and no vote or debate can gather it. It rests not so much upon parties as upon individuals; and it rests upon individuals in no such way as would make it either just or efficacious to visit upon them the iniquity of any legislative act. Looking at government from a practical and business-like, rather than from a theoretical and abstractly-ethical point of view,—treating the business of government as a business,—it seems to be unquestionably and in a high degree desirable that all legislation should distinctly represent the action of parties as parties. I know that it has been proposed by enthusiastic, but not too practical, reformers to do away with parties by some legerdemain of governmental reconstruction, accompanied and supplemented by some rehabilitation, devoutly to be wished, of the virtues least commonly controlling in fallen human nature; but it seems to me that it would be more difficult and less desirable than these amiable persons suppose to conduct a government of the many by means of any other device than party organization, and that the great need is, not to get rid of parties, but to find and use some expedient by which they can be managed and made amenable from day to day to public opinion. . . .

. . . [T]here is within Congress no *visible*, and therefore no *controllable* party organization. The only bond of cohesion is the caucus, which occasionally whips a party together for cooperative action against the time for casting its vote upon some critical question. There is always a majority and a minority, indeed, but the legislation of a session does not represent the policy of either; it is simply an aggregate of the bills recommended by Committees composed of members from both sides of the House, and it is known to be usually, not the work of the majority men upon the Committees, but compromise conclusions bearing some shade or tinge of each of the variously-colored opinions and wishes of the committeemen of both parties.

It is plainly the representation of both parties on the Committees that make party responsibility indistinct and organized party action almost impossible. If the Committees were composed entirely of members of the majority, and were thus constituted representatives of the party in power, the whole course of congressional proceedings would unquestionably take on a very different aspect. There would then certainly be a compact opposition to face the organized majority. Committee reports would be taken to represent the views of the party in power, and, instead of the scattered, unconcerted opposition, without plan or leaders, which now sometimes subjects the propositions of the Committees to vexatious hindrances and delays, there would spring up debate under skillful masters of opposition, who could drill their partisans for effective warfare and give shape and meaning to the purposes of the minority. But of course there can be no such definite division of forces so long as the efficient machinery of legislation is in the hands of both parties at once; so long as the parties are mingled and harnessed together in a common organization.

4   *Senate Rules and the Civil Rights Bill:*
     A Case Study
     HOWARD E. SHUMAN

The rules of the Senate of the United States are only 40 in number and comprise only 49 of the 832 pages of the *Senate Manual.* Yet, when literally invoked they can bring Senate business to a standstill. They are most often ignored or circumvented by unanimous consent in order that the Senate may operate conveniently as a deliberative and parliamentary body. To pass legislation when they are invoked is a formidable enterprise.

Just as the law is said to be no better than the procedures by which it is carried out, so the substance of legislation is shaped and modified by the procedures that may be required under the Senate rules, or by the mere threat to invoke those procedures, for they are compelling. The procedures preceding and surrounding the passage of the first civil rights bill in over 80 years illumine and illustrate the effect of the rules on the substance of legislation as have few other legislative controversies in recent years.

The Senate rules are the product of sectionalism. They were designed to prevent action unacceptable to a sectional minority. Among the more important specific rules with this design are: sections 2 and 3 of Rule XXII—the filibuster rule; section 1f of Rule XXII, which makes a tabling motion not debatable and which, therefore, acts as a "negative" form of majority cloture for, if successful, it can stop talk and kill a bill or amendment without a vote on the merits;[1] Rule XXVI, which requires that all reports and motions to discharge a committee of a bill must lie over one legislative day—in practice this can mean several weeks if the Senate recesses from day to day rather

From Howard E. Shuman, *The American Political Science Review* (December 1957, pp. 955-975), American Political Science Association.

[1] The Senate has no similar form of "majority" cloture which could end debate and bring a vote on the substance of a bill or an amendment.

than adjourns; Rule XL which requires one (legislative) day's notice to suspend the rules; Rule VII, which requires that a petition to discharge a committee be filed in the so-called morning hour, except by unanimous consent; and the same Rule VII which when literally followed requires the reading of the Journal in full, the presentation of messages from the President and reports and communications from executive departments, and numerous other time-consuming procedures in the morning hour, and so may preclude the opportunity for discharge petitions to be reached, for at the close of that hour the Senate must proceed to the unfinished or pending business; and two unwritten rules, first, of seniority, and second, the rule of recognition under which the chair recognizes either the Majority or Minority Leader as against other Senators who are seeking recognition. This can prevent a Senator from making a timely motion or point of order to which the leadership is opposed and so helps give the leadership command of the parliamentary situation.

How these rules affected the course of the civil rights debate and the strategy of both sides in the 1956 and 1957 sessions is now to be shown.

I. THE ABORTIVE CIVIL RIGHTS BILL OF 1956

With only a few days of the 84th Congress remaining in July, 1956, the House of Representatives, by a margin of 279 to 126, passed H.R. 627, a bill substantially the same as H.R. 6127 of the 85th Congress, part of which is now the law of the land. A small band composed of Senators Hennings, Douglas, and Lehman and finally supported by Senators Langer, Ives, and Bender, attempted to gain Senate action on the bill when it came from the House. This move was made notwithstanding the determined opposition of both Majority and Minority Leaders which, in the end, proved crushing.

Senator Douglas was guarding the Senate floor as the House passed the bill, and left his seat to go to the House chamber to escort H.R. 627 through the long corridor from the Speaker's to the Vice President's desk. As he was walking to the House he was passed, unknowing, by a messenger carrying the bill to the Senate. With Senator Douglas outside the Senate chamber and with Senator Hill of Alabama in the chair, the bill, with jet-age speed, was read a first and second time and referred to the Senate Judiciary Committee where its Senate counterparts had languished for two years.

This action took place by unanimous consent and so by-passed the specific provisions of Rule XIV, which require three readings of the bill prior to passage, "Which [readings] shall be on three different days," but state that bills from the House of Representatives ". . . shall be read once, and may be read twice, on the same day, if not objected to, for reference. . . ."

An attempt was then made under Rule XXVI, section 2, to file a petition to discharge the Judiciary Committee from the further consideration of H.R. 627. Except by unanimous consent the petition must be introduced in the morning hour.

On the same calendar day the bill came from the House a unanimous consent request to file the petition was blocked by a motion of the Majority Leader to recess overnight. At the beginning of the next day's session, in what would ordinarily have been the morning hour, the Senator from Georgia, Mr. George, ruled that the petition could not be filed, except by unanimous consent, for the Senate had recessed the previous evening and, in fact, had not adjourned since the evening of July 13, *i.e.*, 10 days previously. Although the date was then July 24, the legislative day was July 16, and thus technically there was no morning hour for the routine business of filing bills, reports, petitions, etc. Individual Senators then objected to further unanimous consent requests to file the petition. The Senate recessed that day and did not adjourn overnight until July 26, the evening before adjournment *sine die*. In the meantime a motion by Senator Douglas to adjourn for five minutes, in order to bring a new legislative day and morning hour, was defeated by the crushing vote of 76 to 6.

In the morning hour on the last day of the session, the discharge petition was finally filed. But a discharge petition, under section 2 of Rule XXVI, must lie over one further "legislative" day. If consideration of the petition is not reached or is not concluded in the morning hour or before 2 o'clock on the next "legislative" day, it goes to the calendar. Then the motion to proceed to its consideration and the motion on passage of the petition are both subject to unlimited debate, unless cloture is applied to each. Such action, even if successful, would only result in placing the bill itself on the calendar, where it in turn must lie for another "legislative" day. The motion to proceed to its consideration and the motion on final passage are also both subject to unlimited debate, unless cloture is applied. Thus the filing of the petition came too late to bring action in the 84th Congress. Even if commenced at the beginning of a session, and even if [67]* votes were obtainable for cloture on each of the four occasions when they are potentially necessary, the process of discharging a committee can be drawn out over several weeks, and even months, if the rules of the Senate are literally invoked.

Although this attempt was abortive the experience was useful to the civil rights proponents in 1957. It brought a familiarity with the rules of the Senate which can only be gained from step-by-step proceedings under them; from it they concluded that action must begin very early in the session if it were to be successful; they saw that the route of discharging a committee meant meeting countless roadblocks, which could only be stormed and surmounted by determined efforts and with overhwelming bi-partisan support; and they concluded that a fight to change Rule XXII was essential because the inadequacy of cloture had either killed previous civil rights bills or brought their death by the mere threat of a filibuster.[2]

II. THE FIGHT TO CHANGE RULE XXII

The effort to change Rule XXII was made at the opening of the 85th Congress in January, 1957. In the past Rule XXII has been the gravedigger in the Senate graveyard for civil rights bills. Section 2 of Rule XXII requires [67] affirmative votes to limit debate and section 3 provides that on a motion to proceed to the consideration of a change in the rules there can be no limit on debate of any kind. The rules of the Senate have carried over from Congress to Congress and changes in them have been made only after a unanimous consent agreement has been reached narrowly limiting the language and amendments which could come before the Senate.

Because of section 3, the only chance of success seemed to lie in a move at the beginning of a Congress that the Senate proceed to adopt new rules, relying on Article I, Section 5 of the Constitution which provides that ". . . each House may determine the rules of its proceedings." Such a motion was made in 1953 and was de-

---

* At time article was written, this figure was 64.—Ed.

[2] Since 1917, or for 40 years, cloture has been successful on only four of twenty-two attempts and never on a civil rights bill. Sixty-four votes have been forthcoming only three times, all in the period 1917 to 1927. Thus, no cloture motion has successfully prevailed in the last 30 years.

[On June 10, 1964, the Senate imposed cloture on a civil rights bill for the first time in history. The vote was 71-29, with a "surplus" of 4 votes. Once the full account of the 1964 Act is written, Mr. Shuman's analysis of the filibuster in Section VI of this article will appear to have been prophetic.—Ed., second edition.]

feated by a vote of 70 to 21. Its opponents argued then that a civil rights bill would be passed, and that the rules should be changed only by ordinary processes of piecemeal amendment.

In 1957 the vote to table the motion to proceed to the considera-tion of new rules was carried, 55 to 38. Three absentees, Senators Neely and Wiley, and Javits, who had not yet taken his seat, opposed tabling and so brought to 41 the total who favored adopting new rules. Thus a shift of seven votes, plus a Vice President's favorable vote or ruling, was all that was now required to change Rule XXII. This was a major gain over 1953, for these 41 votes were obtained over the concerted objections of the leadership of both parties.

The size of the vote and its near success caught Southern Sena-tors on the horns of a dilemma. They knew that any actual and or-ganized use of the filibuster would ultimately bring an end to Rule XXII, and they also knew that if they did not use the filibuster Con-gress would most likely pass a civil rights bill. The fight to change Rule XXII thereby produced a climate in which not only a meaning-ful bill could pass but, it can be persuasively argued, a bill much stronger than that which was actually passed. The arguments and the parliamentary strategy involved in the Rule XXII fight were therefore crucial.

The opponents of the change relied basically on a single argu-ment, namely, that the Senate was a continuing body, and as two-thirds of its members carry over from Congress to Congress, its rules should therefore also carry over from Congress to Congress as they have in the past.

The proponents argued that whatever the Senate had done in the past it had explicit constitutional power to adopt its rules at the beginning of a new Congress. Unlike their course in 1953, when the attempt to adopt new rules was hastily devised, the proponents did not meet the continuing body argument head on, but argued instead that it was immaterial whether the Senate was a continuing body or not. Acceptance of the continuing body argument did not deny to a majority of the Senate the right to adopt its own rules. Proponents also argued that proceedings on all bills and resolutions, as well as on treaties, begin again in a new Congress; that the Senate is newly organized and new committees are appointed; and that the newly elected one-third, even though only one-third, could alter the party alignment and thus provide a new majority and a new mandate which it had the right to carry out.

A second argument by the opponents, less used but probably more telling than the first, was that until the adoption of new rules the Senate would be in a parliamentary "jungle." Senator Russell combined with this argument a threat to proceed to rewrite each of the 40 rules of the Senate.

In rejoinder the proponents argued that the House of Representatives entered and left the parliamentary "jungle" in a very few minutes at each new Congress. They proposed that until the rules were adopted the Senate should proceed under general parliamentary rules including the motion for the previous question under which debate could be shut off by a simple majority. The proponents also relied on the precedents of the Senate to support the contention that majority cloture could be applied, for it was shown that the previous question rule was a part of the Senate rules from 1789 to 1806 and was used to bring debate to a close on several occasions.

The potential parlaimentary moves were extremely involved, but basically the proponents sought to gain a ruling from the Vice President that their motion to proceed to the immediate consideration of the adoption of new rules was in order. This was their strongest position but, in the end, it was not gained.

It was their strongest position for a variety of reasons. To succeed, strong bi-partisan support was needed. The Democratic Party, by its nature, was split on the issue and could not provide a majority of votes. This was true even though the Democrats have traditionally supplied more votes on procedural issues in support of civil rights, and occasionally more on substantive civil rights issues, than the Republicans. In 1953, of the 21 votes for the adoption of new rules, 15 were Democratic. Only 5 Republicans and Wayne Morse, then an independent, voted for the change. That year Vice President Barkley let it be known that he would rule such a motion in order. But he had no opportunity to do so for Senator Taft gained the floor and gave immediate and prearranged notice that he would move to table the motion and thus shut off argument after a short debate. In 1957 with a Republican Vice President and with Republican votes needed to win, it was obvious that the strongest position would follow from a favorable ruling by the Vice President, and on the vote to uphold or overturn his ruling. The Democrats could provide no more than half of their numbers in support of such a favorable ruling. But the Republicans could provide, potentially, almost all of their votes if the issue were one of supporting their own Vice President.

In 1953 it mattered little whether the motion to proceed to the adoption of new rules were tabled, or whether a point of order were made and a ruling sought, for there would still have been a limit to the number of potential Democratic votes on this issue in support of a Democratic Vice President. The Republicans were obviously under no political pressure to support the ruling of a Democratic Vice President who was to leave office in a very few days.

In 1957 it was a different matter. Whether the vote came on a motion to table or on an appeal from the ruling of the Chair was critically important. If a Republican Vice President now ruled favorably, he would no doubt be supported by more than a majority of his own party which, combined with the Democratic support, could provide the winning margin. The proponent group knew that they would make gains over 1953 however the Vice President ruled, but if he ruled for them there was an opportunity for spectacular gains and perhaps a victory.

The strategy was therefore devised that the mover of the motion to proceed to the consideration of new rules for the Senate should also couple with his motion a parliamentary request for a ruling from the Chair that the motion was in order. If this was not done a motion to table would no doubt be made, thereby cutting off debate and bringing an immediate vote. The proponents of a change in Rule XXII not only had more to gain from a ruling from the Chair but also felt that time for debate, which could educate and arouse public opinion, was necessary to the success of the effort. A steering committee representing those who favored adoption of the new rules therefore met with the Vice President to advise him of their proposed course of action. They did not seek nor did they receive the Vice President's opinion as to the merits of their proposal.

They were advised, however, that the Majority Leader had informed the Vice President that immediately following the motion to proceed to the consideration of new rules he would seek recognition for the purpose of tabling that motion. The Vice President then gave his opinion that under the precedents of the Senate a point of order could not be coupled with the substantive motion, and that under the unwritten rule of recognition he must recognize the Majority Leader as against some other Senator seeking the floor. This meant, of course, that once the motion was made the Majority Leader would be recognized to move to table that motion and thereby shut off debate before any other Senator, including the mover of the motion, could raise a point of order.

The unwritten rule of recognition thus brought the vote on the issue of Rule XXII on the least advantageous grounds for the proponents of new rules and an end to the filibuster. It was, however, very ironic that the proponents of unlimited debate should immediately move to shut off debate on the question of changing Senate Rule XXII which, in effect, provides for unlimited debate. Recognition of this anomaly led to a unanimous consent agreement which fixed a limited time for debate on the tabling motion. When the motion to proceed to the consideration of new rules was made, consequently, and was sent to the desk and read by the clerk, the Majority Leader sought and gained recognition. He proposed to table the motion which, but for the unanimous consent agreement, would have cut off debate immediately; as it was, debate was limited and the issue came to a vote as had been planned.

In the course of these events the Vice President gave it as his informal opinion, though not as a formal ruling, (1) that a majority of the Senate could adopt new rules at the beginning of a new Congress if it wished; (2) that Section 3 of Rule XXII was unconstitutional for it allowed a previous Senate to bind a majority of a future Senate;[3] and (3) that until such time as the Senate either adopted new rules or by some action, such as the tabling motion, acquiesced in the old rules, the Senate would proceed under its previous rules except for those which could deny a majority of the Senate the right or opportunity to adopt new ones, or, in short, sections 2 and 3 of Rule XXII.

Thus, the unwritten rule of recognition and the use of the tabling motion as a negative form of majority cloture, not available to the proponents of a motion, bill, or amendment, were decisive parliamentary weapons in the fight over Rule XXII and the filibuster.

Although the fight was lost it nevertheless brought several clear gains to the proponents of the civil rights bill and of majority rule, apart from the dilemma of the Southern Senators over their future use of the filibuster. First, rhetorically, it foreshadowed the end of the effectiveness of the argument that the Senate is a continuing body with necessarily continuing rules. The debate showed it to be irrelevant as well as circuitous to argue that the rules carry over because

[3] It has been asked why, if the Vice President believed section 3 was unconstitutional, Senators did not press the issue later in the session. The answer is that the Vice President's position was that it was unconstitutional to the extent that it bound one Senate by the actions of a previous Senate. However, if the new Senate agreed to be bound, *i.e.*, acquiesced in the old rules as it did when the tabling motion was successful, section 3 would remain in effect throughout the 85th Congress.

the Senate is a continuing body, and that the Senate is a continuing body because the rules carry over. Second, substantively, the episode brought clear bi-partisan gains over 1953; the Democratic vote increased from 15 to 21, and the Republican from 5 to 17. While the press was predicting an overwhelming defeat for the 1957 effort those close to the scene estimated quite accurately that approximately 40 would support the motion to proceed to the adoption of new rules. Third, tactically, this fight gave a political urgency to civil rights legislation which it might not otherwise have had, and improved immeasurably the chances for a meaningful bill.

III. FILIBUSTER BY COMMITTEE

H.R. 6127 passed the House on June 18, 1957. In the Senate its companion bill, as well as some 15 other civil rights bills, still had not been acted on by the Judiciary Committee.

This inaction followed precedent. In the 83d Congress four civil rights bills were reported from the Subcommittee on Constitutional Rights to the full Judiciary Committee, where they died. In the 84th Congress, the Constitutional Rights Subcommittee reported three bills on February 23, 1956 and a fourth bill on March 4, 1956, to the full Judiciary Committee; but they too died following 10 days of hearings by the full committee spread over the 11-week period from April 24 to July 13. In the 85th Congress, after every legitimate attempt by Senator Hennings and his colleagues to gain action on the bills, not one was reported to the Senate during the entire session. A chronology of the efforts to report a bill to the Senate will show how filibuster by committee takes place.

A number of civil rights bills were introduced during the first days of the session. On January 22, Senator Hennings moved in committee that February 18 be set as the deadline for ending hearings on them and that a vote on the legislation and the reporting of a bill to the Senate should not be delayed beyond one further week. This motion was not acted on.

Four days later, on January 26, the 14 bills by then in committee were referred to the Constitutional Rights Subcommittee.

On January 30 Senator Hennings, the chairman, presented an omnibus bill to the subcommittee and moved that it be reported to the full committee. The motion was defeated.

The subcommittee then agreed to hold hearings and Senator Hennings moved that these should begin on February 12 and be limited to two weeks, after which the subcommittee should act on the bills immediately. This motion was defeated.

Hearings by the subcommittee did begin on February 14 and ended after three weeks on March 5. On March 19, the subcommittee approved S. 83 and reported it, along with majority and minority views, to the full committee.

On March 21, Senator Hennings introduced S. 1658; its language was identical with that of H.R. 6127.

On April 1, in the full committee, Senator Hennings moved that the Judiciary Committee dispose of civil rights legislation by April 15. He was unable to obtain a vote on this motion.

On April 8, Senator Hennings intended to renew his motion, but there was no meeting of the committee owing to the absence of a quorum.

On April 15, Senator Hennings moved that S. 83 be voted on by May 6. The committee took no action.

On May 13, at the next meeting, Senator Hennings desired to move that the committee meet every morning and all day, when the rules of the Senate permitted, and in the evenings if necessary, so that a vote on the bill could be taken by May 16. He was unable to obtain recognition to make this motion.

On June 3, the committee added the sweeping "jury trial" amendment to the bill.

On June 10 and June 17, Senator Hennings was unable to gain recognition during committee meetings.

On June 18 the House passed H.R. 6127 and it was sent to the Senate.

How was it possible for the Judiciary Committee, which contained only a minority of Southern Senators, to delay action on civil rights for such a lengthy period of time? Under Section 134 (c) of the Legislative Reorganization Act, "No standing committee of the Senate . . . shall sit, without special leave, while the Senate . . . is in session," Under Section 133 (a) of the same Act, each standing committee is required to fix a regular day on which to meet. The regular meeting day of the Senate Judiciary Committee is Monday. While the Senate is often in recess on other days of the week, it is invariably in session on Monday, because that day is set for the call of the calendar of unobjected-to bills, and because the Constitution provides that neither House may adjourn for more than three days without the consent of the other. Consequently, when the hour of 12 noon arrives or when, as in the latter stages of the session the Senate meets at an earlier hour, any member of the Judiciary Committee may make a point of order that the Committee may no longer sit. This was done, and was one means of postponing action.

In addition, by the chairman's power to recognize an opponent first, and by his power to hold off a vote on a motion until such a member has concluded his remarks on it, it was easy for the chairman either to prevent a motion from being offered or to prevent action on a specific bill during the Committee's normal two-hour meeting. Further, the unwritten rule of seniority has generally placed a Southern Senator in the chair when the Democratic Party controls Congress. While Rule XXIV reads that ". . . the Senate, unless otherwise ordered, shall proceed by ballot to appoint severally the chairman of each committee . . . ," this rule was not enforced either when Senator Eastland was first appointed chairman, on the death of Senator Kilgore, or at the beginning of the 85th Congress when he was reappointed. There was neither a ballot nor a motion to "order otherwise." Finally, on several Mondays it was impossible to muster a quorum.

IV. PLACING H.R. 6127 ON THE SENATE CALENDAR

Faced with this situation, a small group of pro-civil-rights Democratic Senators met a few days prior to the passage of H.R. 6127 by the House of Representatives, to determine on a course of action when that bill arrived in the Senate.

Several possibilities were canvassed. These included: (1) moving to send H.R. 6127 to the Judiciary Committee with instructions to report it to the Senate on a specific date; (2) allowing H.R. 6127 to go to Committee but moving to discharge the Judiciary Committee from further consideration either of that bill or of one of several of the Senate bills; (3) moving to suspend the rules under Rule XL in order to place H.R. 6127 on the calendar; and (4) moving to place the bill on the calendar under Rule XIV.

After consultation with the Senate Parliamentarian the group ruled out the first possibility, of sending the bill to committee with instructions to report it to the Senate on a day certain. Such instructions may be added to a motion to refer or to commit only when the bill itself has been motioned up and is actually before the Senate. Before the bill could come before the Senate it had first to be placed on the calendar, and then to be motioned up. Such a motion is subject to unlimited debate unless cloture is applied. This procedure was therefore evidentally impossible, notwithstanding later statements by Senator Morse who, in justifying his opposition to placing the bill directly on the calendar, asserted that instructions to report the bill on a day certain could have been added after the second reading.

Similarly, as we have already seen, the method of discharging a committee is lengthy, and was probably impossible for legislation as controversial as a civil rights bill. More specifically, the steps involved in this procedure include:

1. Filing a discharge petition during the morning hour.
2. A successful motion to adjourn so that a new legislative day may arrive.
3. Reaching the petition during the morning hour, in which case it would go to the foot of the calendar if debate were not concluded in two hours; or, if it was not reached in the morning hour, motioning it up at a later stage.
4. Moving to proceed to consideration of the petition, after it has reached the calendar, and after one legislative day has elapsed (which requires an intervening adjournment), when such a motion becomes in order.
5. Securing a vote on this motion, which is debatable and requires either unanimous consent or cloture and [67] affirmative votes to bring the debate to an end. Passage of this procedural motion requires only a simple majority.
6. Securing a vote on the next motion, to agree to the petition to discharge the committee. This motion too is debatable and requires cloture.
7. Placing the bill, now discharged from committee, at the foot of the Rule VIII calendar, which follows automatically if the previous steps are successful. It must remain there for another legislative day, which requires another successful motion to adjourn in order to reach a new legislative day.
8. Moving to proceed to consideration of the bill and securing a vote on this motion, which is by now in order, is debatable, requires cloture to end debate, and a simple majority for passage.
9. Moving to agree to the bill and securing a vote on it, after all amendments have been dealt with; this again is debatable and requires cloture.

In the face of determined opposition, and without the help of the party leadership, the procedures outlined here would take a minimum of five to eight weeks even if there were [67] votes in support of action at every stage, which was by no means certain. The group therefore determined that the route of discharging the Judiciary Committee was impractical; indeed, that the votes and physical endurance necessary to break four successive potential filibusters made it impossible.

Suspending the rules of the Senate in order to place the House-passed bill on the calendar was also considered. This procedure is no near cousin of the method of moving to suspend the rules and pass the bill, which is a short-cut frequently used in the House of Representatives and common in state legislatures, where with the backing of the party leadership and a disciplined two-thirds vote at hand an opposition minority can be steam-rolled. In the Senate version it has the advantage merely of reducing from four to three the number of potential filibusters and cloture motions to be met.[4] On the other hand, in comparison with the discharge procedure, it has two immediate drawbacks. First, because the tradition that all matters, unless by unanimous consent, should go to a committee before floor action is rightly very strong, suspension of the rules is open to the charge of by-passing the committee; the discharge procedure at least makes a gesture of giving the committee a chance to act. Second, because the

[4] The steps involved in suspending the rules in order to place the bill on the calendar run as follows: (1) When the bill arrives from the House, either a motion that it be laid before the Senate, or a wait until the presiding officer laid it before the Senate in order to object to the second reading of the bill on the same day. (2) Simultaneously giving notice of an intention to move to suspend the rules, and reading or placing in the *Record* the terms of the motion. (3) Gaining an adjournment to bring a new legislative day. (4) On the new legislative day and after the reading of the Journal, either calling up the motion to suspend the rules, or waiting until the presiding officer laid the bill before the Senate for a second reading. At this time, and prior to the customary referral to committee, gaining recognition to prevent such a reference by calling up the motion to suspend the rules. Since no motion to proceed to the consideration of that motion would be necessary, one potential filibuster is avoided at this point. (5) Securing a vote on the motion to suspend the rules, which is debatable and would require cloture to stop a filibuster. An affirmative two-thirds vote of those present and voting on this motion would send the bill to the calendar. (6) From this stage on the procedure is the same as with the discharge method—an adjournment to bring a new legislative day, when a motion to proceed to the consideration of the bill would be in order; a vote on this motion, which is debatable and would require cloture; disposition of amendments and a vote on final passage, which again is debatable and would require cloture.

suspension procedure has been so rarely used, it is open also to the charge of novelty in procedure—an unorthodox means of gaining an unorthodox end. The steering group of civil rights senators therefore discarded this alternative, and in fact concluded that if a choice had to be made between the two, the discharge route was preferable.

Finally, the possibility of placing the House-passed bill on the calendar under Rule XIV was canvassed. The relevant parts of Rule XIV read as follows:

No bill or joint resolution shall be committed or amended until it shall have been twice read, after which it *may* be referred to a committee; bills and joint resolutions introduced on leave, and bills and joint resolutions from the House of Representatives, shall be read once, and may be read twice, on the same day, if not objected to, for reference, but shall not be considered on that day nor debated, except for reference, unless by unanimous consent. (Section 3, emphasis added.)

Every bill and joint resolution reported from a committee, not having previously been read, shall be read once, and twice, if not objected to, on the same day, and placed on the Calendar in the order in which the same may be reported; and every bill and joint resolution introduced on leave, *and every bill and joint resolution of the House of Representatives which shall have received a first and second reading without being referred to a committee, shall, if objection be made to further proceeding thereon, be placed on the Calendar.* (Section 4, emphasis added.)

Although infrequently used, this seemed to be a relatively simple and direct method of placing the House-passed bill on the calendar. If it could be attacked for by-passing the committee, it was nevertheless a well settled part of the rules of the Senate; and compared with many rules, its meaning appeared to be crystal clear. On that count it was therefore preferable to suspending the rules. And although perhaps less orthodox than discharging the committee, it reduced the potential number of filibusters in finally passing the bill from four to two. It was decided, therefore, that this method had the best, and perhaps the only, chance of success.

On June 14, following press reports that a group of Republican senators, including their leadership, were also considering using Rule XIV to place the bill on the calendar, a group of 15 Democratic liberals issued a statement in which they (1) urged the Judiciary Committee to report out a bill promptly, (2) stated that, while they preferred to act on a Senate bill, if a Senate bill were not reported they would join and cooperate with any other senator or groups of senators on either side of the aisle who wished to place the House bill on the calendar under Rule XIV, (3) gave formal notice of their intention to do so to the leadership and whips on both sides of the aisle, to the Parliamentarian, and to all other Senators, and (4) gave notice that they would not give unanimous consent to any motion to refer the House-passed bill to committee and formally requested that they be notified before the bill was laid before the Senate or referred, so that they might be in their places to ask certain parliamentary questions or to make certain motions. This last request grew out of the experience of 1956, when the House-passed bill was referred to committee while interested Senators were not on the floor. A further important reason for giving notice was that bills from the House as well as bills introduced in the Senate are ordinarily, for the convenience of all, read perfunctorily, not actually laid down by the presiding officer, and automatically referred to committee. Even when a bill is actually laid before the Senate, this can be done at any time and while the floor is unguarded, for under section 7 of Rule VII,

The Presiding Officer may at any time lay, and it shall be in order at any time for a Senator to move to lay, before the Senate, any bill or other matter sent to the Senate by the President or the House of Representatives, and any question pending at that time shall be suspended for this purpose. Any motion so made shall be determined without debate.

Thus with a senator who opposed civil rights in the chair, another senator could move to, or the chair without a motion could, lay the House bill before the Senate and have it referred before another senator could gain recognition to object.

Certain precautionary steps were therefore taken. The first was to try to make certain that a senator in sympathy with the move to place the bill on the calendar, or the Vice President, would be in the chair when the bill arrived at the desk. Teams of senators were organized to guard the floor at all times. Arrangements were made with House members to notify key senators of the step-by-step actions on the bill in the House. Further, it was publicly pointed out that when the bill arrived the Senate would be in executive session considering the Atomic Energy Treaty, and hence that the bill would remain in limbo at the desk until the Senate moved back into legislative session. As the Senate can move back and forth from legislative to executive session by a simple unanimous consent request, attention was called to this fact so that senators would not lower their guard and stay off the floor during executive sessions under the mistaken impression that no action on the bill could be taken. Sheets of instructions were issued to the Democratic senators in sympathy with the move, in which parliamentary details were outlined; these instructed them to object to any attempt to read the bill a second time or to refer it, and to call for a quorum when in doubt. As a result, the rights of individual senators were protected as they had not been in 1956. Agreements were entered into at almost every stage for a specific time when action would take place and motions would be made, so that the rights of each senator could be asserted.

H.R. 6127 was laid before the Senate on June 19. It was read a first time, after which Senator Russell asked unanimous consent that it be read a second time on that day. Objections were heard from Senators Knowland and Douglas.

At this time Senator Russell argued that Rule XXV took precedence over Rule XIV. He claimed that the following procedures under Rule XIV would ". . . throw out the window the laws, the rules, and the Constitution in order to get at 'these infernal southerners' in a hurry." His major argument rested on the premise that the changes made in the rules by the Legislative Reorganization Act of 1946 superseded other rules with which they were inconsistent. In his view the language of Rule XXV, which enumerates the subject matter over which specific committees have jurisdiction, was in conflict with Rule XIV and therefore took precedence over that rule. He quoted Section 101 (a) of the Reorganization Act which reads, in part, ". . . such rules shall supersede other rules only to the extent that they are inconsistent therewith," and Section (k) of Rule XXV which reads:

Committee on the Judiciary, to consist of fifteen Senators, to which *shall be referred* all proposed legislation, messages, petitions, memorials, and other matters relating to the following subjects. (Emphasis added.)

A list of subjects then follows, including "civil liberties." Senator Russell urged specifically that the phrase "shall be referred" is mandatory and superseded sections 3 and 4 of Rule XIV.

The proponents of the move argued that nothing could be clearer than the language of Rule XIV; that Rule XXV was not mandatory concerning referral but merely a specification of the subject matter over which each committee had jurisdiction; that the history of the Legislative Reorganization Act showed this to be true; that there were numerous examples of House bills going directly to the calendar both by precedent and under Rule XIV; and that the phrase "shall be referred," should not now be construed as mandatory when it had not been so on hundreds of other occasions.[5]

Development of the argument brought out examples of House-passed bills which were automatically placed on the Senate calendar when a Senate companion bill was already on the Senate calendar, and examples of a House-passed bill placed on the calendar prior to the Senate bill being placed there, when it was known that a Senate bill would soon be reported. Further, although this point was not made on the floor, it is well known that, especially on the last day of a session, numerous House-passed bills are motioned up on the floor of the Senate when there are no Senate companion bills. There have even been examples of the bill clerk officially referring a bill to a committee and entering that referral in the Journal, only to find that the House bill is motioned up and passed in the last few hours before adjournment. In such cases the Journal has been corrected after the fact to show that the bill was sent to the calendar, in order to be there legitimately when motioned up. These examples added considerable weight to the argument that the phrase "shall be referred" in Rule XXV was by no means mandatory. Since these bills were sent to the calendar by a private decision of the Vice President or his agent, it was argued that what one man could do *in camera* under the precedents a majority of the Senate could do openly under the provisions of a specific rule.

On June 20, Senator Knowland objected to the "further proceeding thereon" immediately after H.R. 6127 was read a second time. Senator Russell raised the point of order that Rule XXV took precedence; and debate on this point, which is not debatable except at the pleasure of the Chair, took place for several hours. One problem concerning the use of Rule XIV bothered some Senators, namely, that a "single" Senator, by objection, could prevent a bill going to committee. The proponents of the move argued that while such a case might theoretically arise, there would no doubt, on an issue of such importance as a civil rights bill, be a point of order, such as Senator Russell

[5] There were only a few examples of a bill going to the calendar under Rule XIV prior to 1946. Since then procedures under this rule were followed once on May 3, 1948 when Senator Downey of California objected after second reading to further proceedings on the Tidelands Oil bill, which then went directly to the calendar. Immediately following that action and on the same day Senator Fulbright attempted to do the same thing to the oleomargarine tax repeal bill. . . .

raised; and that a majority of the Senate would, in fact, decide whether the bill should go to the calendar or to the committee.

Senator Case of New Jersey was particularly concerned about a single Senator's objection sending the bill to the calendar, and felt that greater support for the move could be obtained if some method were found to decide the issue more directly by majority vote. He proposed that, after the second reading, a motion rather than an objection should be made, to send the bill to the calendar. He had numerous discussions with the Vice President on this point and prepared a detailed memorandum outlining his views. The Vice President's opinion on the Russell point of order reflects, to a considerable extent, these original views of Senator Case.

The leaders of the liberal Democratic group, while sympathizing with Senator Case's position, believed that if a specific motion were made to place the bill on the calendar following the second reading, rather than an objection by a single Senator under Rule XIV, such a motion would be debatable and hence would require [67] affirmative votes and cloture to end debate. If this were true then the attempt to place the bill on the calendar could not succeed.

This point was overcome by the opinion of the Vice President, who stated (1) that Rule XXV did not require a mandatory referral to committee; (2) that if objection were made under Rule XIV and no point of order were raised the bill would go directly to the calendar; but (3) that if a point of order were raised the effect of it would be to put the substantive question, "Shall the bill be referred," in which case the issue would be decided by a majority vote. A filibuster at this stage was precluded when the Vice President went on to state that a motion to table could lie against the point of order. A simple majority, therefore, could end debate by moving to table the point of order. No such tabling motion was made, but the fact that it could be made allowed the Senate to vote on the substantive issue, "Shall the bill be referred?" The vote was 35 to sustain Senator Russell's point of order and 45 who opposed; and the bill went to the calendar.

Major Results of the Maneuver. There were at least three major, and perhaps historic, results of this action. In the first place it was probably the only method by which a civil rights bill could have been placed in a position to come before the Senate. Without it the civil rights bill would no doubt have languished again in the Senate Judiciary Committee until the end of the Congress. This procedural move was a major and essential step towards the final passage of the bill.

Secondly, for the first important occasion since 1938, the coalition of Southern Democrats and conservative Republicans was shattered. The *quid pro quo* of that coalition has long been that Southern Democrats would provide enough votes to defeat liberal social and economic legislation while the conservative Republicans provided the votes to defeat civil rights moves. Now, for the first time, a coalition of Northern Republicans and liberal Northern Democrats had acted together on a procedural issue to further the progress of a civil rights bill. This was all the more significant for, in the past, the conservative Republicans had furnished their votes in support of the South mainly on procedural rather than substantive issues, such as the 1949 appeal from the decision of the chair and amendment to Rule XXII which made it even more difficult than before, to shut off debate. They provided just enough votes or absentees so that cloture could not be applied to previous civil rights bills. They opposed and defeated the 1953 and 1957 attempts to adopt new rules of the Senate at the beginning of a new Congress. In that way the Republicans hoped to avoid the charge of opposing civil rights, for they professed their willingness to support, at least in part, the bills themselves on which, in almost every case, they prevented action. This was playing both sides of an issue and, because procedural niceties are little understood by the public and even more difficult to explain, they avoided condemnation for opposing civil rights which was the real affect of their actions.

In place of this coalition two new coalitions emerged. One was the Knowland-Douglas Axis, as Senator Russell referred to it, on the civil rights issue. This coalition is probably limited to civil rights and was more the result of public opinion, of the Republican gains in the Negro districts in 1956, possibly of the personal Presidential ambitions of individual Senators, and of the effective filibuster by committee, than the basis for any agreement or tacit arrangement for mutual support on other issues.

The other coalition was a revival of cooperation between the Southern and Western Democrats together with the remaining hard core of the Republican right wing. In many respects this coalition was not new for it had operated for years on such economic issues common to both areas as legislation on sugar cane and sugar beets, rivers and harbors and reclamation projects, the wool tariff, the silver subsidy, aid to the Western mining industry, and similar matters. As the course of the civil rights debate continued, this combination became dominant and civil rights, apparently, was added as a part of the bargain.

A third and most important effect of the vote was that for the first time in many years the Senate asserted a disciplinary jurisdiction over one of its committees. In theory, at least, committees of the Senate should be the servants of the Senate as a whole. Notoriously, in practice this has not been so. Examples include the unwillingness of the Senate to deal with the excesses of investigating committees; the tacit arrangement whereby the leadership, committee chairmen, and those Senators who are within or who are seeking admittance to the "inner circle" join to provide 52 to 55 votes to defeat motions and amendments on the floor when offered by individual Senators who are not members of the committee; and the unwritten rule of the Senate leadership that it supports the substance of committee action without regard to opposition by what may be even a majority of the party. In this respect, placing the civil rights bill on the calendar was unique and precedent setting. Although committees will no doubt continue to operate substantially as they have in the past, the possibility or threat of similar action may well serve to allow action by the full Senate on controversial bills of great importance for which there is overwhelming support and which otherwise would die in a committee stacked against them.

V. The Debate on H.R. 6127

Although the vote to take up the bill was 71 to 18, the new Southern-Western coalition proved powerful enough to effect major changes in the bill itself. They forced the delection of Section III of the bill and they added a jury trial amendment to the voting section which, as it passed the Senate, would have made the bill least effective in those areas of the Deep South where it was most needed.

Apart from the coalition, two other major factors operated towards weakening the bill. The first was the press conference statement of the President on Section III, saying that it was not his intention that the Attorney General should have the power to initiate civil rights suits under that Section and the 14th Amendment. The second was the fact that the press centered its coverage almost wholly on the contest—the strategy and maneuverings in connection with the bill—and avoided, almost completely, the moral and substantive grounds for supporting it in the first place. For example, Senator Douglas placed in the Record a detailed legal brief on the jury trial amendment and contempt proceedings, showing that no "right" to trial by jury was being denied by the provisions of the bill. This was ignored by the press. County-by-county figures on Negro registration in the South were also detailed, as were the various subtle methods by which Negroes are denied the franchise; and these too were largely, although not entirely, ignored. Further, Senator Javits and others made lengthy and even brilliant rebuttals of the attack on Section III of the bill which were little reported and went almost unnoticed even by such papers as the *Washington Post* and the *New York Times*.

On three further occasions after the bill was taken up the rules of the Senate, together with other internal and external factors, affected the substance of the bill materially. These include the abortive attempt on the part of the Knowland-Douglas forces to modify Section III when it was clear, following the President's press conference, that it would otherwise be stricken; the various revisions of the jury-trial amendment; and the successful use of the unanimous consent device to bring a third reading and deny the possibility of further amendments at the late stages in the debate.

Striking Out Section III. Once the bill was before the Senate, Senators Anderson and Aiken moved to strike out Section III. This section would have permitted the Attorney General to seek injunctive remedies under the equal rights provisions of the 14th Amendment in cases affecting the use of schools, busses, public parks, etc., either on his own initiative, or at the request of an aggrieved party, or at the request of local public authorities which, in practice, would generally have meant school boards. Despite repeated claims to the contrary during the course of debate, the bill gave him no power to issue court orders or to decide how fast school integration must proceed. The remedies sought were milder in form, though easier, it was hoped, to obtain, than the criminal penalties now available against those who deny rights guaranteed under the Constitution; they were to supplement, not supplant, these penalties. The Little Rock, Arkansas case has since shown something of the potential effectiveness of the injunctive remedies. But the Attorney General was able to act in that case only because the original court order was sought by the Little Rock School Board, and because the court then invited him to intervene. Section III would have given the Attorney General the right to take the initiative.

When it was clear, after the President's press conference, that Section III would be deleted, the Knowland-Douglas forces sought to reach agreement on some substitute which could gain majority support. The Knowland position was that such an amendment should allow the Attorney General to intervene only when he was requested to do so by the local school boards or officials. The Douglas group's position was that the amendment should enable the Attorney General to intervene in these cases and also when an aggrieved party sought his intervention. Both versions abandoned the provision for the Attorney General to initiate action on his own and without specific request.

The parliamentary situation was that the amendment to strike out Section III could only be decided after perfecting amendments to the section in its original form had been offered and voted on. Under the rules even though the motion to strike out was offered first its priority for purposes of voting was last. The Knowland forces were unable to agree to the Douglas amendment, largely because they felt they could not push beyond the President's position; but the two groups tried to work out a strategy whereby they would fall back step by step, attempting to pick up strength as they did so. They decided that Senator Knowland should first offer his amendment, and that Senator Douglas would then move to substitute his own amendment for it. In this way they hoped that the liberal Democrats and other supporters of the stronger position could vote for the Douglas motion and when defeated, as they no doubt would have been, they could join the Knowland position as the next defensive move.

Because of the rules and precedents of the Senate this strategy had eventually to be abandoned. The supporters of the Douglas position were willing to fall back a step at a time, but could not agree to support a weaker provision when it was presented against a stronger position. They could vote for the Douglas motion as against the Knowland motion. They could vote for the Douglas or the Knowland motion as against the Anderson-Aiken motion to strike out Section III. They could not vote for the Douglas or the Knowland motion if either were to lie against Section III.

The parliamentary situation made it impossible to carry out their strategy. Once the Douglas motion was defeated there was no way in which the Knowland motion could be made to lie against the Anderson motion to strike Section III. The issue would have been between the Knowland motion and Section III, in which case the liberal Democrats and some Republicans would have felt compelled to vote against the Knowland motion. This was true because of the precedent that a motion to strike is only voted on after the perfecting amendments to the basic provisions of a section have been disposed of. Efforts to substitute a weaker provision for the existing Section III were therefore abandoned at this stage. It was decided to let the vote come on the Anderson motion to strike, and to offer a revised Section III at a later stage, preferably following a victory on some substantive issue.

The Moving Target. Yet another example of the effect of the rules of the Senate on the substance of legislation may be seen in the successive revisions of the jury trial amendment. It is a cardinal principle of most parliamentary procedures that once a motion is offered it belongs to the full body and not to the mover. The parliamentary body determines what action should be taken, *i.e.*, to amend, commit, refer, etc. This is not true of the Senate of the United States. An amendment, even after it is offered, belongs to the mover of the amendment and until such time as the yeas and nays have been ordered, he may amend it, revise it, or change it as he sees fit. In this fashion the jury trial amendment was changed almost from day to day, not by any vote of the Senate but by offering or acceptance of revisions on the part of its mover, Senator O'Mahoney. As Senator Douglas said on the floor, the opponents of the jury trial amendment were "shooting at a moving target." The initial point at issue was the definition of the criminal contempts to which a jury trial would be made applicable —an exceedingly intricate technical question.

The first version met strenuous objection. The distinction it drew between civil and criminal contempt was whether or not questions of fact were at issue. As any good defense lawyer could raise a question of fact, the effect of this version was to allow a jury trial in all contempt cases.

The second version attempted to distinguish between civil and criminal contempt on the basis of whether or not the act committed was a crime. The traditional distinction between the two types of contempt, often hard to draw in practice, turns on whether the action of the court is for the purpose of compelling compliance with a previous court order, or for the purpose of punishment for failure to carry out the order. Thus in a voting case, a local registrar could be held in contempt for failing to carry out the court's order, but so long as he could remove that contempt by compliance with the order it would be civil contempt. Once the day for election had arrived and passed, and the defendant was no longer able to remove his contempt by compliance, then the contempt would be criminal, for the court could send him to jail or impose a fine only for the purpose of punishment. Since almost all obstructive actions connected with voting in federal elections are criminal, the effect of the second version was to grant a jury trial in contempt cases arising from interferences with voting.

In the third version of the O'Mahoney amendment the orthodox distinction was finally drawn between civil and criminal contempt. In an attempt to gain more widespread support for it, however, the amendment was broadened to apply not only to voting cases but to all contempt actions under federal law. At least 40 other statutes were affected, but primarily this revision was aimed at gaining labor support, particularly from the Railroad Brotherhoods and the United Mine Workers who were sensitive about past abuses of labor injunctions and who, in turn, influenced a number of key votes in the Senate. This provision was a most radical departure from existing procedures. Like the second version, it was merely accepted on the floor by Senator O'Mahoney, and no vote was taken on the question of substituting it for the previous version.

At this stage the question of passage of a jury trial amendment was touch and go. Those opposed to it still appeared to be in the majority. Finally, a fourth version was offered to meet the complaints over the absence of Negroes from Southern juries, and so to pick up a few more votes. Federal law sets certain standards for service on Federal juries, but also provides that no one may serve on a federal jury who is incompetent to serve on the grand or petit jury under the laws of his state. As one must be a voter or qualified elector in Texas, Arkansas, Mississippi, South Carolina, and the Parish of New Orleans in order to be eligible to serve on a local grand or petit jury, and as Negroes are largely excluded from voting in these states, this means that by law Negroes are also excluded from federal jury service there. The fourth version, offered by Senator Church, repealed the provisions of the United States Code which excluded those from federal jury service who could not meet state qualifications. The effect of this final version was to provide the margin of strength to pass the jury trial amendment. However, as Negroes are excluded from jury service in other Southern states, in practice and by other means, it is doubtful that this change will have much practical effect.

The right to revise and modify an amendment at the will of its sponsor played a large part in attaching a jury trial amendment to the bill, for had the vote come on the first, second, or possibly the third version, it appears fairly certain that the amendment would have been defeated; and that, once defeated, the forces favoring it could not have recovered enough strength to pass even a greatly modified new amendment.

Unanimous Consent. The final instance in which parliamentary practice affected the substance of the bill occurred following the jury trial amendment vote and prior to the vote on the remaining amendments. Senator Russell referred to it in a speech on August 30, after the bill had passed, in which he justified and explained the failure of Southern Senators to filibuster the bill and took great credit for watering it down. He had this to say on the floor:

When we had arrived at this particular stage of the proceedings in the Senate I happened to learn that a determined effort would be made to revive some of the provisions of Part III that had been stricken from the bill. The new amendment appeared harmless on its face, but if it had been adopted it would have placed the stamp of congressional approval on the erroneous, if not infamous, decision of the Supreme Court requiring the mixing of the children in the public schools without regard to the wishes of the parents of either race. We, therefore, quickly closed the bill to amendments in order to assure that none of the victories that we had gained would be snatched from us.

What happened was that a bi-partisan group determined to try to revive a part of the Section III previously stricken. Before they could offer their amendment a unanimous consent agreement was reached, at a time when there was general commotion on the floor, limiting further proceedings to those amendments which had already been offered and printed and confining the time for debate to 30 minutes on each amendment. Senator Douglas was within minutes of offering the revised Section III amendment and was prevented from doing so by Senator Johnson's unanimous consent request which was made and agreed to at a time of confusion when his request could not be heard in the chamber. Apparently a gentlemen's agreement had also been reached that all further amendments would be voted down by voice vote and without a roll call.

VI. The Filibuster: A Paper Tiger?

One final point should be made concerning the effect of the rules of the Senate on the substance of the civil rights bill. A number of highly competent journalists who were not close to the debate, or who have since been misled by the interpretations placed on it by some, have asserted that the absence of a filibuster at any stage in the proceedings on the floor represented a willingness on the part of the Southern opponents to accommodate themselves at least to the voting rights provisions of the bill. A closer view leads to the opposite conclusion, that the passage of the bill represents no compromise or accommodation on the part of the Deep South Senators at all. Rather, the failure to filibuster may be regarded as a carefully calculated decision to avoid consequences which would have been worse, from the Southern point of view, than those of the bill as it passed the Senate.

Throughout the debate, and preceding the votes on Section III and the jury trial amendment, the threat of a filibuster was used to gain support for both these amendments. Senator Russell has since frankly admitted what many on the inside felt sure of at the time, namely, that the South would not filibuster and that the thread of doing so was more effective than the reality would have been. Notwithstanding the arguments made earlier in the year, that no meaningful civil rights bill could be passed unless Rule XXII was changed, the filibuster, after the Rule XXII fight and after the bill was placed on the calendar became a paper tiger. In retrospect it seems clear that the Southerners did not dare to use it because they feared the results would be the loss of Rule XXII and the passage of a much stronger bill than was passed. They were sufficiently convinced that a filibuster would so outrage the country and the Senate that they had more to lose than to gain by its use. This accounts for the severe condemnation of Senator Thurmond by his Southern colleagues following his 24-hour "talkathon."

The Southern group decided, instead, to attempt to filibuster the bill to death in committee. In this they were successful; they could have kept it throttled there indefinitely. However, as a result of the great increase in votes for a change in Rule XXII and the vote to place the bill on the calendar, they knew they could not successfully transfer that filibuster to the floor. In Senator Russell's words:

In years gone by, it has been a great source of pride to me that our group was able to defeat bills of this nature when they were forced to the consideration of the Senate. In the case of H.R. 6127 we were from the outset faced with greater odds than ever before. . . .

There was not a man among us who was not willing to speak against this iniquitous bill until he dropped in his tracks. We would have done so, but for the conviction, growing out of our knowledge of the Senate and the experience of many years in this body, that a filibuster was certain to make a bad bill infinitely worse. . . .

Our group held numerous meetings and the wisdom of launching a filibuster was often discussed. All members of the group were living with the problem from day to day, defending the things dearest to our heart while under heavy fire. At no time did any member of our group declare in any of our meetings that it was his belief that a filibuster was advisable, much less that one could be successfully waged. The contrary view was expressed on innumerable occasions. . . .

They therefore decided to avoid a filibuster while using the threat of it to gain their points. They decided also to keep debate relevant, and with one or two very glaring exceptions this was done. With the wholehearted support of Senator Johnson, the Democratic leader, they then pressed for the two basic amendments which, from their point of view, would gain the least offensive result. In this, too, they were successful. They took this course not from any desire for accommodation or willingness to compromise but because a different course would, from the Southern position, "make a bad bill infinitely worse."

Although the filibuster was not used, the existence of Rule XXII made it still possible for Senator Russell to claim that:

. . . the fact that we were able to confine the Federal activities to the field of voting and keep the withering hand of the Federal Government out of our schools and social order is to me, as I look back over the years, the sweetest victory of my 25 years as a Senator from the State of Georgia.

Because of the filibuster rule, the unwillingness of some professed supporters of civil rights to see that the South dared not filibuster at this time, the consequent surrender to the mere threat of its use, and the skillful tactics of Senators Russell and Johnson, the bill as passed by the Senate was largely a victory for the forces of segregation. As civil rights proponents saw it, all their sweat and struggle to overcome the parliamentary obstacles had led to a bill which, except for a few minor gains, was almost form without substance. They took what consolation they could in watching the House revise it enough to make it a modest forward step.

5   *The Seniority System in Congress*
GEORGE GOODWIN

The seniority system ordinarily rates no more than two or three pages in books devoted to Congress. There is likely to be a brief description and a weighing of the arguments, pro and con, followed generally by the conclusion that the system is a poor one; occasionally an author will defend it stoutly. Regardless of the conclusions, the analyses are rarely thorough. This article attempts to fill a gap in the literature on Congress by describing and analyzing various aspects of its seniority system.

It is well to remember at the outset that very few human institutions ignore seniority entirely. Champ Clark, in his autobiography, noted that it is observed in all the affairs of life:

No sane man would for one moment think of making a graduate from West Point a full general, or one from Annapolis an admiral, or one from any university or college chief of a great newspaper, magazine or business house. A priest or a preacher who has just taken orders is not immediately made a bishop, archbishop or cardinal. In every walk of life "men must tarry at Jericho till their beards are grown."

Yet, as George Galloway states, "in no other place, perhaps, does seniority or length of service carry so much weight as it does in the Congress of the United States." It is more than a means of choosing committee chairmen; it is a means of assigning members to committees, of choosing subcommittee chairmen and conference committee members. It affects the deference shown legislators on the floor, the assignment of office space, even invitations to dinners. In short, "it is a spirit pervading the total behavior of Congress." Its significance for constituencies was expressed by Senator Byrd, who, when he was persuaded to run again for his seat, explained that "seniority of serv-

From George Goodwin, Jr., *The American Political Science Review* (June 1959, pp. 412-436), The American Political Science Association, Washington.

ice and committee rank have importance over and above the capabilities of the members." The system seems absolute in the assignment of office space, and nearly absolute in the choice of committee chairmen. Yet in other areas, it is often bypassed to a surprising degree. Our concern here is seniority as it relates to the standing committees of Congress.

I. WORKING RULES

As might be expected, seniority is not mentioned in the House or Senate rules, although it has drastically changed their effect. Senate Rule XXIV states simply, "in the appointment of standing committees, the Senate, unless otherwise ordered, shall proceed by ballot to appoint severally the chairmen of each committee, and then by one ballot, the other members necessary to complete the same." House Rule X reads, in part, "at the commencement of each Congress, the House shall elect as chairman of each standing committee one of the members thereof. . . . All vacancies in the standing committees of the House shall be filled by election by the House."

A distinction should be made between Congressional and committee seniority. Taking the former first, senators are ranked according to the length of uninterrupted service, dating in most cases from the opening day of the Congress to which they are elected. If they are elected or appointed to fill an unexpired term, different provisions prevail. The appointee starts accumulating seniority on the date on which a governor certifies his appointment. If a special election has been held, however, seniority commences on the day on which the new senator takes the oath of office, if the Senate is in session; or if it is not in session, then on the day after the election. Those entering on the same day are listed alphabetically, with the same rank number. House procedure is similar, except that greater credit is given for non-consecutive service. Those with three non-consecutive terms are ranked above those with two consecutive terms, for example. Congressional seniority is followed on social occasions, in the allocation of office space, and in making assignments to committees.

Committee seniority is established by consecutive service on a given committee. If two or more members go on a committee at the same time, note is taken of previous political experience, preference being given to former senators, to former representatives, and finally to former governors. If previous political experience is equal, they are likely to be ranked alphabetically; in the House they may draw lots.[1]

When the committee party ratio changes because of a change in the party ratio of the house, members of the minority party with the least seniority may thereby lose their committee assignments. Otherwise the right to remain on a committee and to move up the ladder is generally unquestioned. A study of the committee assignments of Senate party bolters since 1925 shows only two examples of removal from a committee regardless of seniority (Frazier in 1925 and More in 1953) and four examples of members remaining on their committees but losing seniority (Ladd, Brookhart, Frazier, and LaFollette in 1925). In all other cases, including those of 1948 when Senator Eastland supported the Dixiecrats and Senator Taylor ran on the Progressive ticket, no retaliatory committee action was taken.

If a ranking member leaves a vacancy because of transfer to another committee or retirement from Congress, all his fellow party members on the committee who were beneath him move up in rank. The career of Representative Sabath, to cite a case, gives a unique illustration of what can be accomplished by transfer, if it is combined with longevity. He entered Congress in 1907, transferred to the Rules Committee in 1929, after 22 years of service, became its chairman in 1939 after another ten years, and remained the ranking Democrat on the Committee for 13 more years.

A member who is defeated or who fails to run, and later returns to Congress again, loses his congressional and his committee seniority. He is likely, however, to receive more important committee assignments than the average freshman. Alben Barkley, for example, after a tour of duty as Vice President, was reassigned to his former committees, Finance and Foreign Relations.

In short, to become a chairman, a legislator must remain continuously on a given committee longer than any other fellow party member, and be of the majority party. It is not uncommon to find men on a given committee of higher House and Senate rank than the committee chairman. This is partly a matter of luck and partly a feeling on the part of some that it is better to be second or third on an im-

[1] So John M. Vorys of Ohio lost the draw to Robert B. Chiperfield of Illinois in 1939 when both were assigned as Republican freshmen to the House Foreign Affairs Committee. Twenty years later, when Vorys retired, though he had been for most of that period the Republican mainstay on the Committee, he was still only second ranking minority member—Chiperfield's district was as safe as his, and the seniority order once established was not disturbed.

portant committee than chairman of a minor one. In the 85th Congress, for example, fourteen Democratic senators who were not chairmen had seen greater service in the upper house than Senator Hennings, the Rules Committee chairman, and sixty-one Democratic representatives who were not chairmen had seen greater service in the lower house than Congressman Burleson, chairman of the Committee on House Administration. But other members will stay with an early assignment, preferring to be bigger fish in smaller ponds.

Although they have no power to determine who shall be committee chairmen, party committees-on-committees in the House and Senate make important decisions on initial committee assignments and transfers from one committee to another. There is great variety in these committees, as can be seen from Table I, which describes the situation prevailing in the 85th Congress (1957-1958). House committee-on-committee members are chosen in a way that would seem to make them less subject to party leadership control than Senate members; however, there is no doubt that the House party leaders

TABLE I. *Committees-on-Committees in the 85th Congress*

No. of Members	Senate Democrats	Senate Republicans	House Democrats	House Republicans
	15	23	15	38
How Chosen	By Floor Leader (Johnson*) called Steering Committee	By Conference Chairman (Saltonstall) with Conference approval	Democratic members of Ways & Means, *ex officiis*, who are chosen by Democratic Caucus	Each State Republican delegation chooses one member, with as many votes as state has Republican Congressmen
Chairman	Floor Leader (Johnson*)	(Bricker) designated by Conference Chairman	Ranking Democrat on Ways & Means (Cooper, followed in '58 by Mills)	Floor Leader (Martin*)

*Johnson was replaced by Senator Mike Mansfield in 1961. Joseph Martin was replaced by Charles Halleck in 1959, and Halleck was replaced by Gerald Ford in 1965.—Ed.

can influence the appointment of these members when they find it advisable.

In working out the "giant jig saw puzzle" of committee assignments certain limitations are generally observed by these committees-on-committees. They must, of course, be guided by the number of vacancies and by the number of applications for transfer. Care is taken to attain geographical distribution, if not balance.[2] Attention is paid to group desires[3] and to the experience and training of individual legislators. And balance among the various factions of the party is sought. Beyond these more or less objective factors, being in the good graces of the party leader is certainly important in getting on a major committee.

The House Republican Floor Leader presides over his party's committee-on-committees, and, while Speaker (or, in the 80th and 83rd Congresses, Floor Leader) Rayburn does not preside, "his presence is felt in the deliberations." Important positions are most likely to go to those who display party regularity or, at least, support for the party leader, as the following ditty tells:

> I love Speaker Rayburn, his heart is so warm,
> And if I love him he'll do me no harm.
> So I shan't sass the Speaker one least little bitty,
> And then I'll wind up on a major committee.

This party control, which is expected in the more tightly knit House, is also found, though perhaps to a lesser degree, among the Senate Democrats. The so-called "Johnson Rule," initiated in 1953 [when President Johnson became Democratic majority leader], allows for departures from seniority in making appointments and, in so doing, leaves room for the application of less automatic criteria. According to the rule, no Senate Democrat is entitled to a second top committee assignment until every party member, no matter how junior, has one top position.

For all the committees-on-committees "it is handy to have the seniority system to pull them out of a dilemma"; but seniority has not been a controlling factor in the making of initial appointments and transfer, except among the Senate Republicans. Until the 86th

[2] In the Senate, for example, there may not be two senators of the same party from the same state on any committee, a practice that is convenient on other grounds, since it eliminates what otherwise might be a source of intrastate jurisdictional disputes between the two senators.

[3] Farm state representatives dominate the agriculture committees, for example, and only lawyers are seated on the judiciary committees.

Congress this group, however, placed the utmost emphasis on making the appointment process entirely automatic. Seniority was carefully measured, previous government service weighed and, if all else failed, the alphabet was resorted to in order to solve the committee assignment problem on an impersonal basis. In 1959, the Senate Republicans moved far in the direction of the "Johnson Rule," after considerable discussion in the Policy Committee and the Committee on Committees.

In making initial appointments and transfers there is room for choice and for favoritism, but there is almost no room for this in choosing committee chairmen. Becoming a chairman is a matter of party luck and of individual endurance. Once a member becomes a committee chairman, nothing but a change of party control or removal from the Congress is at all likely to force a change.[4] Chairmen have great powers. They subdivide the work of the committees, arrange the agenda and the work schedule, control the staff, preside over committee meetings, manage floor debate, and dominate conference committee proceedings, to mention only their more obvious activities.

Seniority also plays a part in the appointment of conference committee members and subcommittee chairmen. It is difficult to generalize about the former, because there is great variety in practice: but if the legislation involved is important, the chairmen of the committees which handled the bill originally, the ranking minority members and other senior members, will in all likelihood make up the conference committee.

Subcommittee chairmen are generally the senior members of the majority party on a given committee. In the 85th Congress, for example, every senior member had his own subcommittee on 12 of the 34 committees (three had no standing subcommittees at all). On 19 committees, one or more of the senior members of the majority party was passed over in favor of a junior. In most cases a reason for this variance from seniority was obvious. The member, for example, may have been a party leader or the chairman of another committee. Yet in a number of instances there was no evident "automatic" reason

[4] The voluntary abdication, early in 1959, of Senator Theodore F. Green of Rhode Island, then well into his nineties, as chairman of the Foreign Relations Committee, in order to make room for J. William Fulbright of Arkansas in that post, was a startling exception widely hailed as a tribute to Johnson's persuasive powers. Thomas S. Gordon of the House Foreign Affairs Committee relinquished his chairmanship during the 85th Congress on account of ill health.

for ignoring seniority. (One can guess at the reason why House Education and Labor Chairman Barden of North Carolina passed over Representative Adam Clayton Powell in favor of more junior members.)

II. Historical Development

Historians of the House and Senate are not entirely clear as to when the seniority system, as we now know it, developed. This is not surprising, since it is a custom enforced by opinion, rather than by written rules. Seniority undoubtedly evolved first in the Senate, for this body was reluctant to give its presiding officer, the Vice President, the appointment power. He was thrust upon them by the Constitution, not chosen by the senators, and was not treated as a member of the Senate. Appointment power was vested in the president *pro tem* and in the majority leader, from time to time; but apparently the seniority system became firmly established with the development of standing rather than select committees, and with the crisis of the Mexican War. Since then, although there is no definitive listing, at least five departures from the seniority rule in choosing or displacing committee chairmen apparently have occurred in the Senate. In 1859 Stephen A. Douglas was denied the chairmanship of the Committee on Territories; in 1871 Charles Sumner, the chairmanship of the Committee on Interstate Commerce; in 1913 Benjamin R. Tillman, the chairmanship of the Appropriations Committee; in 1924 Albert Cummins, the chairmanship of the Agriculture Committee; and in 1925 Edwin F. Ladd, the Committee on Public Lands.

In the House the power of making committee appointments evidently gravitated early to the Speaker, who, unlike the Vice President, was a member and the choice of his peers. It remained there until the revolt against Speaker Cannon in 1910 and 1911, when the seniority system took full hold. Even prior to this, however, seniority was a factor to be taken carefully into consideration. In carrying out the complex task of making committee assignments, the Speaker inevitably sought to regularize his work. One study, for example, notes that seniority prevailed in four-fifths of Cannon's appointments during the 58th through the 61st Congresses.

In 1910, insurgent Republicans, working with Democrats, managed to take away many of the Speaker's powers, including the appointment of committee members and chairmen. Congressman Norris proposed that this power be given to a newly constituted

Rules Committee which would represent the entire country and every interest in the country, and which would not include the Speaker. The Democrats, however, would not go along, and the system as we know it today developed instead.

Norris felt that "committee assignments were the rawhide used to promote party subserviency and to crush any spirt of independence." He was willing to take any lessening of the Speaker's powers on which he could reach agreement with the House Democrats, but he regretted the fact that he could not get support for his proposed committee on committees. Still unrepentant, he wrote in 1944, "If we had adopted this rule, as I originally proposed it and as agreed to by all the Insurgents, the seniority rule would not be here to trouble us now."

III. The Pros and Cons of Seniority

The debate over the seniority system generally centers on the choice of committee chairmen. The favorable arguments stress the harmony which results from the system, the emphasis which it places on experience, and the lack of any more suitable alternative. The unfavorable arguments stress the effect of the system on party responsibility and Presidential leadership, the lack of any dependable relation between seniority and qualified leadership, and the fact that the committee leaders in Congress are by no means representative of many of the dominant interests either in the party or in the nation.

The most telling argument of the proponents of seniority is that the system promotes legislative harmony. It prevents hurt feelings on the part of those passed over in the struggle for appointment, and incidentally, it keeps pressure groups out of this struggle. As a result, it helps to create a more cooperative atmosphere, both in the legislative body as a whole, and on the various committees. Committees can act as more of a unit, and in a more nonpartisan manner. Roland Young makes this point in this fashion:

The adjustment of rival claims must precede the adjustment of major conflicts without being permitted to divert attention for long from the larger task at hand. Some harmony within the legislature—including agreement on the location of internal authority—must exist before the legislature can itself promote harmony between conflicting groups.

Senator Barkley spoke in similar terms, when he opposed the Morse-Lehman attempt to prevent Senator Eastland from becoming Judiciary Chairman in 1956:

The element of favoritism would come into play, and there would be log-rolling and electioneering for the votes of the committee members by those who wanted to be committee chairmen . . . Jealousies, ambitions, and all the frailties of human nature would crop out in the electioneering methods of men who wanted to be chairmen of committees.

Another argument of the proponents is that the system produces experienced chairmen—experienced both in the subject matter of the committee on which they have served so long, and in legislative procedure. They may also be better acquainted with the officials at working levels in the executive branch with whom they have to deal than the more transient department heads, who come and go with changes of Presidents. Robert Luce suggests that "though not the only factor in deciding merit, experience is the most important factor."

Finally, the proponents argue that the system is better than the alternatives, which range all the way from the even more arbitrary automatic proposals once made that the chairman be the member of the committee from the most Northern state, to one in which the President is responsible for the appointments. They take the essentially conservative position that there is no reason to change from a system that is working satisfactorily to a system about which the results are largely unknown. Some wonder if the system has not turned out to be a "rather handy scapegoat for Congressional inertia."

People on both sides of the fence tend to agree that when and if Americans turn toward party responsibility, "seniority will be an early casualty." The proponents of seniority, as one might expect, emphasize the harmonizing, rather than the issue-defining role of political parties, while the most outspoken critics of seniority favor responsible parties. They emphasize the diffusion of leadership among the 36 standing committees of Congress,[5] and the fact that there is no adequate way of integrating their various programs. In fact, they hold, the people most likely to become chairmen, the people from one-party constituencies, are the ones most likely to be out of tune with the party's program:

A chairmanship, after all, is the position of a quarterback on a football team. It should not be given to someone who refuses to be part of the team or who might even carry the ball across the wrong goal line.

[5] Two new standing committees were created by the 86th Congress, bringing the total to 36. These are the Senate Committee on Astronautical and Space Sciences and the House Committee on Science and Astronautics.

The system, the critics argue, is no guarantee that chairmen will be well qualified. A hardy constitution and the ability to get re-elected in the home district do not necessarily fit a man to preside over committee meetings or to defend committee reports on the floor. If the system puts so much emphasis on experience, why, they ask, is a man who leaves to take an administrative post, but who returns later to Congress, given little or no credit for his previous experience? There have been examples, also, of chairmen who were too senile to be effective. When Senator Capper became chairman of the Agriculture Committee he could neither make himself understood, nor understand others. "The seniority principle is followed mainly because the seniors are pleased with themselves and see no sufficient reason for consigning their powers to others."[6]

Finally, the critics suggest that the system produces a large number of chairmen who are representative of only one element of the party, and that, generally, a minority element. They represent "stagnant" districts made safe by restrictions on voting, by a one-party monopoly, by the ascendency of a major interest group, or by an effective rural or urban political machine. Thus, the leaders of Congress, produced by the seniority system, are almost guaranteed to oppose the President, regardless of party, and a new non-constitutional dimension is added to our constitutional system of separation of powers.

IV. Some Effects of the Seniority System

Although it is impossible to prove the correctness of many of these appraisals of the seniority system, some can be analyzed statistically. Charges have been made, for example, that chairmen are approaching senility, that certain sections enjoy a disproportionate share of the chairmanships, that chairmen come from districts which are socially and politically stagnant, and that they vote against their party and the President a great percentage of the time.

The statistics concerning seniority in this section cover the years 1947 through 1958. This period from the 80th through the 85th Congress is a logical one to take for analysis, for the committee pattern has remained essentially unchanged since 1947 when the Legislative Reorganization Act cut the total number of committees from

[6] This was phrased differently to the author by Senator Saltonstall, as follows, "The longer I stay in Washington, the more sympathetic I become with the system."

80 to 34. The period includes two Republican Congresses (80th and 83rd) and four Democratic Congresses. There were a total of 60 Democratic and 30 Republican chairmen in the Senate; 76 Democratic and 38 Republican chairmen in the House of Representatives, counting each chairmanship for each Congress separately; altogether, 114 individuals occupied these 34 places during the time covered.

It is certainly true that chairmen are older than their colleagues, although perhaps not as markedly so as is commonly believed. The spread, greater in the House than in the Senate, averages 11 years in the former and six in the latter. Table II shows the age distribution of all chairmen at the commencement of each of the six Congresses studied. A greater percentage of Senate chairmen have been in their fifties than in any other ten-year period, while a greater percentage of House chairmen have been in their sixties. The youngest chairmen in the period studied were Representative Velde (42) and Senator McCarthy (43), both in the Republican 83rd Congress. The oldest chairmen, both Democrats, were Representative Doughton (87) in the 82nd Congress and Senator Green (89) at the commencement of the 85th Congress.

It is also true that the South provides a large percentage of the chairmen when the Democrats are in control, as the Middle West does when the Republicans are in control. . . . [Table III] Taking both parties together each of the four regions has had a reasonably equal number of chairmen, except for the West, which has produced few House chairmen. However, over half the Democratic chairmen from the House and the Senate have come from the South, and over half the Republican chairmen from the Midwest.

TABLE II. *Age Distribution of House and Senate Committee Chairmen*

Age Range	House		Senate	
	Number	Per Cent	Number	Per Cent
40-49	9	8	6	7
50-59	32	28	29	32
60-69	43	38	28	31
70-79	24	21	20	22
80-89	6	5	7	8
	114	100	90	100

TABLE III.   *Percentage Distribution of Committee Chairmen by Geographical Regions*

	Senate			House		
	Democrats and Republicans	Dems.	Reps.	Democrats and Republicans	Dems.	Reps.
East	20	12	37	33	17	31
Midwest	19	2	53	33	17	66
South	36	53	0	41	62	0
West	25	33	10	4	4	3
	100	100	100	100	100	100

There are a number of ways of attempting, very roughly, to identify the more "stagnant" states to see if they tend to produce the greatest percentage of chairmen. Presumably, in our urban-industrial society, rural states and states with low total personal income should fall into this category. Furthermore, in this two-party country, one-party states and states with low voter turnout should also fall into this category.

Table IV relates the degree of urbanism of the states, grouped in quartiles, to the percentages of committee chairmen from the states so grouped, during the period under study. The Senate, particularly under Democratic control, has drawn its chairmen from the more rural states. The 24 least urban states have had 67 per cent of the Democratic and 40 per cent of the Republican chairmen. In sharp contrast, the House chairmen have tended to come from more urban states, but with a similar differential between the two parties. The 24 most urban states have produced 79 per cent of the Republican and 43 per cent of the Democratic chairmen. The House results are very different, however, when the analysis is made by congressional districts instead of states.[7]

Another test of the social and economic characteristics of the states which have produced chairmen is found in Table V. The states

[7] This perhaps more meaningful approach is to divide the 435 Congressional districts as nearly as possible into four quartiles. According to this breakdown, made for the 85th Congress only, the 109 most urban districts produced 21 per cent of the House chairmen, and 108 next most urban produced 5 per cent, the 110 next most urban 16 per cent, and the 108 least urban 58 per cent. See *Congressional Quarterly*, 1956, p. 790, for raw data.

TABLE IV. *Percentage Distribution of Chairmen from States Grouped According to Degree of Urbanism*

| | Senate | | | House | | |
	Democrats and Republicans	Dems.	Reps.	Democrats and Republicans	Dems.	Reps.
1st Quartile	11	5	23	46	31	76
2d Quartile	31	28	37	9	12	3
3d Quartile	25	28	17	21	21	21
4th Quartile	33	39	23	24	36	0
	100	100	100	100	100	100

TABLE V. *Percentage Distribution of Chairmen from States Grouped by Total Personal Income**

| | Senate | | | House | | |
	Democrats and Republicans	Dems.	Reps.	Democrats and Republicans	Dems.	Reps.
1st Quartile	17	5	40	53	41	80
2d Quartile	18	27	0	37	51	7
3d Quartile	40	48	23	10	8	13
4th Quartile	25	21	37	0	0	0
	100	100	100	100	100	100

* Department of Commerce, *Survey of Current Business,* August, 1957, p. 8. Less recent total income figures make relatively little difference in the grouping of the states into quartiles so that it seems justifiable to use the 1956 figures for the entire period. The first quartile includes states which had between 2.16 and 11.96 per cent of the total national income, the second quartile between 1.23 and 2.15 per cent, the third between .51 and 1.22 per cent and the 4th between .18 and 50 per cent.

are divided into quartiles according to total personal income for 1956. In the Senate, in line with the general criticism of seniority, 65 per cent of the chairmen of both parties have come from the 24 states with the lowest income. In the House, on the other hand, more than half of the chairmen have come from the 12 states with the highest income.

Turning to more clearly political classifications, Table VI di-

TABLE VI. *Percentage Distribution of Chairmen from States Grouped by Their Party Systems*

	Senate			House		
	Democrats and Republicans	Dems.	Reps.	Democrats and Republicans	Dems.	Reps.
1-Party Modified	33	47	7	21	32	0
1-Party	17	5	40	28	33	18
2-Party	50	48	53	51	35	82
	100	100	100	100	100	100

vides the states into those with one-party (10), with modified one-party (12), and with two-party systems (26). Almost exactly half of the House and Senate chairmen have come from two-party states, the remaining half being divided fairly evenly between one-party and modified one-party states. There are marked party differences, however, the most obvious being the fact that a greater percentage of Republicans come from two-party states. This is particularly noticeable in the House.[8]

A final test to see if chairmen tend to come from the more "stagnant" states, as is so often claimed, is to divide the states into quartiles according to the percentage of the adult population voting in the 1956 election, and relate this classification to the distribution of chairmen. The results are presented in Table VII. Because of the difficulty of obtaining data for previous elections, and the considerable variations in turnout over the years, this analysis was made for the 85th Congress only. A fairly even division among the four quartiles appears when both parties are combined, but a marked difference shows up again between the two parties. A considerable

[8] Another way to look at party strength is to determine what percentage of the members of Congress come from safe districts (districts which give them 60 per cent or more of the 2-party vote), fighting districts (districts which gave them between 55 and 59.9 per cent of their vote) and doubtful districts (those which gave them less than 55 per cent of their vote in the most recent election). Data for the 85th Congress show, as might be expected, that there are more safe House than Senate districts. Seventy-one per cent of House chairmen or ranking minority members have come from safe districts, while the comparable figure for the Senate is 44 per cent. More Democrats than Republicans have come fom safe districts.

TABLE VII. *Percentage Distribution of Chairmen and Ranking Republican Committee Members from States Grouped according to Voting Percentage of Population, 85th Congress*

	House			Senate		
	Democrats and Republicans	Dems.	Reps.	Democrats and Republicans	Dems.	Reps.
1st Quartile	20	20	20	24	11	37
2d Quartile	17	13	20	16	5	26
3d Quartile	33	7	60	31	26	37
4th Quartile	30	60	0	29	58	0
	100	100	100	100	100	100

majority of Democratic House and Senate chairmen come from the 12 states with the lowest voter participation, nearly all of them Southern.

Now, turning to voting records, Figure 1 charts the chairmen's performance in voting with the rest of their party. A "party unity" score is used, which indicates the percentage of times that a member votes in agreement with a majority of his party when a majority of the other party votes in opposition. The graphs compare the average party unity scores of the chairmen, of all members, and of the floor leader of the majority party in the Senate and House. They also make these comparisons within the Democratic and Republican parties. When a party is not in control of a given Congress, the score of the ranking minority members of the committees is given. The chairmen's score is not far out of line with the average party member's score. It averages 3 per cent below in the Senate and 6 per cent below in the House. In the Republican-controlled 80th and 83rd Congresses, the House chairmen actually had a party unity score higher than the member's average.

The usual view is that the chairmen's party unity score would be higher if these key Congressional leaders were chosen by the party leaders, as is the practice in a majority of state legislatures. Yet even under the seniority rule, the average is not so much lower than the score of the party leader as is commonly supposed. The chairmen's average is 16 per cent lower than that of the party leader in the

Senate

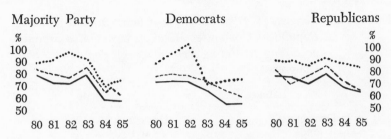

Majority Party   Democrats   Republicans

House of Representatives

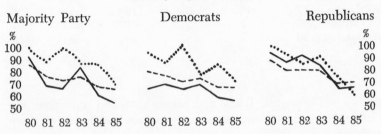

Majority Party   Democrats   Republicans

Fig. 1. Party Unity Score for Chairmen (or Ranking Minority Members) Compared with Score for Party Members and for Floor Leader, 80th-85th Congresses.*

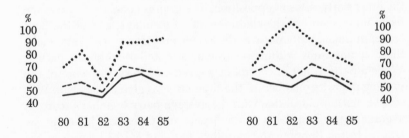

Fig. 2. Presidential Support by Members of the President's Party.*

Key ———— Chairmen's (or ranking members') presidential support score

-------- Presidential support average of all members of President's party

. . . . . . Presidential support score for President's floor leaders

* Data for these charts are taken from the appropriate volumes of *Congressional Quarterly.*

House and 12 per cent lower in the Senate.[9] The Congressional floor leaders, however, often have relatively low unit scores. Party leaders, for example, voted on an average of 8 per cent below the highest individual party unity score in the House and 10 per cent below in the Senate. Well over half the chairmen are close to the top in party unity. Their average, however, is pulled down by the party mavericks who by seniority win one or two chairmanships in most Congresses.

Voting records also lend themselves to analysis of the degree of support that party chairmen, or ranking minority members, have accorded their President. Figure 2 compares the support given the President by the chairmen or ranking committee members of his party, by all the members of his party and by his party leaders in the House and Senate.[10] The chairmen's or ranking members' score is not far below the average party member's score. It averages 4 per cent below in the House and 5 per cent in the Senate. The House chairmen's, or ranking member's, score averages 24 per cent below that of the floor leader, while the gap in the Senate is 21 per cent.

In conclusion, a comparison should be made between the seniority system as it operates in the House and as it operates in the Senate, as well as a comparison of its operation under Democrats and Republicans. Turning first to its operation in the two houses, the analysis above shows some interesting similarities. The House and the Senate are about equally likely to get Southern committee chairmen, and voting participation in the states furnishing chairmen and ranking Republican committee members in the 1956 election showed a remarkably similar pattern. Further, there is a close similarity in the House and Senate party system patterns with 50 per cent of the Senate and 51 per cent of the House chairmen being chosen from two-party states.

However, House chairmen come from more urban states (46 per cent from the most urban quartile while only 11 per cent of the Senate chairmen came from these states) and from states with higher total personal incomes (with 53 per cent from the first quartile com-

[9] This quite obviously does not give the full measure of a chairman's relationship to his party's stand. He can do a great deal in his committee to keep things he does not like from coming to a vote on the floor.

[10] During the 80th Congress there was a Democratic President and a Republican Congress; during the 81st and 82nd both President and Congress were Democratic; during the 83rd both President and Congress were Republican, and during the 84th and 85th there was a Republican President and a Democratic Congress.

pared to 17 per cent for the Senate). It is tempting to hazard a guess, therefore, that House chairmen, with a generally more urban-industrial background, should tend to be more closely aligned with their party and with a President of their party. The statistics presented on the voting records of chairmen fail to show this conclusively, however.[11] House chairmen and ranking members voted on an average 2.8 per cent more with their President than did Senate chairmen (60.8 per cent compared to 58.0 per cent for the Senate), but Senate chairmen voted, on the average, .7 per cent more with their party than did House chairmen (79.2 per cent compared to 78.5 per cent).

More marked differences show up in the backgrounds of the chairmen as between the two parties than as between the House and Senate chairmen; and a prediction of probable voting behavior based on these backgrounds is borne out. Democratic chairmen come from states which are more Southern and more rural, which have lower incomes, which tend more strongly to one-partyism and which have a lower voter turnout. It might be expected, consequently, that a greater percentage of Democratic chairmen would be out of line with their party and their President. In the period studied Senate Republican committee leaders supported their President 22.0 percent more often than Democratic committee leaders supported theirs (70.7 per cent as compared to 48.7 per cent). They also showed slightly greater party unity than the Democrats (77.8 per cent as compared to 76.3 per cent). In the House, Republican presidential support was only 1.0 per cent greater than Democratic presidential support (61.3 per cent as compared to 60.3 per cent), and Republican party support was 3.0 per cent greater than the party support of Democratic leaders.

This statistical analysis does not make as clear a case against seniority as many of the critics of the system seem to claim. Chairmen are older on the average than their colleagues, and yet with luck a number of younger men are singled out for chairmanships. The districts which produce chairmen are not as stagnant as is often suggested, and the degree of party unity and presidential support among chairmen is not as low as many believe. The picture, however, is far from the ideal held by the proponents of majority rule. . . .

---

[11] It must be remembered that much of the information concerning House chairmen applies to the entire states from which they come, and not to the specific congressional districts which may be atypical of the states.

6   *The Making of a Senator*
WILLIAM S. WHITE

The old definition of the Senate as "the most exclusive club
in the world" is no longer altogether applicable, as perhaps it never
was. It *is*, however, both a club and a club within a club. By the newly
arrived and by some of the others the privileges are only carefully
and sparingly used. To the senior members—and sometimes they are
senior only in terms of power and high acceptability—privilege is in-
exhaustible and can be pressed to almost any limit. I have seen one
member, say a Lehman of New York, confined by niggling and almost brutal Senate action to the most literal inhibitions of the least
important of all the rules. And again I have seen a vital Senate roll
call held off by all sorts of openly dawdling time-killing for hours, in
spite of the fact that supposedly it is not possible to interrupt a roll
call once it is in motion, for the simple purpose of seeing that a delayed aircraft has opportunity to land at Washington Airport so that
a motorcycle escort can bring, say a Humphrey of Minnesota in to be
recorded.

Lehman was, of course, a member of the Outer Club, which is composed of all the Senate. But Humphrey is, in part by the mysterious
operation of acceptability-by-association, in or very close to the Inner Club. The inequality indicated here has nothing to do with political belief or activity; both Lehman and Humphrey are liberal Democrats and both have records of distinction. Humphrey simply got
along better. . . .

. . . As a reform Mayor of Minneapolis he had become the hero of
a liberal movement indigenous to the upper Middle West and as a
delegate to the 1948 Democratic National Convention in Philadel-

phia he was shortly to become one of the heroes of the liberal movement nationally.

At that convention, the Democratic party appeared even to its oldest and most loyal partisan leaders to be in very poor shape for the Presidential contest shortly to come.

It had, two years before, lost Congress to the Republicans for the first time in half a generation and less recently it had lost its greatest modern leader, Franklin Roosevelt. The then President, Mr. Truman, had not by that time been recognized for the major contributions to history that he had made, as he is now fully recognized for these and the other contributions that later he made. No political estimate was more general than the estimate that the Democrats were very likely to lose the 1948 elections and that such a loss would become a moral certainty if the convention further inflamed a Democratic South-North division over civil rights.

All was accordingly arranged among the party leaders, in both factions, to deal softly in the platform with this highly sensitive issue. The platform committee duly brought out a carefully diluted document. Humphrey, a member of the committee and then only an aspirant to the Senate, would have none of this. He took to the convention floor, where it could not and did not lose, an appeal for a civil rights plank far more acceptable to the North than to the South.

Many will recall what followed: the angry march out into the rain of some of the Deep Southern delegations, the enfevered scene on the convention floor which even the most faithful considered a sure prelude to Democratic disaster in the following November. It did not, to be sure, turn out that way: Mr. Truman won after all and the Democrats regained Congress.

The point now, however, was that Humphrey, even before reaching the Institution in that November, . . . had broken the most underlying of all the unwritten rules. He had rejected the greatest political *raison d'étre* of the Institution, the function of political compromise, and in the process he had made rude gestures toward those who were shortly to be his powerful Senatorial elders.

The road lay lonely and hostile before him, in consequence, when he appeared in the Senate to take the oath of office. The Outer Club was open to him only in the sense that all who belong to the Institution must belong to it. The Inner Club, at this point, lay immeasurably beyond any reckoning of hope for him.

What then, in the pursuit of this particular case history in the making of a Senator, saved Humphrey—or, more specifically, what was it that from this beginning made him a good Senator after all? Primarily there was the fact that though he had beyond doubt outraged the essential Doctrine of the Concurrent Majority these things, at least, *could* be said of him: His intolerable activities at Philadelphia had in any case occurred before he had been schooled in the Institution. Thus it could be urged in his behalf, by those who wished to give him a chance, that his had been an unconscious rather than a willful heresy. And it had to be admitted that his issue, however painfully he had insisted upon drawing it, was not a merely trifling or truly un-Senatorial one. (The Senate's instinctive memory could not wholly dismiss the fact that something akin to young Mr. Humphrey's issue in fact had been quite prominent in its affairs in another century, in the time of Webster and Calhoun.)

Finally, to a body of old men Humphrey was quite young and there was a certain tendency to forgive error in the young.

More important than all these considerations, however, his slow ascent to grace was the clear, but far from simple, fact that he had in him so many *latently* Senatorial qualities.

Not long had he been around before it became evident that, notwithstanding his regrettable past, he had a tactile sense of the moods and the habits and the mind of the place. Where another newcomer of the class of '48, Kefauver of Tennessee, seemed somehow usually to do the wrong thing at the right time, Humphrey seemed progressively to do things right. Where, for example, Kefauver suffered from a sad-eyed ebullience of highly personal effort that however worthy was notably disparate—from investigating crime to supporting some unlikely project like Atlantic Union—Humphrey unerringly set his purposes to be in harmony with the forms and spirit of the place.

He did not at all abandon his liberal designs (though as to civil rights the unyielding facts of life in the Senate forced him to move upon a zigzag course). He largely confined himself, however, to such suitably traditional liberal issues as higher farm subsidies and more generous labor laws. But he pursued these in complete awareness that in this body the best of motives will languish away unless one is able to marshall for them at best the support and at worst the fairly benevolent neutrality of at least some of the true Senate types.

Having recognized the nature of the problem Humphrey went about finding the human means with which to meet it. Unhurriedly—

easy does it—and more or less naturally he fell into the habit of fore-gathering with the Democratic leader, Senator Johnson of Texas, and through Johnson there shortly developed a line of communication, however strained at first, with the other Southerners. With these Humphrey kept up a running and good-humored private debate, in the Senate lounges and on private occasions.

As he came really to know them, and particularly the able Senatorial politician who is Johnson, he began to suspect that there was, even on such matters as civil rights, less of blood-in-the-nostrils to their approach than he had supposed. And they came to suspect the same thing about him.

Slowly, by this means, Humphrey began to be taken into the informal and decisive deliberations of the Democratic hierarchs, if only as a spokesman among these centrists of a liberal view that did not characterize either his party there or the Institution itself. To be brought one way or another into this sort of deliberation is indispensable to becoming a good Senator, for such recognition foreshadows recognition for assignment to the committees from which one draws the greater part of his power in the Senate.

It is, however, a recognition that does not and will not come to those who fail to seek it or, seeking it, lack the peculiarly perceptive touch first to solicit perquisite without seeming to hunger for it and second to exercise perquisite without seeming to abuse it. (Abuse of perquisite is left to the long-established in the Senate; and in their case it is deemed no longer abuse but only the free exercise of what are regarded as the inherent and inalienable powers of the seniors in the Inner Club.)

Indeed, Humphrey had found, and now he illustrated, one of the ultimate truths of the Senate. This is that one *cannot* forever refuse there to make any compromise at all and remain a good, or effective, member. The art of high negotiation is an absolutely necessary part of Senatorial equipment. For the Institution, as it was at its beginning, is something more than a parliamentary body engaged upon parliamentary work. It is likewise an assemblage of diplomatists, in which each State in a sense sends Ambassadors to the Federal Republic, and the function of Ambassadors is not to reach proud, violent disagreement; it is, of course, to find acceptable agreement.

To accomplish this and yet not to let down one's principles, one's side, one's State—this is the unique achievement of a good Senate man. Because this is the highest requisite, it follows that this is no place for the man who has *only* principle; for every genuine political fanatic is simply awash with principle as he understands the term.

Humphrey, in short, as well all others new to the Senate, had found, and quite honestly found, that the career he had prefaced by scorning at the Philadelphia Convention the concept of necessary compromise would proceed in the Senate only to the degree that he accepted the inevitability, and even the desirability, of just that concept. The vehement heretic of yesterday had now embraced, perforce and indeed happily as his understanding grew, the Doctrine According to the Senate.

The tolerance of dissent—to a degree practiced in no other parliamentary body—that is characteristic of the place had now enabled Humphrey to find his home. In the process there had been a mutual erosion of views—his earlier views had to some extent been altered by the conservative views at which he had chipped. And those views had been somewhat altered by his.

By the year 1956 this circumstance had been interpreted by some of his more advanced liberal friends as a surrender to "reaction." And these, who had exulted when he took the lead on civil rights at Philadelphia, now began to fall away from him. It cannot readily be denied, however, that the more moderate Humphrey of the late fifties had, in consequence of all that had happened to him, put himself in infinitely better position to bring the Senate to adopt *some* bill in that area.

Because he was no longer looked at doubtfully by the Senate types (for an important illustration of this point) he was able in the Eighty-fourth Congress to bring off, by a *unanimous* Senate vote, one of the most cherished objectives alike of the liberals and of the true conservatives. This was the establishment, over the initial opposition of the Eisenhower Administration itself, of an independent commission to review the operations of the Government's loyalty security program. A man not so acceptable simply could not conceivably have done this, however fine might have been his bill.

Thus, the making of a good Senator involves several intangibles: a credible emanation of ultimate good faith in what he is about, one of the main criteria of good faith being the absence of petty exhibitionism. An understanding acceptance of the requirement of compromise, and therefore a willingness to abide dissent. A concentration upon the coherent and important and an avoidance of the diffuse and doubtful. A deep skill in sensing what may and may not be done. A gift if not for friendship at least for amicable association with other minds and with the interests of others.

And then, of purely human qualities there are yet more. The really good Senator must be a man of such sensitivity, a sensitivity not expressed by mere softness, as to be able to perceive those odd surges of feeling that mysteriously move among men generally, sometimes informing and sometimes obscuring the true meaning of issues before the Senate. He need not be particularly skilled in every kind of human relationship but this instinct of high discrimination is indispensable. It is, sometimes, the only quality that stands athwart hysterical action.

Then he must have a considerable essential ardor for life, an *élan vital* that is constant if not necessarily intense, to survive in a trying and hazardous way of life. This was the sort of quality that enabled Mr. Truman, an old Senate man, to go doggedly forward in 1948, refusing to be discouraged, while associates on his very campaign train were quite certain that he was finished. It was the quality that permitted Senator Taft, dying a rushing death from cancer, to go on working to the end, accomplishing in the weeks of his last illness more than he had accomplished before.

THE POLITICAL PROCESS IN CONGRESS

7   *The First Richard Nixon*
      EARL MAZO

Nixon registered as a voter in 1938. He was twenty-five and had missed four voting years. But his job as assistant city attorney of Whittier was a political plum, so to speak, and therefore he had become, in effect, a politician. But it was the late fall of 1945 before he went into politics in earnest.

Whittier and its environs, then the 12th Congressional District of California, was stanch Republican territory. Yet in 1936 it elected a Democrat for Congress, and kept re-electing him. Jerry Voorhis, the Congressman, was mild mannered, conscientious, likeable, and extremely popular. He was respected by fellow Congressmen and the press corps in Washington. He worked hard at his job, answered his mail promptly, dealt with personal problems of his constituents on an eagerly nonpartisan basis, and when Congress was not in session he seldom passed by opportunities to be guest teacher of Sunday-school classes or to address church and civic groups. Furthermore, the Congressman faithfully remembered births, anniversaries, and other happy occasions in his district. And, of course, that kept his name in the minds of many voters. In short, Jerry Voorhis was a smart politician.

As was customary for candidates in the crazy quilt of California politics, Voorhis always sought both the Democratic and the Republican nomination. He never ran as an out-and-out, partisan Democrat.

In fact, the word "Democrat" rarely appeared in his advertisements and other paraphernalia (just as the word "Republican" almost never showed up on the material of his opponents). Several Republican organization leaders were among Congressman Voorhis' loyal supporters. This galled other rock-ribbed Republicans because, well known to the party faithful, Voorhis was no ordinary Democrat. He was raised in well-to-do circumstances, and that made him all the more sensitive to the woes of the poor. After graduating Phi Beta Kappa from Yale, he took a factory job at 39 cents an hour, worked as a freight handler in a railroad yard, where he saw two fellow workers killed for lack of adequate safety equipment, toured Europe, where he witnessed hunger everywhere, and then, after failing to get a job in a southern textile mill, and working awhile on a Ford assembly line, he married and with financial help from his father, opened a school and home for orphaned boys. In the mid-twenties Voorhis was a LaFollette Progressive. Then he became an active Socialist. And in the early depression years he embraced the "End Poverty in California" program of Upton Sinclair and ran for assemblyman on the ticket which Sinclair headed for governor. By 1936 Voorhis had become a bona fide Democrat and ran for Congress as a follower of Franklin D. Roosevelt. Although he grew increasingly conservative in Congress and became an energetic foe of Communism, his record as a whole was bitter medicine for most stalwart Republicans. Worst of all to them was his espousal of co-operatives and a Voorhis plan for altering the monetary system. They called the latter a "funny-money scheme."

When all else failed, the Republican hierarchy in California turned to the 1940 census for salvation. Since the legislature was Republican, the plan was to gerrymander Voorhis and several other Democratic congressmen out of office simply by redefining their districts. Two communities which Voorhis normally carried by a ratio of 5-1 were sliced from his district. Even so, Voorhis was re-elected in 1942 by a 13,000 vote majority and again in 1944, for a fifth term, by the same impressive margin. Other Democrats also survived the gerrymander. Therefore, in 1945, Republican professionals agreed to let complaining amateurs try their hand. These, most of them successful business, industrial, and professional figures, traced the trouble to low-grade candidates, known in the trade as "turkeys." It was decided to form a Fact-Finding Committee of leading citizens in each troublesome district. This committee would interview potential candidates,

weed out the perennials and the misfits, and support with all available resources "sound-thinking, articulate, and respected" individuals, preferably newcomers. Murray M. Chotiner, a resourceful Bev-
erly Hills lawyer-politician whose enterprises included a public
relations firm, was designated by the party organization to help the
amateurs. Chotiner had masterminded several exceptionally successful campaigns for Republicans, including Governor Earl Warren,
and later was to become Richard Nixon's political manager.

Meanwhile the citizen fact-finders in the 12th District bestirred
themselves well ahead of schedule. In the late spring of 1945—a full
year and a half before the target election—a group met in Arcadia.
Stanley Barnes, an attorney who has since been appointed to the
United States Circuit Court of Appeals, as chairman and Frank E.
Jorgensen, a vice-president of the Metropolitan Life Insurance Company, were the spark plugs. Later, to assure unity, leaders of various
regular Republican party organizations were added to the committee
in time to hear the first aspirants for nomination. As might be expected, none of the eight applicants were satisfactory. In fact, Jorgensen and his group already knew the man they wanted. He was Walter
Dexter, a former president of Whittier College who had become California's superintendent of education. To run for Congress Dexter
would have had to resign his state position and, as Jorgensen recalls,
"he couldn't afford to risk the financial loss that would result if he
was not elected." Dexter therefore suggested one of his former students, Richard M. Nixon, whom he described as one of the most
promising young men he had ever known. Jorgensen and two associates, Boyd Gibbons and Rockwood Nelson, drove over to the Nixon
grocery store to make inquiries. Frank and Hannah Nixon were more
than willing to talk about their oldest living son. They noted that a
good friend in town Herman L. Perry, manager of the local Bank of
America branch, also had mentioned that their son would be an ideal
candidate.

Perry telephoned Nixon in Baltimore, where he was renegotiating
Navy contracts while awaiting release from the service. Nixon flew to
California, and on December 4, 1945, he formally accepted the fact-
finding committee's endorsement in a letter to Roy O. Day, district
Republican chairman. It was evident from his letter that the 32-year
old Nixon was eager to be out of uniform and running for office. "I
am going to see Joe Martin and John Phillips and try to get what
dope I can on Mr. Voorhis' record," he wrote, in part. "His 'conserv-

ative' reputation must be blasted. But my main efforts are being directed toward building up a positive, progressive group of speeches which tell what *we* want to do, not what the Democrats have failed to do." The neophyte politician advised Day to "bring in the liberal fringe Republicans. We need *every* Republican and a few Democrats to win. I'm really hopped up over this deal, and I believe we can win."

In January Nixon was released from active duty, and he came west with a satchelful of ideas and a set of electioneering pictures from which he learned a fundamental political truth. It was that the great majority of veterans had been enlisted men for whom a politician campaigning in the uniform of an officer held little attraction. The photographs were thrown out, and the simple words "Dick Nixon" or just "Nixon" replaced "Lieutenant Commander Richard M. Nixon" on proposed literature. Nixon began his active campaign immediately. Shortly thereafter the Nixons' first daughter, Patricia, was born, and within three weeks Mrs. Nixon left the child with her mother-in-law and joined her husband.

Murray Chotiner was the principal professional member of Nixon's campaign organization. Chotiner was Senator Knowland's southern California campaign manager, in itself a full-time job. Roy Day retained him as publicity director for Nixon, on the side, at a fee of $500.

Voorhis and Nixon took advantage of California's peculiar cross-filing system to become candidates for the nominations of both parties. But, while Nixon worked at it energetically, Voorhis sent word that he was very busy looking after the people's welfare in Washington and therefore could not spare the time to campaign in the spring primaries. As usual, that was fine strategy. Voorhis won the Democratic nomination, got a substantial vote in the Republican primary, and gained the psychological advantage of beating Nixon by 7,000 votes in the over-all count. Normally this would have meant sure victory in the November general election. But Nixon's morale went up when a Los Angeles political reporter pointed out that Voorhis' vote, 53.5 per cent of the total, was quite a drop from 1944, when he polled 60 per cent.

"Keen political observers . . . thought we ran a darn fine race, and this was the best Republican primary showing in years," Nixon wrote Chairman Day. "Frankly, Roy, I really believe that's true, and it is time some of the rest of the people began to realize it. All we need is a win complex and we'll take him in November."

The general election campaign flared up early in September, much like many others being fought throughout the country that year of meat and housing shortages, labor unrest and general postwar disenchantment. The Republicans were the "outs," and their battlecry was "Had enough?" The theme of the 12th District campaign followed the national pattern in most respects—that is, the incumbent Democrat was branded as a tool of Sidney Hillman's CIO-Political Action Committee, a promoter of controls, and an enemy of free enterprise who would socialize America.

But the Voorhis-Nixon battle developed distinctive nuances of bitterness. The veteran Congressman had never before been confronted by a buzz-saw opponent, and the tenderfoot candidate had never before debated so totally for keeps. Both candidates electioneered on three fronts. Most exciting to them and the voters were five debates. Meanest of the three fronts was a battle of newspaper advertisements and statements. Most strenuous for the candidates were handshaking and coffee-hour tours.

While Voorhis believes, in retrospect, that he would have lost anyway, Nixon believes the turning point for him, as the underdog, was the first debate. "It was tough," Nixon says. "I was the challenger, and he was the experienced incumbent. Once that debate was over, I was on my way to eventual victory." Nixon went into the debates against the wishes of all his advisers except Chotiner. The others feared Voorhis was too experienced and Nixon too green. Chotiner insisted the gamble had to be taken because, at worst, Nixon would lose and, at best, he might strike the spark his campaign needed so badly.

The first debate did just that—thanks to a Political Action Committee endorsement of Voorhis which is still the subject of controversy. There had been a small Nixon advertisement which declared, in part, "A vote for Nixon is a vote against the Communist-dominated PAC with its gigantic slush fund." Voorhis vigorously insisted he had not sought and didn't have the endorsement of the regional Political Action Committee of the CIO. At this Nixon leaped to his feet, drew a paper from his pocket, and read a report in which the Los Angeles chapter of the *national* Political Action Committee recommended that the national group endorse Voorhis. Nixon also read off the names of officers of the national organization's chapter who were also officers of the regional group. Then, dramatically, he thrust the paper at Voorhis.

Shortly afterwards Voorhis issued a long, poignant statement declaring that, while he cherished the support of labor, he didn't have and didn't want the backing of the California CIO because "under present top leadership of the CIO in California, there is at least grave question whether the Communist Party does not exercise inordinate if not decisive influence over state and county organizations."

A few days later he telegraphed the national Political Action Committee demanding that it withdraw its "qualified endorsement" of him.

For the remainder of the campaign Voorhis expended much of his time and energy denying that he was the CIO's errand boy, while Nixon jabbed or punched, as the occasion demanded, with observations about "lip-service Americans" and high officials "who front for un-American elements, wittingly or otherwise, by advocating increasing federal controls over the lives of the people." In mid-October Nixon warned voters against being "fooled" by the "very conservative" tone Voorhis was adopting. "In the last four years, out of forty-six measures sponsored by the CIO and the PAC, my opponent has voted against the CIO and PAC only three times," declared Nixon. "Whether he wants it now or not, my opponent has the PAC endorsement and he has certainly earned it. It's not how a man talks, but how he votes that counts."

The PAC controversy reached its shrill peak three days before the election, when Republican campaign headquarters issued a statement in behalf of a former lieutenant governor accusing Voorhis of "consistently voting the Moscow-PAC-Henry Wallace line in Congress." The statement also mentioned "the insolence of Moscow in telling the American voter to elect PAC candidates, such as Mr. Voorhis," and it pronounced Candidate Nixon to be "a man who will talk American and at the same time vote American in Congress . . . and fight in and out of Congress to perpetuate American ideals and American freedom."

There were, of course, other issues in the campaign, and in the context of those times it is not unlikely that some were more decisive with voters than exchanges about the PAC. There was, for example, the veteran issue. Nixon pointed to his own wartime service (and indirectly to Voorhis' civilian status) in an often-repeated promise "to preserve our sacred heritage, in the name of my buddies and your loved ones, who died that these might endure." For his part, Voorhis referred to his opponent at times as "the Lieutenant Commander" and the "subtlety" escaped no one.

As an "in," Voorhis was compelled to harp on only one positive theme. It was that he had achieved seniority and experience and to turn him out for a newcomer "wouldn't be good sense and would be damaging to popular government in these critical days."

On the other hand, as an "out," with no record to defend, Nixon was free to attack and promise at the same time. Thus he became "thoroughly committed to a program of federal tax reduction" and promised that a Republican Congress would solve the meat, housing, and controls problem.

(It was during this first campaign that Nixon developed the knack of repeating verbatim questions asked of him from the floor. It requires the vocal apparatus to operate on one track while the thinking apparatus operates on another. Nixon does it to give himself time to think of the answer.)

Voorhis had 296 inches of campaign advertising and Nixon 162 inches, in the *Post-Advocate*, the daily newspaper of Alhambra, largest city in the district. It is noteworthy that not one line in a Nixon manifest mentioned the fact that he was a Republican, and none of Voorhis' alluded to his membership in the Democratic party.

Nixon won by a vote of 65,586 to 49,994, and was one of seven Republicans to unseat incumbent Democrats in California. All told, the Republicans picked up fifty-five House seats and won control of the Eightieth Congress. In reflecting on the campaign twelve years later Nixon said the race was, in effect, a contest between a well-known New Dealer and a conservative Republican. "Voorhis lost because that district was not a New Deal district," he said. "Our campaign was a very honest debate on the issues." . . .

At the outset Nixon's favorite work was as a member of a small subcommittee that drafted the Taft-Hartley Labor Law. That was where he became quite friendly with a freshman Democrat from Massachusetts named John F. Kennedy. Nixon and Kennedy were on opposite sides of the Taft-Hartley question, and in the spring of 1947 they went to McKeesport, Pennsylvania, to debate the issue. (Nixon still considers Kennedy "a good personal friend" and says, "I have a very high regard for him as an able senator and campaigner; he's very attractive and formidable." Kennedy does not now reciprocate those feelings. In fact, his attitude toward Nixon is that he would like very much to run against him for president.)

Meanwhile Nixon's interest in the Un-American Activities Committee was not very great. But it warmed up on August 3, 1948, when Whittaker Chambers, a former Communist, listed among his one-time fellow conspirators a man named Alger Hiss. . . .

8   *The Representative and His District*
LEWIS A. DEXTER

We talk frequently of a Representative or Senator "representing" or "failing to represent" his constituents. This is shorthand. The fact is the congressman represents his image of the district or of his constituents (or fails to represent his, or our, image of them). How does he get this image? Where does it come from?

On numerous important policy matters, he hears nothing from his constituency. But whether he hears anything on an issue, what he hears, whom he hears from, or how he interprets what he hears all vary depending upon the kind of person he is, the kind of associations he has had and has in the constituency and in Washington, the public image of his interests and concerns, and the background information or misinformation which he possesses. . . .

A good many congressmen believe that their districts feel very strongly on this, or the other issue, and that they are constrained therefore to vote a certain way. The more sophisticated realize, of course, that legislative procedures and processes are so complex that it is more often than not possible to go through the motions of conforming to such views without helping to enact them, when they believe the public preference to be wrong. On most issues, out of a de-

From Lewis Anthony Dexter, *Human Organization* (Vol. 16, No. 1). Reprinted by permission of Lewis A. Dexter.

sire to serve the district or from indifference, many congressmen
do go along with any view which they believe "the district" holds
strongly. When the chips are down, and they have to declare themselves, some will vote against their convictions and for their constituents' (presumed) preferences.

This situation has led to a series of classical utterances on the
moral problem of the representative: *Should he sacrifice his judgment to his constituents' inclinations as he conceives them or not?* It
would be more accurate to emphasize the ways in which representatives' beliefs about constituent preference are functions of the channels of communication and the special processes of transaction between constituents and representatives rather than of anything else.

If this is in fact so, more students of representation and representatives would concur with Congressman Veteran's interpretation of the
representative-constituent picture. The latter has for years been at
the center of the legislative issues which provoke the most comment
by critics of "pressure," and he told me early in my study of reciprocal trade:

You know I am sure you will find out a congressman can do pretty
much what he decides to do and he doesn't have to bother too much
about criticism. I've seen plenty of cases since I've been up here where
a guy will hold one economic or political position and get along all
right; and then he'll die or resign and a guy comes in who holds quite
a different economic or political position and he gets along all right too.
That's the fact of the matter.

*The first difference between some congressmen and others is how
(consciously or unconsciously) they define their responsibilities.*

Many of the congressmen interviewed about both tariff and defense matters referred to a personal conception of what they owe
their job, of what in some circles would be called "professional obligation." A few made explicit and many apparently hold implicit theories of representation. These theories of representation were not,
except for a few instances, so far as I could tell, directly derived from
philosophical or academic sources. They resulted from the experiences of men facing the actual moral complexities of a job.

Some members expressed themselves in terms of their obligation to
select the right course, regardless of the views of their constituents.
For instance, Congressman Stubborn has for a good many years represented a district which (according to interviews with business interests in the district and from an economic analysis of its industrial

situation) is inclined to favor the reciprocal trade program. Nevertheless he says:

Oh, knowing my stubborn characteristics, no one ever thinks he can change me, you know . . . some of my people say, "You may not agree with this man, 'Stubborn,' but you know where he stands."

Mr. Stubborn agreed that if fate were to select as his successor a Clarence Randall type "free trader," such a man would be able to vote for a reciprocal trade program without much difficulty, but Stubborn interrupted an effort to probe this point further by declaring:

That's because they (my constituents) do not really understand the matter. During the twenty-one years reciprocal trade has been in effect, it has had . . . [and he named various alleged or actual consequences which he regards as evil] . . . There isn't any use trying to change me!

Congressman Emphatic on the other hand voted the same way as Mr. Stubborn on the Reciprocal Trade Extension Act of 1955 because of a quite different definition of his responsibility. He said:

My first duty is to get reelected. I'm here to represent my district. . . . This is part of my actual belief as to the function of a congressman. . . . What is good for the majority of districts is good for the country. What snarls up the system is these so-called statesmen—congressmen who vote for what they think is the country's interest . . . let the Senators do that. . . . They're paid to be statesmen; we [members of the House] aren't. (This was said sarcastically, but without humorous intent.)

Mr. Leader, as strong a supporter of reciprocal trade as Mr. Stubborn is an opponent of it, comes fairly close to Mr. Stubborn in his attitude towards constituent opinion. Said Leader:

You're not identifying me on this of course? It's strictly confidential? Always bear in mind there are those in Congress who lead their districts and those who are led by them. . . . It makes a lot of difference. . . . The "ruanga" growers of my district never opposed me on reciprocal trade. . . . The answer is government stockpiling for them. . . . I think I have convinced these men that a program of high tariffs would not assist them and I think my viewpoint has gained general acceptance from them.

Several times he spoke of himself as having "straightened out" people who had seen the matter "wrongly." . . .

Mr. Fourth represents a district in which there is vociferous antireciprocal trade sentiment. This district also has strong economic reasons for supporting reciprocal trade and a particularly influential number of intellectuals predisposed toward reciprocal trade. Mr.

Fourth showed how a portion of the district can influence a man when he said:

My impulses when I came down here were in favor of trade not aid, until I started to hear all sorts of things from my district. . . . So, actually, when you stack all these things together, well you're in favor of trade not aid, but, goodness, there comes a time . . . if trade means wholesale layoffs in your district. . . . . I've got any number of letters against it . . . carpets, imported rugs . . . there've been around 300 layoffs in a local bicycle plant . . . textiles . . . chemicals . . . electrical equipment . . . glass salesmen. It's difficult to get figures. I assume the Randall Commission report has them. . . . I haven't had time to read it. I don't know. . . . I assume that the people I hear from exaggerate the seriousness of the situation but still that it is serious.

Mr. Fourth ultimately voted against reciprocal trade on the key votes; the decisive factor appears to have been his unwillingness to separate himself from several members from his state, also of junior status, who were definite in their opposition to reciprocal trade. Mr. Fourth, according to his colleagues was wavering as late as two hours before the vote. Had the Chairman of his state delegation (who strongly supported reciprocal trade) personally requested his support, he might well have voted the other way. But he was obviously uncertain, *on the reciprocal trade issue,* whether to adopt the role of servant of his district (as he conceived its desires) or to think in terms of the ideology, implied by the phrase "trade not aid." How he would vote was therefore completely unpredictable. Had he stumbled into any one of three congressmen with strong pro-reciprocal trade views in the lobby or the corridors just before the vote, he might have voted the other way .

Congressman Fourth's vote was unpredictable because on this particular issue he does not have a clear conception of what his obligations are. On some issues—flood control or taxes affecting the major agricultural product of the district—one can predict that he would see his responsibility as being almost exclusively to the district. On others—particularly those under consideration by the very important subcommittee of which he is a member—he would be strongly inclined to emphasize national interest in some form as against district concern.

Congressmen tend to see their obligations as being either to the nation or to their constituency—other equally possible obligations are seemingly not considered.

Obligation seemed to be conceived as national interest versus district interest (district interest was often, as in the case of Mr. Emphatic, related to reelection and therefore to self-interest). No congressman interviewed indicated any feeling of moral obligation to our allies or to any other country, although our allies are regarded instrumentally as means. This is contrary to a theory sometimes expressed that Americans tend to adopt some favorite foreign country as "theirs." Also, reference to representing a region (the South, the West, New England) was very slight. . . .

A congressman's conception of his district confirms itself, to a considerable extent, and may constitute a sort of self-fulfilling prophecy.

Early in my study of reciprocal trade, Congressman Veteran told me:

You know I am sure you will find out a congressman can do pretty much what he decides to do and he doesn't have to bother much about criticism.

Within the limits of the morally and sociologically conceivable (no congressman from Alabama in 1942 could have advocated integration for instance!), a congressman has a very wide range of choices on any given issue, *so far as his constituency is concerned!* His relationships in the House or Senate and with party leadership, of course, limit these choices severely. It is a fact, however, that there is no district viewpoint as such to be represented on the overwhelming majority of issues. A few will care one way and a few the other, but the issue will be insignificant or unknown to the great majority. Indeed, in many districts, only a fraction of the voters know the name of their congressman, let alone how he voted on a particular issue.

A congressman of my acquaintance took about 100 letters which he received on a particular issue and checked the registration of the writers. He found that almost three-quarters of them were not registered in his district. What difference then would their views make with respect to his prospects for reelection? Mr. Emphatic who insisted that he was representing his district's desires, was led nevertheless, by my questions, to admit that more than likely none of the workers presumably represented by him actually knew how he had voted. . . .

Actually, most of the letters Mr. Emphatic received and most of the comments he heard originated in three large plants in the district and they represented less than 7% of the voters of the district. These plants are organized by national unions which, ironically enough, in chalking up Mr. Emphatic's score in 1956, were inclined to regard his vote against reciprocal trade as an anti-labor vote. Fortunately for him, his stand on other matters and his personal contacts offset this factor. Of the groups in the district, only members of the League of Women Voters wrote to him in favor of reciprocal trade. "They aren't," he averred, "God knows, a potent political force; and all their letters are damn stilted, right out of the same handbook." Actually, however, it was likely that the League members would remember in 1956, and perhaps again in 1958, how he voted. And, because of the "racial" and academic composition of the district, League members may have some influence outside their own membership. It would have been perfectly possible for Mr. Emphatic to take the reverse position favoring reciprocal trade and still to regard himself as representing his district—particularly since the area also has a strong port interest. . . .

A congressman has great difficulty in deciding what the viewpoint of the district is even on such an issue as reciprocal trade. Most persons with an interest or belief in the tariff will have interest or beliefs in other issues as well. Thus, the most effective representation of their overall interests may necessitate concessions on some matters, in order to get along with party leadership, colleagues, or prominent committee members in Congress. "Joe Martin and Charlie Halleck in their heart of hearts," said a prominent Republican, "certainly go along with us, not with the White House on this; and they can swing twenty-five votes, at least, anytime they want; we lost by less than twenty-five votes, so they beat us." Martin is the Republican leader; Halleck is his likely successor as Republican leader or Speaker when he steps down. Is a congressman doing a better job of representing his district when he keeps in the good graces of such powerful men (and thereby helps to get a bridge or a new post office or a dam for his district) or when he opposes them on an issue, the details of which no one will remember six months later? The Republican who told me this is one of the most persistent enemies of reciprocal trade in the party and he is probably the most effective in a quiet way. He is opposed to reciprocal trade in part because of its "harmful" effect on his district. However, he cheerfully admitted, "It wouldn't make any difference what my congressman does on this matter," insofar as his re-election is concerned. Afterwards he qualified this by saying that perhaps the incumbent ought not stick his neck out strongly *for* reciprocal trade, but there is no call for activity of any kind.

A congressman hears most often from those who agree with him.

A congressman's relationships with his district tend to be maintained through a small group whom he knew before he was elected or through a group who have since then worked closely with him. Generally speaking, the views of those whom he knew prior to his election tend to be more like his than do the views of the "average" voter. It is a well-known fact that we tend to be like the people with whom we associate and vice versa. Also, most of the people who have worked closely with the congressman since his election—because he is a congressman—have a particular axe to grind. They will naturally tend therefore to stress agreement with him on issues about which they are not concerned—just as salesmen typically do not disagree with their customers on politics. For several years, I wondered about the unfavorable references congressmen frequently made to the League of Women Voters and several times to delegations from labor unions. Ultimately, it occurred to me that these two groups are probably the only ones which seriously, on a face-to-face basis, year after year, go over with a congressman the issues on which they disagree with him. Because their efforts cannot be entirely discounted as "politics," they make congressmen uncomfortable. . . .

Some men automatically interpret what they hear to support their own viewpoints.

Mr. First of New Hungary does not think he hears much about foreign imports. Mr. Second, coming from the same sort of district in the same city, says:

It's either the first or second most important issue with me. Unemployment is the other. And, of course, they're really the same thing.

The last sentence is the clue to why Mr. Second hears so much more than Mr. First about foreign imports. When Mr. First hears about unemployment, he hears just about the invidious differential effect which accelerated amortization and certain other tax provisions have had on industry in the area. In fact, when I talked to him about the tariff, he advised me that I really ought to study accelerated amortization. Mr. Second, however, interprets almost any statement about unemployment as a plea for relief from foreign imports. Sometimes it is, but sometimes it isn't. So, seeing the same men and hearing the same things said, Mr. Second will "hear" about tariff matters, Mr. First will not. (Mr. Third, their colleague from an adjoining district, is vitally interested in wilderness preservation, hunting, and fishing. He sees many of the same men, but they are likely to talk to him about his interests, and if they do talk to him about unemployment, he is less likely to draw any special conclusions from the talk.) . . .

In more general terms, what congressmen hear and how they interpret what they hear depends on who they are.

Conventional discussion of the relationship between congressmen and constituents assumes that the kind of man the congressman is does not influence what he hears from the district and that the question is whether he follows or contravenes district sentiment. The notion of the congressman representing "the" district at least needs restatement *in terms of a particular congressman* who represents what he hears from the district as he interprets it. And his interpretation results from his being the particular kind of person he is and is reputed to be. . . .

Pressure is how you see it.

"Pressure" and "pressure politics" are regarded by most "sophisticated" people today as "explaining" a great deal that happens. But it was frequently impossible to find any admission of or apparently any awareness of "pressures." That was not because shrewd and worldly politicians were concealing what really goes on from this naive and innocent interviewer and his naive and innocent colleagues.

The reason is explained by Senator Service's assistant:

There are very few people actually pressuring us, even if you count all we hear about all issues. Seriously, the sense of being pressured is a matter of reaction. Other people who get no more mail than we do in this office would say, "See how much pressure is on me." We don't feel it. . . . Sure, you get mail. It's just that so-and-so makes more 'phone calls than somebody else. The result is purely physical. It isn't a representation of what or how or when people are going to vote in elections. My personal opinion is that members of most organizations make up their minds on what they read in the papers without reference to organizations.

With this theory of voting behavior, Senator Service's assistant naturally will not be too much worried by a good deal of effort to get him or his boss to change policies—he simply will not regard it as pressure.

Congressman Widesight amusingly illustrated the point made by Service's assistant. Mr. Widesight has moods when he reaches way out into left field looking for things to worry about, things which might possibly defeat him. One day, discussing reciprocal trade, he said that things were very bad indeed. His reason was that he was getting "so much" mail against it. "I, whom they never used to bother at all." When I checked with his secretary later, I found he couldn't possibly have received more than 50 letters (representing glass, electrical equipment, and 2 or 3 bicycle interests) opposing reciprocal trade. This was only a fraction of the mail Senator Service receives on the same matter. It was also a fraction of what Congressman Widesight himself has several times heard on other matters such as postal pay increases. However, Widesight is accustomed to communications on that issue and he wasn't accustomed to them on the reciprocal trade issue. . . .

Even where there is a considerable amount of what the outsider would consider pressure, the point made by Senator Service's assistant is entirely valid. What you call pressure . . . or what you feel to be pressure . . . depends on how thick your skin is. Mr. Second, for instance, told me that he had been subject to no "pressures—that is, no threats." To many men in politics threats alone represent the only real pressure because they know very well that few votes are actually lost on any one given issue such as reciprocal trade. But, of course, what is a threat to one man is not a threat to another. (For comparison, we should have studied some explosive issues like "McCarthyism" or *humane slaughtering* or perhaps some issues in which the profit-and-loss relationship is clearer like the question of pay increases for postal employees.)

The most strongly felt kind of pressure on the reciprocal trade issue came, apparently, from Speaker Rayburn and the Democratic leadership against the potentially recalcitrant Democrats. Speaker Rayburn attended a breakfast for freshmen congressmen shortly before the vote and said, in effect, that he'd discovered that those who go along, get along. One new member regarded this as pressure—a threat. Another new member (actually probably more vulnerable in terms of his factional position and his position within the delegation) did not. Both of them failed to "go along." Aside from this speech, most of the "pressure" on the doubtful members seems to have come through the grapevine or from their own apprehensions as to what might happen if they bolted the party leadership.

One reason why fairly few members seem to have felt pressure on this matter is to be explained in terms of their background and associations in local politics. In many states, "pressure" on matters like highway contracts or patronage or even for or against gubernatorial programs, must be relatively heavy—that is, threats are far more common at the state level than they are in Washington. Many congressmen come from such a background and a good many are still involved in local conflicts about patronage, contracts, etc. As a result, Washington to them seems very mild.

Nagging may also be called pressure, whether done by mail or in person. When a congressman has definitely announced his stand and does not intend to switch it, he resents being bothered by avoidable pleas (pressures) to change. The resentment point, obviously, is highly individual so one man's pressure is another man's routine. . . .

9   *Party in Congress: Whip Organizations in the United States House of Representatives*
RANDALL B. RIPLEY

Author's Note: The changes made in this version of the paper are intended to make more clear the central point of the piece: that the whip organizations in the House are now (and have been increasingly so for 30 years) the core of the two parties in the House. Both in terms of structure and in terms of activity the whip organizations are the parties. This is particularly true of the majority Democratic whip organization. The whip, chosen formally by the Majority Leader with the advice and approval of the Speaker, works closely with those two party officials in making and executing party policy. The Republican whip, chosen by his party's Committee on Committees, works with the minority leader and they both in turn work with the Republican Policy Committee in determining what the minority stance will be on legislative proposals and how best to engineer success.

I

Champ Clark, Speaker of the House for eight years (1911-1919), described the whips as "the right hands of the two leaders," and stated that the principal duty of a whip "is to have his fellow politi-

From Randall B. Ripley, "The Party Whip Organizations in the United States House of Representatives," *The American Political Science Review* (September, 1964, pp. 561-576), American Political Science Association.

cal members in the House when needed." Clark's comments are still accurate, although the functions performed by the whips have become more diversified in recent years. The whips are 1) responsible for the presence of their fellow party members, but they must also 2) transmit certain information to them, 3) ascertain how they will vote on selected important pieces of legislation, and 4) guide pressure to change the minds of the recalcitrant and stiffen the wills of the wavering.

Most of these functions have been performed on a disorganized basis in the House since 1789, although the name "whip" was not formally applied to a party official in the House until the end of the nineteenth century.[1] Throughout most of the nineteenth century members functioning as whips were in evidence only in connection with important legislation and only when the division between the parties was close enough to necessitate a device that would help gain a high degree of party regularity. Many of these members who acted as whips were men who volunteered to act in that capacity only for a given floor fight.

Both parties began to designate their whips formally for an entire Congress around the turn of the century. By the late 1920's and the beginning of the party battles that predated the New Deal struggles the whips became even more prominent in the House. Both parties were eager to maintain disciplined lines either for or against far-reaching legislation after the 1920's. The top-heavy Democratic majorities of the 1930's began to be plagued by dissenting Southerners and Westerners, which increased the need for machinery aimed at a high degree of party unity in voting. Republicans desired to produce a united opposition.

Gradually the House began to recognize not only the importance of the individuals serving as whips but also the importance of the whips as institutions. The House provided space in the Capitol and money for staff assistance. From 1911 until the present the Republican whip has had an office in the Capitol, unless he chose to operate from his congressional office. The Democratic whip had an office in the Capitol in the 63rd Congress (1913-1915) and has had an office there since 1919. Since 1913 the House has provided for at least limited staff help to be appointed by the whips. The sum was

[1] The name "whip" derives from the British fox-hunting term "whipper-in," which was used to describe the man responsible for keeping the hounds from leaving the pack. It was first applied to the British Parliament about 1770.

to be used for a messenger for each whip until 1947. In that year provision was also made for two clerks. In 1953 the party whips were given administrative assistants. By 1963 the office of each whip had a budget of about $40,000.[2]

II

The whip organizations of the parties grew in size and complexity through the years of this century. By 1963 both party whip organizations were large, formal organizations that performed a variety of tasks.

The Republican Organization. John Dwight (1909-1913) was apparently the first Republican whip to have assistants. There is no evidence that any Republican until Carl Bachmann (1931-1933) again used assistant whips. Bachmann organized the Republican whip system on essentially the same basis that is still in use. He divided the country into two divisions and appointed Joseph Martin of Massachusetts (later Minority Leader and Speaker) to be in charge of the Eastern Division and Harry Englebright of California (himself whip from 1933 to 1943) to be in charge of the Western Division. He also designated a "key man" in each state with Republican members. When a poll of the Republican members was necessary Bachmann asked Martin and Englebright to get reports from the key men about their state delegations. When Englebright became Republican whip in 1933 he retained the pattern of assistant whips (increasing them to three in number) and "key men" in the state delegations.

The Republican whip from 1944 to the present, Les Arends of Illinois, formalized and expanded the key man system. By 1963 he had a deputy whip, three regional whips, and 12 assistant whips. After the chief whip is chosen he has a free hand in appointing all of his assistants.

The Republican whip organization performs the four functions mentioned earlier which involve attendance, information, polling, and pressure. The Republican whip keeps records of Republican

[2] The value of the party whip organizations was widely enough recognized in the House by the late 1950's for a portion of the Democratic membership to imitate the political parties and establish a third whip organization. In 1957 a loose alliance of liberal Democrats was formed in the House under the leadership of Representative Eugene McCarthy of Minnesota. This group immediately established a whip organization, which functioned at least sporadically. In 1959 both the Democratic Study Group and its whip organization were formally established. The Secretary of the DSG also serves as its whip.

members' voting on teller votes as well as on roll calls. This the Democratic whip does only informally and sporadically, without notes or records being kept.

The Republicans have developed no pattern of leadership succession. Joe Martin had been an assistant whip before becoming Minority Leader and Speaker but no whip has ever become the Republican floor leader. Similarly, when Speaker Martin was forced to become Minority Leader in 1949 and 1955 the Republican whip kept his job, rather than surrendering it to the former Majority Leader.

The Democratic Organization. On the Democratic side Oscar W. Underwood of Alabama, the first Democratic whip (and later Majority Leader in the House and Minority Leader in the Senate), had an assistant whip in 1900. But by the 1921-1928 period William A. Oldfield of Arkansas had no assistant whips. John McDuffie of Alabama (1929-1933) had two assistants. The great expansion in the Democratic whip organization, which had come in 1931 in the Republican party, came in 1933 under Arthur Greenwood of Indiana (1933-1935). He organized a system of 15 assistant whips. Each of the assistants was responsible for the Democrats in a specific zone. The zones were identical with those established for the Democratic Steering Committee, which was also created in 1933. The Steering Committee withered quickly but the whip zones remained. The initial 15 zones were similar in composition to the present 18 zones.

Greenwood's successor, Pat Boland of Pennsylvania (1935-1942), worked diligently to perfect the functioning of the organization. During his tenure of seven years the press and other Democratic leaders began to take public notice of his operations.

The Democratic deputy whip, who is especially active on the floor in checking attendance and voting, is appointed by the whip. The Democratic assistant whips are either appointed by the dean of the delegations for which they are responsible or they are elected by the members of those delegations. This contrasts with the centralized method of appointment (by the chief whip) used by the Republicans.

The assistant whips are responsible for a small number of Democrats, averaging between 14 and 15. The whips, or staff members designated by them, make the regular contacts with all of the Democratic members' offices. When the Democratic leadership in the House makes a decision to transmit information to all Democrats or elicit information from them the chief whip's office contacts the 18 assistants. In this way all Democrats can be alerted to come to the floor in 15 to 20 minutes. The leadership can ascertain the sentiments of virtually every Democrat in the House on a given bill in a day or two.

III

The Democratic whip organization has worked as an arm of the majority party for all but four years (1947-1949 and 1953-1955) since 1933. Its functions are described in the following detailed analysis of the Democratic organization in 1962 and 1963. These were years of especially great activity for the Democratic whip organization. In the 1930's Boland greatly expanded the use of the organization. Rayburn, who was a strong leader and had never been whip himself, used the whip organization less than the weaker Speakers of the 1930's.

But in 1962 and 1963 the new Speaker, John McCormack, began to use the whip organization for a greater number of formal polls. McCormack had been whip as had the new Majority Leader, Carl Albert of Oklahoma. Hale Boggs of Louisiana, the new whip, had been deputy under Albert. Thus the top three Democrats in the House all had an appreciation for the potentialities of the whip organization—both formally and informally. These three men, joined by D.B. Hardeman, Administrative Assistant to Boggs, and the deputy whip, John Moss of California, functioned as a small, close-knit group dedicated to attaining the most favorable voting outcomes on Administration bills. This group met with White House and Departmental officials on legislative matters throughout 1962 and 1963.

The Office of the Democratic whip was composed of four people —Boggs, Hardeman, a secretary, and an intern—during the entire time period studied. The office had contacts—generally a staff member—in the offices of each of the 18 assistant whips. Information and poll requests were transmitted by telephone in conversations between the whip's office and the offices of the assistant whips. Occasionally the whip's office would contact all Democratic members of the House directly, either on substantive legislative matters or urging them to be present.[3] The whip's office, located in the Capitol,

[3] An unusual instance of this occurred in the drive for adjournment in October, 1962, when the leadership was having difficulty in keeping a quorum in Washington. The whip's office called or sent telegrams to all missing Democrats from east of the Mississippi at their homes asking them to return to Washington. A similar situation, even more acute, developed in 1963 as the House struggled until Christmas eve to pass a foreign aid appropriations bill acceptable to the President.

served as a meeting place for White House and Departmental congressional liaison officials interested in the success of a particular bill.

The whip during these two years was Hale Boggs of Louisiana, a loyal Administration supporter on most matters. The deputy whip, John Moss of California, was even more loyal to the Administration. The assistant whips, who were the primary direct contacts with rank and file Democratic members, varied in their voting loyalty to the Administration. Table I shows that the assistant whips tend to be more loyal to the Administration than all Democrats and that variations in individual loyalty tend to reflect the normal variations by zone.

The problem of "disloyal" assistant whips is troublesome. The power to appoint and replace assistant whips rests exclusively in the hands of the Democratic delegations involved. But even if the whip had the power to remove assistant whips the roll-call voting record of the assistants would not be an infallible test of performance. For example, in 1962 one assistant whip supported the Administration only rarely and yet did an excellent job as assistant whip, not only in reporting accurately but also in indicating the weak point of each member through which he might be induced to change his mind and support the Administration on a given bill. Loyalty is less important ᵗhan accuracy and thoroughness. The Democratic assistant whips are expected to perform the functions involving attendance, information, and polling but they have a great deal of discretion in deciding whether they also wish to pressure their zone members to vote the Administration position.[4]

The four main tasks of both party whip organizations have been designated as involving attendance, information, polling, and the guiding of pressure. An analysis of how the Democratic whip organization performed these four functions in dealing with the major legislation acted on by the House in 1962 and 1963 will form the bulk of this section. "Major legislation" here indicates those measures on which the House leadership decided a poll should be taken, on which the poll was taken and completed, and on which the House

[4] The Republicans, starting with a base of greater party agreement on issues, look on their assistant whips as definite agents of the leadership. The method of appointment for Republican assistant whips—by the chief whip himself—insures some accountability to the leadership. On the Democratic side Boggs obviously cannot assume that the assistant whip appointed by Howard Smith will be an avid Administration supporter.

TABLE I. *Voting of Democratic Assistant Whips and Members of Their Zones, 1962-1963*

The first column under each of the two years gives the percentage of pro-Administration votes cast on 17 key roll calls by the assistant whips as individuals. These men were the same in both years except in the starred zones. The second column under each of the two years gives the percentage of pro-Administration votes cast on the 17 key roll calls by all Democrats whose districts are located in the various zones. The 17 votes used are listed in Table II.

	1962		1963	
States in Whip Zone	Assistant Whip	Zone Members	Assistant Whip	Zone Members
Mass., Conn., R.I.	100	95	100	97
N.Y.	100	95	100	97
Pa.	100	98	90	95
N.J., Del., Md.	100	92	100	99
* Va., N.C.	43	53	60	56
Ga., S.C.	86	62	89	74
Mich., Wisc., Minn.	100	97	100	97
Indiana	100	96	100	97
W. Va., Ohio	57	83	100	93
Tenn., Ky., Ark.	71	81	90	90
* Miss., La.	86	41	100	53
* Alabama, Fla.	67	62	78	70
Mo., Iowa	100	80	100	81
* Illinois	100	98	100	98
* Texas	29	51	100	70
Okla. (Kans. & Mont. in 1962)	100	78	90	90
Wash., Ore., Alaska, Hawaii, Ariz., N.M., Utah, Colo., Ida., Nev. (Mont. in 1963)	67	86	100	92
California	100	98	100	97
Average	84	79	94	85

acted either favorably or unfavorably by roll call vote. This definition includes seven bills in 1962 and ten bills in 1963.[5] The 17 votes include 14 which the Administration won and three which the Administration lost.

[5] The specific issues are given in Table II.

The first function of the whip organization is to insure maximum Democratic attendance on the floor when critical votes are taken. Getting the best attendance is a matter both of keeping the members in Washington and getting them to the House chamber when the vote comes. To facilitate its work in keeping a maximum attendance the whip's office uses a variation of a poll called an attendance check. In this procedure the assistant whips simply ask the members if they will be in town "next Wednesday" or "next Wednesday and next Thursday." By asking these questions the whip can identify members who should be asked to change their plans and stay in town. Or, if the leadership has a choice in scheduling it can estimate on which one of two or three days the attendance and absence situation will work most in the Administration's favor.

On the day of a vote on the floor the whip's office checks its attendance poll against the absentees on the first quorum call of the day to indicate what members need to be contacted or may need pairs. The whip's office is particularly anxious to arrange live pairs—whereby an anti-Administration vote actually present is nullified by an absent pro-Administration vote.[6] As the time of the vote or votes approaches a series of whip calls goes out from the whip's office, specifying what is being voted on and indicating that the Speaker, Majority Leader, and whip would like the member's presence on the floor.

The whip's office goes to great lengths to guarantee the presence of members on crucial votes. In April, 1963, votes on a medical student loan provision and on the feed grains program were scheduled for the same week. The whip's office contacted one Democratic member who was on the West Coast to make a long-scheduled speech and arranged for her to fly back for the votes. It contacted another member touring his district with the Argentine Ambassador and asked him to return to Washington. In the May, 1963, fight over increasing the limit on the national debt the whip's office was instrumental in arranging for two Democrats to attend the session in wheel chairs. Occasionally, faulty timing lost a vote. In the June, 1963, vote on the

[6] Pairs are used to record the position of absent members on a roll call. A regular legislative pair is an agreement to neutralize the votes of one absent member on each side of a question. A live pair results in a net gain of one vote for one side or the other. A member is most likely to give a live pair when he is in sympathy with the other party's position but feels unable to vote that position because of pressure from his own leadership and whip organization. There are also "general pairs," which have no legislative value in that no position is announced for either of the absent members.

Area Redevelopment Act amendments a member was told that the vote would be taken about two hours later than it actually came. Consequently he was at the Washington Airport when his vote was needed.

The promotion of optimum attendance can also involve some selectivity. On the day of the Area Redevelopment vote in 1963 the Air Force was scheduled to take 19 members to an air show in Paris. The whip's office contacted the Air Force to get assurances that the plane would not leave until one hour after the final vote on the bill. Then it contacted the six Democratic members known to be friendly to the bill who were also scheduled to go on the trip and told them of this so as to insure their presence on the floor.

In the August, 1963, debt limit fight the whip's office was especially active in working on attendance. Those Democrats friendly to the bill not answering the quorum call on the day before the vote received telegrams from Boggs urging them, in the Speaker's name, "to make every effort to be present Thursday." On the day of the vote the whip's office called the offices of 15 Democratic members who had not answered the quorum call that morning. Despite the previous stress on attendance seven of these members had absented themselves without informing the leadership and did not come to vote.

In late August, 1963, there was a long, bitter floor fight over the foreign aid authorization bill. The whip organization made a concerted effort to get all Democrats to the floor and keep them there. A series of teller votes was anticipated on Wednesday and Thursday. Thus on Tuesday a meeting was held in the whip's office which was attended by all but one of the assistant whips (or their representatives), the Democratic House leadership, Executive liaison personnel, Under Secretary of State Harriman, and AID Administrator Bell. Harriman and Bell explained the provisions of the bill and the necessity of defeating crippling amendments. The leadership stressed that all assistant whips should be on the floor during the entire voting period (which consumed 10 to 12 hours) and should keep track of the members from their zones.

The appeal was effective in that all 18 assistant whips were on the floor during both days of teller votes. Yet two early votes were lost because of absentees and thus a whip call directed at friendly assistant whips (15 of the 18 on this issue) stressed the necessity of winning the first teller vote on the next day.

The attendance on voting on the tax bill in 1963 was almost perfect. On the most important vote (that on the Republican recommittal motion) only one Democrat was unexpectedly absent. The other four Democratic absentees had been identified for several days. Three of them were in the hospital. Special efforts were made to get everyone else. For example, two Democrats flew back from a conference abroad specifically for the vote.

No statistical measure can judge *precisely* the effect of the Democratic whip organization on attendance for roll call votes. Yet some inferences can be drawn from looking at a few figures. On the 17 bills in these two sessions on which the whip organization was fully active total Democratic voting attendance was 94%. This can be compared with the Democratic attendance on all roll calls: 83% in 1962 and 84% in 1963. This higher attendance was partially a function of the importance of the bills. Yet the specific instances recounted above suggest that the whip organization had some effect in producing a high voting turnout.

The second function of the whip's office is providing information to Democratic members on upcoming measures. At the most mechanical level the whip's office is responsible for informing all Democrats what is scheduled for floor action week by week. But the office also provides information more directly related to legislation which is highly important to the Administration and to the House leadership. In May, 1963, during the struggle over the increase in the debt limit the whip organization distributed sheets of information on what defeat of such an increase would mean to the country and to all Democratic members. A more neutral communication was sent to all Democrats directly from the whip's office with reference to the June, 1963, Area Redevelopment amendments. The content of this letter was an outline explanation of the provisions of the bill. A similar letter—signed by Albert and Boggs—was sent in connection with the cotton bill late in the 1963 session.

In 1963, prior to the passage of the foreign aid authorization bill, an effort at informing the assistant whips on specifics of the program was made at the meeting described above. As a result of the meeting AID prepared two memoranda which were then distributed to the assistant whips through the whip's office.

Before the voting on the tax bill in 1963 the whip's office was instrumental in helping Chairman Mills distribute a short summary of the bill to all Democratic members. It was accompanied by a brief letter urging support for final passage and defeat of the recommittal motion because "this bill is essential to our national well-being." The letter was signed by Mills, the Speaker, Albert, and Boggs.

The third function of the whip's office is ascertaining how the Democratic members of the House will vote on certain pieces of legislation central to the Administration's program.[7] The major device used to get information on the future voting of Democrats is the poll. The whip's office does not take a poll until the leadership decides one is needed. This is usually during the period between the time the bill has been reported from the committee and the time it is scheduled for action on the floor. This means that the poll must be finished in a period lasting from two days to two weeks. Naturally the longer time periods produce greater accuracy in results. Likewise, the more clear and specific the question asked of the members the more accurate the result. If the legislation is extremely complex a simple response for or against the legislation may hide important feelings about amendments. The most effective assistant whips probe their members for feelings about specific provisions. If a current of opinion develops against a certain provision in the legislation it may be changed in time to save it from defeat. In 1963 a poll was started on a bill extending the Export-Import Bank and allowing it to continue direct borrowing from the Treasury. The initial poll results revealed a strong feeling against such backdoor financing and the Banking and Currency Committee changed the bill to eliminate such financing.

The question which the assistant whips are to ask members is precisely framed. Ambiguous questions produce ambiguous answers. The question is not always on the final passage of the legislation. Often it is on the recommittal motion to be offered by the Republicans if the "instructions" in this motion can be discovered in advance

[7] The Democratic whip's office also relays to the leadership whatever information it receives about Republican voting probabilities. Such information may come from lobbyists, Executive officials, or through personal contacts between Democratic and Republican members. The Republican and Democratic whips' offices do not, of course, trade information. Information on Republican voting tends to be quite unreliable when it reaches the Democratic whip's office. For example, during the debt limit fight in May, 1963, it was supposed that at least eight to 10 Republicans would vote for the increase. Only one did. When the Administration lost the Area Redevelopment bill in June, 1963, the whip's office had received information that 21 Republicans would vote for the bill. Only 15 did. During the 1963 struggle over enlarging the Rules Committee six Republicans who finally voted with the Democratic leadership had been written off as lost to Halleck and Judge Smith.

of the vote. At other times a specific amendment is the subject of a poll.

The results of the polling process are supplemented by and checked with officials from the White House and the Executive Department involved. Occasionally group lobbyists provide some information. It should be noted that without a sensitive and knowledgeable interpreter of the poll data the results could be highly misleading. Fortunately for the Democratic leadership such an interpreter was in charge of the office during the period studied. He could tell when a report from a member was of dubious validity and when it could be accepted at face value.[8] He had a "feel" for contacting the proper members.

How accurate were the final poll results which were submitted to the leadership? Accuracy is important because decisions about provisions in the bill, scheduling the bill for floor action, and attempts to change Democratic votes are based partially on the poll results. To judge the accuracy of the whip poll the final complete poll presented to the leadership which still left time for any of the actions indicated above (usually two days before the vote) was checked, individual by individual, against the final roll call embodying the issue on which the poll had been taken. The results are summarized in Table II. This shows the percentage of members reported correctly by the poll and also shows the number reported correctly and incorrectly and the number whose positions could not be ascertained. As can be seen, the whip's office increased in accuracy in 1963 as compared with 1962. Apparently the refinement of techniques and the lessons of experience were put to good use.

Probably the most important use for the poll results is in helping the leadership determine where to apply pressure. Meetings of the Speaker, Majority Leader, whip, Administrative Assistant to the whip, deputy whip, White House and Departmental liaison officials, and the relevant Committee Chairman begin during a period between three weeks and three days before a bill comes to the floor. At these

---

[8] There are several reasons for a member's making an inaccurate report of his position. He might want to avoid leadership pressure by not alerting anyone to his opposition. He might be annoyed at the inconvenience of repeatedly reporting his position. Finally, he might use the report of opposition as a bargaining device. For example, on the poll on the debt limit increase in May, 1963, a loyal Administration supporter from the midwest reported "doubtful" and, at the same time, indicated his eagerness for final Treasury confirmation that a new Internal Revenue Service installation would be in his district.

TABLE II. *Accuracy of Democratic Whip Polls*

Bill	% Correct	No. Correct	No. Incorrect	No. Unknown
1962: Urban Affairs	87	226	15	19
1962: Tax Bill	81	212	26	23
1962: Debt Limit	90	237	18	7
1962: Farm Bill	82	216	36	10
1962: Trade Expansion	92	241	15	6
1962: Public Works	87	228	23	10
1962: U.N. Bonds	87	227	24	10
1963: Rules Committee	96	247	2	8
1963: Public Works Approp.	91	233	8	15
1963: Medical Student Loans	94	240	0	16
1963: Feed Grains	84	214	16	26
1963: Debt Limit (May)	93	239	9	8
1963: Area Redevelopment	91	232	17	6
1963: Debt Limit (Aug.)	85	218	32	6
* 1963: Tax Bill	96	246	6	4
1963: Debt Limit (Nov.)	92	235	19	2
1963: Cotton Bill	84	214	34	8

* The recommittal motion on the 1963 tax bill did not fully meet the criteria of "major legislation" given on pp. 98-99 because part of the poll on this motion was taken through the Democratic members of the Committee on Ways and Means. The 15 zones used by these men when acting as the Democratic Committee were employed in the poll and the results were channeled first to Chairman Mills and then to the whip's office. Aside from this deviation, however, the whip's office performed its normal functions during the struggle. Since the bill was one of the most important to the Administration and the House leadership in 1963 it was thought a more accurate picture of the whip system could be given by including it.

meetings a division of labor is made, on the basis of the whip poll. Thus a more thorough and accurate poll produces fewer wasted contacts and enhances the probability that the contacts that are made will be with members who may be persuaded.

This fourth function of the whip's office—that of directing pressure—is, in some ways, the most important of the four. The goal of the office is, after all, to produce votes for the President's program. There is no precise systematic or statistical way of charting the effectiveness of this whip-guided pressure. But some incidents involving the legislation studied in this article will give a sample of the work done and its effectiveness.

The whip's office was effective in 1962 in identifying the trouble spots on the tax bill of that year. One particularly dangerous area was the New York delegation, which was finally brought into line, losing only three votes. Several Southern delegations were initially opposed to the bill but a caucus of the North Carolina delegation, plus the effective work of the assistant whip for Texas, helped hold Southern losses on the bill to 15 votes. At the last minute, during the floor debate, the secretary in the whip's office discovered that some of the members from a Midwestern state might be wavering in their support for the bill. This message was transmitted to Boggs on the floor and he proceeded to escort one of the delegation's members to the Speaker's office where both the Speaker and the President (on the telephone) convinced him that he should support the bill.

During the 1962 prelude to the vote on increasing the national debt limit the whip's office was instrumental in enlisting Francis Walter of Pennsylvania to use some of his credit with the Southerners to convince one major Southern delegation to vote for the bill. As a result, only three Democrats from that state voted nay.

During the week of June 25, 1962, the whip poll began to show that the Republican motion to recommit (kill) the trade bill might attract as many as 80 Democratic votes. Frantic activity on the part of the President, Chairman Mills, Secretaries Goldberg and Hodges and their Under Secretaries, the Speaker, the Majority Leader, the whip, and others on Tuesday and Wednesday of that week reduced the eventual Democratic losses on the recommittal motion on Thursday to 44.

During the 1963 Rules Committee fight, after the whip poll was relatively complete, the Speaker, Majority Leader, and whip each took a list of members to call. Of the 17 called about their vote seven finally voted with the leadership.

The events leading up to the passage of the debt limit increase in May, 1963, provide another illustration of the use made of the information supplied by the whip poll. At a meeting five days before the vote the results of the poll were discussed. During this meeting the Speaker, Majority Leader, and Larry O'Brien of the White House called and talked to several members either about their opposition or possible absence. Those members still considered doubtful or open to persuasion were divided among the leadership for further work. Chairman Mills asked that the latest whip poll be given to him the day before the vote so that postponement of the bill could still be announced if it appeared that defeat were likely.

A week before the final vote the Speaker saw an early version of the poll and, on the basis of that, persuaded six members reporting doubtful to commit themselves to voting for the bill. By the time of the floor action the poll indicated that the vote would be extremely close. On the basis of that information the leadership received promises from 13 Democrats who were planning to vote against the legislation that they would vote for it if their votes were needed to change defeat into victory.

The passage of the second debt limit increase of 1963, in August, was the occasion for a substantial amount of whip-directed activity. The Secretary of the Treasury persuaded one Southern Democrat to vote for the increase after the whip poll had shown him to be vacillating. The Speaker contacted 15 wavering Democrats directly and, as a result, persuaded 10 of them to vote for the bill. Chairman Mills was especially effective in getting Southerners to vote for the bill. Again, as in May, the leadership had ten "pocket votes," that is, men who preferred to vote nay but would vote aye if necessary to pass the bill.[9]

In summary, the whip's office performs its four functions in such a way as to enhance the chances of Democratic victories on floor votes in the House. No absolute figures can be given on votes won that would otherwise be lost. Yet the weight of evidence is that the efforts to insure a maximum attendance, inform the Democratic membership of undesirable effects on the country if an Administration proposal is defeated, ascertain voting behavior with great accuracy in advance, and direct pressure to the precise spots where it will do the most good result in some small, yet definite, net gains for the Democratic majority in the House.

IV

David Truman has commented that "the persistent reality of party in the functioning of the [House] chamber is unmistakable." Julius Turner stated that "Party pressure seems to be more effective than any other pressure on congressional voting." Yet neither they nor any other commentators on Congress using primarily statistical indices based on roll call votes have been able to be more specific about the nature of party activity in the House. The indices describe the *results* of the activity. But the *activity itself*—the "reality" of Truman or the "pressure" of Turner—cannot be caught by voting indices.

[9] Seven of these 10, largely at the urging of Mills, voted aye even though not needed. Mills was anxious to have a respectably large margin of victory. He was trying to set a precedent for November, when another debt limit increase would be necessary.

The whip organizations are at the core of party activity in the House. This is particularly true of the Democratic party. Thus the data which have been presented on the whip organizations are also data on parties in the House. These data can be analyzed to provide a broad range of generalizations about party activity in the House.

(1) The Democratic whip organization has become the focus of a corporate or collegial leadership in the House. Truman concluded that the evidence provided by record votes shows no collegial leadership,[10] although he indicated that the individual elective leaders in each party showed somewhat more unity. But analysis of roll call votes does not fully describe actual activities of the party leaders. Observation of the Democratic whip organization suggests that the pattern of leadership in 1962 and 1963 was for the Speaker, Majority Leader, whip, deputy whip, and relevant Committee Chairman to work closely together in the effort to pass a given piece of legislation. To expect a greater degree of corporate leadership—including *all* major Committee Chairmen on every separate piece of major legislation—is unrealistic. Each Chairman has time to be concerned only about the legislation produced by his Committee. The major missing participant that one would expect to find in a collegial leadership is the Chairman of the Committee on Rules, who has a legitimate interest in all major legislation.

(2) Truman found that the voting structure of the parties in Congress "was focused upon one or a pair of positions: the Floor Leaders, joined at times, particularly on the Democratic side, by the Whips and, among the House Democrats, impliedly by the Speaker." For House Democrats the operation of the whip organization offers some clues why this focus is not mere coincidence. Even if the assistant whips do not uniformly "pressure" the members of their zones they do inform them of the voting preferences of the Speaker, Majority Leader, and whip. This information, as universally distributed to all Democrats, is one of the "triggers" that precipitates action.

(3) The Democratic whip organization, coordinated with the leadership offered House Democrats by the President, helped the House Democrats to cohere on the major votes in 1962-1963. Truman suggests that the majority party has a natural basis for greater cohesion than the minority party. Again the whip organization is important in explaining the implementation of that basis. Similarly, the

[10] David B. Truman, *The Congressional Party*, New York, 1959, p. 245.

whip organization is an important institutional device for helping the House leadership perform a mediating role between the President and the rank and file membership of the Democratic party in the House. The elected legislative leaders of the President's party have a stake in his success in the House. The whip organization thus has a similar stake and also provides machinery for improving the President's chances.

(4) An important function performed by the Democratic whip organization is the carrying and recording of various bargains struck between party members on legislative matters. Within whip zones and even between whip zones both explicit and implicit bargains are made between individual members. The whip organization then provides a framework for channeling the information on the bargains to a more central location—either the whip's office or the relevant Committee Chairman or one of the leaders individually. The transmission of information is incomplete but it is more complete than totally unorganized gossip.

(5) The operations of the Democratic whip organization, especially as highlighted in points 2 and 4 above, suggest that information can be as important and as effective as "pressure" of the classic mold. Information about legislation and about the intentions of individual legislators can be used to trigger or cue voting behavior favorable to the President and the leadership.

(6) The growth in the strength, complexity, and importance of both party whip organizations in this Century suggests a growing sense of party and party solidarity within the House. After all, the whip organizations now involve 16 Republicans and 20 Democrats directly. These 36 men and women have made a commitment of time —which members of the House must necessarily hoard—to work for their respective parties within the House. Unless they felt that party work was worth doing a sufficient number of such commitments might not be made.

(7) The history of the party whip organizations suggests that the importance of the whip is partly dependent on the mode of leadership exercised by the Speaker or Minority Leader. Strong, solitary leaders like Rayburn have relied less on the whip than leaders who seek and need the active help of others. Leaders with fewer resources, like McCormack and Halleck, necessarily rely more on others in the leadership circle—including the whip and his organization.

(8) The contrast between the place of the Democratic whip orga-

nization and the Republican whip organization in 1962-1963 provides material for broader generalizations about the differences between the two parties in the House. The Democratic whip in these years was firmly lodged in a three-man leadership circle. His influence was great and his prospects for eventual advancement to Majority Leader were good. The Republican whip, however, would never obtain another leadership post. In addition, he had to work not only with the Minority Leader but also was subject to the decisions of the 35-man Republican Policy Committee, of which he was but one member. The majority leadership appeared to be substantially more compact than the minority leadership.

(9) At the same time several features of the two party whip organizations suggest that the customary characterization of the Democratic Party in the House as a loose coalition of disparate groups without many central allegiances and of the Republican Party in the House as a closely knit body of men dedicated to common principles may be at least partially correct. The Democratic assistant whips are regarded primarily as informing agents rather than as pressuring agents, although individual assistant whips may choose to pressure their zone members. The Democratic whip's office keeps no systematic voting records with which to confront the less loyal members. The Republican assistant whips, however, are expected to work for a solid Republican vote in accord with the dictates of the Policy Committee. The Republican whip's office keeps voting records, even on teller votes, so that the whips may berate the goats and praise the sheep when the occasion demands. The method of selection of the assistant whips, as noted earlier, is also an important difference. The Democratic whip is presented with assistants he may not want. The Republican whip picks his own assistants.

In short, the data suggest that a change is necessary in the typical description of the House which attributes, in the words of Professor Hugh Bone, "no consistently great influence in policy directing or in establishing party accountability for legislative program" to the party machinery. As important pieces of party machinery the whip organizations possess such influence. How great and how consistent the influence are still open questions. This article has attempted to provide some tentative answers to those questions.

EXECUTIVE AND CONGRESS

10 Planning the President's Program
RICHARD E. NEUSTADT

Early in 1954, President Dwight D. Eisenhower presented to the Congress—and the country and his party—some 65 proposals for new legislation, over and above appropriations. This presentation was a massive affair. First came six weeks of well-publicized preliminaries: cabinet deliberations, congressional briefings, press conferences, and a fireside chat. Then, in three annual messages to Congress —a State of the Union Address, a Budget Message, and an Economic Report—the President set forth his bundle of proposals, elaborating certain aspects, outlining the rest. Along with these came seven supplementing special messages, each filling in details on some particular: Taft-Hartley, farm price supports, social security, health, housing, atomic energy, foreign aid, and trade. And following the messages Administration-approved bills, conveyors of the ultimate details, were introduced in Congress.

Throughout, one theme was emphasized: here was a comprehensive and coordinated inventory of the nation's current legislative needs, reflecting the President's own judgments, choices, and priorities in every major area of Federal action; in short, his "legislative program," an entity distinctive and defined, its coverage and its omissions, both, delimiting his stand across the board. And—quite explicitly—this stand was being taken, this program volunteered, in order to give Congress an agenda, Republicans a platform, and voters a yardstick for 1954.

From Richard E. Neustadt, *The American Political Science Review* (1955, Vol. XLIX, No. 4), American Political Science Association, Washington.

Thus, one year after his inaugural, Eisenhower espoused a sweeping concept of the President's initiative in legislation and an elaborate mechanism for its public expression; developments which no one seemed to take amiss. Both in governmental circles and in the press, the whole performance was regarded almost as a matter of course, a normal White House response to the opening of Congress. The pattern, after all, was quite familiar; the comprehensive program expressed in ordered sequence, with some sort of publicized preliminaries and detailed follow-up, had been an annual enterprise in Truman's time. Indeed, while Eisenhower had undoubtedly improved upon the earlier mechanics, his 1954 procedure seemed expressive less of innovation than of reversion to accustomed practice. In 1953, he had been criticized in many quarters for failing to produce a defined program of this kind; now that "failure" was made good, a general expectation satisfied in the "customary" way.

Customary, perhaps; yet as recently as 1946 an informed observer had remarked, accurately enough, on the "absence of cohesion in the legislative program of the chief executive—absence, in fact, of a program clearly designated as such." Presidential reports and recommendations to Congress were as old as the Constitution; presidential sponsorship of specific measures, high-lighted in special messages and spelled out in Administration bills, had been a commonplace in Franklin Roosevelt's time and by no means unknown much earlier. But the elaborate paraphernalia of a comprehensive and specific inventory, contents settled and defined as regards substance no less than finance, *presented in detailed fashion and packaged form at the opening of each session of Congress*—this was a "custom" scarcely nine years old, a postwar phenomenon evolving under Truman and now carried forward under Eisenhower.

Here is an institutional development of no mean proportions, with a great preparatory effort obviously involved in advance of every session. Three questions are suggested: First, currently, what are the mechanics of this program preparation; how is the job done and by whom? Second, historically, what gave rise to such institutionalization in the postwar decade; how did it evolve and how did it survive the change of Administration? Third, prospectively—and speculatively—what may the whole development imply regarding powers, opportunities, of President and presidency in the legislative process? This paper attempts answers to these questions; its starting point is the making of the Eisenhower program of 1954.

I. Preparing the Eisenhower Program of 1954

"The presentation of a legislative program," wrote Truman in his farewell message to the Congress, "falls properly to my successor, not to me . . . and I would not infringe upon his responsibility to chart the forward course." This was easier said by the outgoing President than done by the incoming, with his first Congress already in session (courtesy the Twentieth Amendment). In 1953, for the first time in years, there was no "legislative program," no charting of the course in the specific sense conveyed by Truman's words and prior practice.

At the outset, Eisenhower did present to Congress his own report on the State of the Union, but he chose throughout that address to keep most of his legislative references general to the point of homily. The new regime, while reducing appropriations requests—as in the case of the Air Force—forebore to present a complete new budget document and message; while revising some economic policies—as in the case of credit and controls—it attempted no new Economic Report. During the spring of 1953, a number of Administration stands on legislation were developed and expressed, piecemeal, in special messages or bills, or both. But for the most part these encompassed only inescapable necessities—like foreign aid, taxation, reciprocal trade—where scheduled expirations of authority forced the presidential hand. More characteristic were the surveys, investigations, and study groups brought forward by the President or his subordinates in lieu of action recommendations on numbers of great issues, foreign and domestic.

What accounts for this lack of firm programming in the congressional session of 1953? . . .

. . . [W]hatever Eisenhower's personal position, there seems no doubt that certain members of his entourage were then distinctly predisposed against a comprehensive program presentation along anything like Truman's lines. "We always meant to have a program," appears a considerable overstatement, at least if "we" refers to the whole White House entourage in 1953. Conciliating Congress was the order of the day; by some, apparently, this was interpreted as *not* doing whatever Truman might have done. Moreover, some of the new White House aides appear to have been seriously concerned about the constitutional proprieties; others disturbed about the range of Democratic intervention in domestic spheres; still others doubtful of the need for further emphasis on lawmaking, *per se*. Such attitudes as these add up to general bearishness toward widespread volunteering of firm presidential stands on current or prospective legislation—especially when controversial. "Let Congress struggle with it; keep us out·" Here was, reportedly, an often-sounded White House theme through most of the first session of the 83rd Congress.

Yet scarcely five months after that session's close, there came the Eisenhower legislative program of 1954. Whether as an outcome of deliberate plans, or of changed attitudes, or both, this represents a distinct alteration in approach from one session of Congress to the next. How did it come to pass? How was the newness tempered, the bearishness reduced, the program put together?

In May, 1953, the Bureau of the Budget sent to the multilith machines—in preparation for June 30 distribution—its annual call for estimates from Federal agencies, in this case for fiscal 1955. Included in that document as an instruction to each agency was section 86, entitled "Legislative Program":

A statement will be submitted [September 15] describing the preliminary legislative program of the agency for the forthcoming session of Congress. This statement should include *all* items of legislation [other than appropriations] which the agency contemplates proposing during the ensuing twelve months. . . .

The statement should be in three parts:

1. Those items in the President's legislative program which have not yet been enacted . . . limited to proposals . . . specifically identified by the President as part of his program, or specifically held [by Budget through central clearance] to be "in accord with the program of the President."

2. Legislative proposals not included in part 1 . . . which would cause no increase in budgeting requirements.

3. Legislative proposals not included in part 1 . . . which would cause an increase in budgeting requirements . . . arranged to reflect relative priority among items on the list and also . . . with respect to other portions of the budget. . . .

With respect to each item of proposed legislation, this statement should set forth (1) the subject matter . . . together with a summary statement of the objectives . . . and the need . . . (2) the state of readiness of legislative drafts and other supporting material; (3) a reference to the numbers of pertinent bills and . . . reports [in recent sessions] . . . together with a brief appraisal . . . (4) a forecast of both the appropriations and the expenditures required . . . and (5) the names of other [interested] departments and agencies. . . .

This language was identical with that included in the 1952 call for estimates issued a year earlier before the close of Truman's term. Indeed, section 86 and its requirements had been a feature of each Budget call since 1949. Their renewal in 1953 marks not an Eisenhower innovation but a bureaucratic continuum, an attempted restoration of routines, an action taken on the Budget's own initiative without advance assurance as to either agency response or ultimate White House reaction.

This was a venture with no guarantees attached; it was, however, something more than a leap in the dark. The Budget Bureau's renewal of section 86 was powerfully reinforced by two other acts of initiative, one preceding, one following preparation of the new call for estimates.

The first of these involved the agencies. As early as January, 1953, the new Budget Director, Joseph M. Dodge, had corralled cabinet colleagues, one by one, for orientation briefings by his career aides. In a number of cases these sessions were held even before Inauguration Day, providing several cabinet members-designate their first glimpse from inside into the complexities of their new assignments. And at each briefing Budget staffers took occasion, with Dodge's assent, to inform the department head about "his" legislative program (compiled the preceding fall), its existence in form and fact, its usefulness for orientation, its potential for planning and control, its liability to renewal on Budget's call.

Thereby, a piece of left-over machinery idling in the departmental depths was impressed on the consciousness of new department heads at a uniquely favorable moment. This had its due effect; by late summer 1953, when lower-level bureaucrats began preparing agency responses to Budget's new call, their top superiors, in almost every case, were reasonably well acquainted with the departmental "program," quite acclimated to its presence as a fact of departmental life, and quite prepared to oversee it renovation and renewal in advance of 1954.

Meanwhile the Budget had taken a further act of initiative, this time involving the White House. Early in July, 1953 President Eisenhower had voiced some concern about means to bring together, well in advance, data and suggestions for his January, 1954 State of the Union message. Budget aids were asked to brief him on his predecessor's practice; they took the opportunity to urge some White House recognition for the programming requirement in section 86 of the new call for estimates. In Truman's time it had been customary for the President to write each agency in early autumn, requesting message data and, at the same time, reiterating over his own signature the main terms of section 86. Message and program requests had long been joined; that was made clear to the new President.

The result was an identical letter to each cabinet officer over Eisenhower's signature and bearing signs of his own dictation. Dated July 30, 1953—a month after formal issuance of Budget's call—the letters asked for substantive ideas appropriate to the State of the Union Message, these ideas to be based on a "thorough rethinking of the mission of your department and the . . . means to achieve it." And, quite explicitly, that review was to "complement attention you are giving the 1955 budget and the formulation of a carefully planned, specific legislative program."

If there were any doubts remaining at top departmental levels about the propriety—and the priority—of Budget's legislative call, this missive from the President appears to have resolved them. By mid-September, 1953, agency legislative programs were flowing to the Budget. By early October, departmental message memoranda were en route to the White House, many of them referencing or appending these programs to concretize suggested points of emphasis. The President had called for a "thorough rethinking." Here, in this double-barrelled presentation, was the visible response.

Cumulatively, it was an astonishing response, at least to those White House staffers disinclined toward executive initiatives in legislation. For here were departmental declarations of intent to sponsor literally hundreds of measures great and small, *most of which the President was being asked to make his own by personal endorsement in a message.* And among these were dozens of proposals, espoused now by one or another of Eisenhower's own department heads, closely resembling—in general purpose, if not always precise form— predecessor measures urged in Truman's time and bearing then a Fair Deal label: an expansion of social security, an increased minimum wage, a revision of immigration laws, a broadening of unemployment compensation, and many more. Mostly these represented improvements in going programs long advocated by career administrators (and their clientele) to modernize or clarify the application of public policies in their charge. Agency legislative programs in 1953 were not sheer replicas of those in 1952 and earlier—some items were stricken, others added, still other revised—but their content makes plain that mixed with the rethinking from on high was a good deal of educating from below.

For eight years past—save only 1953—there had been a presidential charting of the course in Truman's terms: an executive inventory of specifics (agenda and yardstick both) for action by the Congress. Now, in October, 1953, these agency submissions forecast that some such executive charting would be done in 1954—if not by Eisenhower comprehensively, then by his cabinet members piecemeal; if not in his name, then in theirs. At his own invitation they had defined their ambitions, drawn their plans, and these now turned out to encompass controversial innovations of national concern, inextricably involving the President's position and prestige. Were he therefore to influence scope, scale, priorities, and presentation, he needs must act upon their requests for endorsement, thereby asserting his own rule in program-making, *his* plans, *his* charting of the course as against theirs.

The implications were not lost for long upon the presidential staff. . . .

Within the White House . . . there was no escaping action upon agency submissions. By mid-October it was generally conceded that whatever major issues they might raise would have to be acknowledged in some form or fashion—negatively, at the very least—by or before Eisenhower's annual messages. This necessitated first of all a close look at the contents of the pile well in advance of message preparation. And by early November, such examination was preoccupying half the members of the White House entourage.

Their initial "look-see" became a rather elaborate affair. Under the aegis of the Assistant to the President, Sherman Adams, with his deputy, Wilfred E. Persons, and the then Special Counsel, Bernard M. Shanley, actively in charge, anywhere from six to ten members of the entourage—depending on subject-matter—joined in an item-by-item review around the conference table; over a two-week period this involved some 12 meetings of two to three hours apiece. . . .

[From mid-October through December of 1953, program-making went through various stages, briefly summarized here. With the help of Roger Jones, career chief of the Budget Bureau's Office of Legislative Reference, the staff sorted through some 33 "major" proposals, pros and cons of each were sought from congressional and "outside" sources and priorities among the proposals were established. From late November through mid-December several cabinet presentations were made, consensus was sought, with Eisenhower actively participating. This served educative and co-ordinative purposes and also as a dress rehearsal for what was to be many cabinet members' first full-scale approach to a legislative committee.—Ed.]

In the course of these various proceedings late in 1953—staff reviews, presidential briefings, cabinet presentations, and attendant negotiations—the White House grew increasingly committed to an Eisenhower legislative program, the more so as its practicable scope and character came clear. By the end of November there was no longer any question that a program would ensue, or that it should appear in annual messages, or that it should be at once comprehensive and concrete. Amidst the concentration on specifics, these things came to be taken for granted. In part, this is attributable to the sheer momentum of those staff and agency proceedings once started on their way. In part, it seems related to the intra-party power struggle in which Senator McCarthy had engaged with increasing directness since the death of Senator Taft the preceding summer. On December 2 and on December 16 the President at press conference took pains to assert that his own forthcoming program, *not* McCarthy's chosen issue, would measure Republican performance in the election year of 1954; this hard upon the Senator's press statements to the contrary. The presidential program, once, perhaps, a questionable undertaking or a necessary chore, was now become a prime political imperative, its relative readiness a godsend, one expects, to the regime. . . .

On December 17, 18, and 19, 1953, Eisenhower formally unveiled his program to the Republican congressional leadership, in an unprecedented series of carefully staged briefings at the White House. With the President presiding, these ran a full eight hours daily, covering a subject-matter agenda fixed in advance and rigidly enforced from the chair. The Vice-President, the Speaker, the Majority Leaders, and the Whips were in attendance at all times, as were most members of the cabinet and the White House entourage. Committee chairmen and their ranking (Republican) associates participated when their subjects were discussed, arriving and departing on a pre-determined schedule; so did a number of executive officials below cabinet rank. In deference to Eisenhower's own communiques, issued each afternoon, and honoring his personal request, those moving in and out avoided detailed comment to the press; thereby, the White House got ideal publicity in presidential terms—headlines about Eisenhower and his program but no scoops on particulars. . . .

Less than three weeks intervened between these leaders' meetings in December, 1953 and the President's State of the Union Address to Congress; it was a busy season for the message drafters. In policy terms there was by this time little left to be decided, but the contents of the several messages remained to be coordinated, their relative scope and coverage fully defined, specific drafts agreed upon—or, indeed, written—and final language snarls worked out. In carrying these matters forward, actual drafting of the Budget Message was left largely to the Budget Bureau, the White House checking mainly general tone and precise wording of concrete proposals. Similarly, drafting of the Economic Report remained largely in the hands of the Economic Council chairman, himself a prime participant in earlier staff consultations. But for the psychologically most important annual message, the President's personally delivered State of the Union Address, the drafting was from first to last a White House undertaking. . . . the first consolidated State of the Union draft was so crowded with specifics that it would have taken some three hours to deliver. In consequence, large portions were pulled out to form the first five of Eisenhower's 1954 special messages, his personal address becoming in the end a sort of preparatory note and table of contents for the supplementing documents to follow·

Meanwhile, the departments concentrated on bill drafting in order that each definite proposal conveyed by these messages might be backed promptly by a detailed draft of legislation bearing an Administration label and ready for transmission (formally or not) to Congress. . . .

Neither by content nor tone were documents like these well suited to the task of dramatizing for the country and his party the President's own personality and purposes. Yet if there was but little drama in the messages themselves, there was, perhaps, much to be gained by focussing attention on their presentation as a collectivity, seeking dramatic impact in the sheer fact of "program," aside from the nature or the statement of its parts. To this the White House—President and staff together, it appears—devoted a great deal of thought and care during December, 1953.

In the five weeks before the State of the Union Address, there emanated from the White House a steady stream of press communiques and dope stories concerning the program's preparation. Specific plans were guarded rather carefully—the aim, no doubt, to generate suspense—but generalized official comments on the special cabinet sessions, and in particular the legislative leaders' meetings, were arranged and facilitated by the White House press office with all the fanfare usually reserved for first-rank international conferences. After the conclusion of those meetings, December 19, the President removed to Georgia over Christmas, whence came almost daily stories of last-minute conferences on the impending messages with officials flown down from Washington. On January 4, 1954, all this was capped by a radio and television address to the nation, in which Eisenhower plugged his program and urged everyone's attention to its imminent unveiling. In dramatic appeal this discourse was scarcely an unqualified success; trying to reach the country in the evening hours without depriving Congress of its first crack at details, he avoided scooping his congressional address at the expense of overgeneralizing. Nevertheless, the notion that something portentous impended, Eisenhower's own, received top billing once again in newscasts and the press.

On January 5, the President met minority legislative leaders at the White House for a courtesy preview of his recommendations; thereby the press got one last "program" story before the opening of Congress. Then on Thursday, January 7, came the President's State of the Union Address to the Congress, another radio and television presentation, if at noon. There followed on three successive Mondays and Thursdays no less than seven of his supplementing messages, spaced for optimum press play and in a sequence obviously intended to strengthen the impression of a vast executive creation, highlight its most generally appealing features, blur the rest: Taft-Hartley and farm messages sent up at the same time on the same day (with a Korean defense treaty sent the Senate simultaneously); social security, health, and housing messages each featured in a separate package on a separate day; housekeeping and limited-interest requests buried by the dozen in the Budget Message; tax reduction dominant in the Economic Report. . . .

II. LEGISLATIVE PROGRAMS AND PRESIDENTIAL LEADERSHIP

Survival is the acid test of institutional development within the White House orbit. At this writing, in 1955, the Budget's call for estimates for fiscal 1957 has just gone to the agencies, a section 86 included as before. The President may now abandon letters of request for message data—in 1954, a reminder at cabinet table served instead —but there is every expectation in his entourage that 1955's budget and message seasons will proceed along the lines of prior years, with

January, 1956's annual messages conveying to the Congress and the country a comprehensive program presentation, Eisenhower's third—thus marking the tenth anniversay of Truman's trial compendium of 1946. . . .

Traditionally, there has been a tendency to distinguish "strong" Presidents from "weak," depending on their exercise of the initiative in legislation. The personal appearances in the hall of the House, the special messages, the drafted bills, the public appeals, so characteristic of contemporary program presentation, have all been represented in the past—no farther back than Franklin Roosevelt's time—as signs of a President's intention or capacity to "dominate" the Congress. If these were once relevant criteria of domination, they are not so today. As things stand now they have beome part of the regular routines of office, an accepted elaboration of the constitutional right to recommend; as such, no more indicative of presidential domination than the veto power, say, in Herbert Hoover's time.

Indeed, from the congressional point of view, "service," not domination, is the reality behind these presidential undertakings. In practical effect, they represent a means whereby Congress can gain from the outside what comes hard from within: a handy and official guide to the wants of its biggest customer; an advance formulation of main issues at each session; a work-load ready-to-hand for every legislative committee; an indication, more or less, of what may risk the veto; a borrowing of presidential prestige for most major bills—and thus a boosting of publicity-potentials in both sponsorship and opposition.

That Congress wants these things and finds them useful for its purposes may be judged from the almost total absence nowadays of vocal criticism or surprise at annual presentations of the President's program; an indicator reinforced by irritated comments, privately expressed on both sides of the aisle, when Eisenhower stayed his hand in 1953. Outcries against "dictatorship" and "speeches-from-the-throne" have long been stilled in responsible quarters. In 1947, Senator Taft told a Budget aide that as a matter of orderly procedure Republican committee chairmen *ought* to have the Democratic President's own views across-the-board and in detail, else the committees would lack solid ground from which to gauge the pleadings of departments and their clientele. In 1953, the very senior chairman of a major House committee reportedly admonished an Administration witness, "don't expect us to start from scratch on what you people want. That's not the way we do things here—*you* draft the bills and *we* work them over."

As that remark suggests, the Congress deals not in abstract ideas but in bills. It comes to grips with substance in terms of phraseology. The process cannot start without a draft. And since executive expertise is often indispensable, while executive wishes are data to be weighed—though quite conceivably ignored—a "downtown" draft has tangible advantage as the starting point. But more than drafting service is provided by contemporary presidential programs. Annual programming serves also to identify, to render timely, in effect to choose, most *legislative* issues on which serious attention is to center at a session; the President becomes agenda-setter for the Congress, the chief continuing initiator of subject-matter to reach actionable stages in committee and on the floor, whether or not ultimately passed. Of course, as Lawrence Chamberlain and others have made plain, most major measures are the product of long germination, much cross-fertilizing. Quite so; the service of contemporary Presidents has been less creativity than crystallization; a matter less of seeding new terrain than of tracing new lines in old ground, thereby to mark the field for current cultivation.

In this respect, the presidency is performing for the Congress a task apparently beyond that body's institutional capacity to carry on its own account. When one looks at the legislative record of the last decade, the major controversial measures brought to focus, debate, and near-passage, or enactment on congressional initiative *alone*, are small scatteration relative to those highlighted by—or with assistance from—the President: most prominently, perhaps, the Taft-Hartley Act, the two McCarran Acts, and the perennial Bricker Amendment.[1] Of these, at least Taft-Hartley may be ascribed actually to a reverse sort of presidential initiative—Truman choosing *not* to propose action in an area where momentary public sensitivity was certain to evoke response of some sort from the 80th Congress. . . . presiden-

[1] Other items which reached the point of passage include the tax reduction measures of 1947 and 1948, the first tidelands bill in 1947, and the natural gas and basing point bills of 1949. Of course, there have been infinite numbers of amendments to, adjustments in—and sheer denials of—Administration proposals, over the years, as matters of distinct congressional initiative, oppositional to presidential purposes or claimed intent. But these are in a different category. The fact that Presidents are now so largely raisers of the issues does not signify that they are safe from penalties for having done so; quite the contrary, both in and out of Congress.

tial silences no less than statements may serve to delineate the action-able issues.

But note that setting an agenda is not the same thing as enforcing it; selecting issues for consideration is not equivalent to having bill enacted into law. For evidence one has but to review the course of any recent congressional session. As a matter of fact, the most institu-tionalized aspects of the President's involvement in the legislative process are precisely those least concerned with actual campaigning for his program once presented: legislative programming and legisla-tive clearance, *not* legislative in-fighting and signal-calling, day-by-day. To be sure, periodic White House meetings with congressional party leaders have become the norm; agendas prepared for the Presi-dent in Truman's time; minutes kept as well in Eisenhower's. And Eisenhower has established in his entourage an Army-type liaison operation, its several staff aides covering each corner of the Hill on regular patrols. But formal leaders' sessions tend to be ambassadorial encounters; organized liaison tends to create its own chores, if not, indeed, to confuse liaisoners' loyalties. So far as one can judge from the outside, it remains true in Eisenhower's time—as in Truman's and F.D.R.'s before him—that when the chips are down, there is no sub-stituting for the President's own footwork, his personal negotia-tion, his direct appeal, his voice and no other's on the telephone. Naturally, such methods cannot guarantee success; to overwork them would be self-defeating; to institutionalize them may well be impossi-ble. Yet these, not programming devices, must bear the weight, pro-vide the test, of presidential "domination" over Congress.

Indeed, a presidential purpose to control the congressional *prod-uct* may actually be impeded, not advanced, by legislative program-ming as presently evolved. Those massive, annual presentations have a tendency to blur the public impact of particulars, scatter attention, divert interest—as with Eisenhower's messages of 1954, or Truman's, year by year. Regularized repetition tends to dilute the dramatic, fo-cussing effects of personal appearance and appeal. White House spon-sorship spread wide tends to reduce the import of each presidential label. Manifold commitments tend to complicate the task of striking particular bargains. Multi-item programs tend to encourage score-keeping by parties, press, and public, ordinarily with the result of stressing losses over gains on a strict by-the-numbers basis. . . .

But whether or not always advantageous in those terms, the annual presidential inventory and its attendant mechanics have now become so rooted in responsibilities of office, so customary in the view of press and public, so satisfactory to the Congress, so institutionalized in the executive, that major alteration of the present pattern, much less its permanent abandonment, would appear no light matter for a President, nor likely. . . . And these are backed now by accustomed practices each year becoming more entrenched—not only as responses to congressional and public expectations, but as prime means to policy decision and control in the executive. To disavow them now might be to trade more flexibility with Congress for fewer hand holds on departments—this difficulty among others. . . .

11   *The Purge of 1938*
WILLIAM RIKER

As the primary campaign started that year it did not seem to differ significantly from earlier primaries. President Roosevelt did, it is true, try to smooth out intra-party disagreements. For example, he persuaded Representative Disney of Oklahoma not to run in the primary against Senator Thomas. He repeatedly and unsuccessfully urged John L. Lewis and the party regulars in Pennsylvania to support the same candidates in the primary; but he was unable to prevent a vicious, mud-slinging campaign fight between the two factions, a fight disastrous to the Democratic ticket in the fall. He took much trouble to help two Southern New Dealers, Senators Pepper of Florida and Hill of Alabama, in the spring primaries—for Pepper, the President's eldest son formally announced "we are interested" in seeing him return. Early in March, Roosevelt took a part behind the scenes of the Kentucky primary, persuading erstwhile supporters of Governor Chandler, who coveted Senator Barkley's place, to desert

From *Democracy in the United States* (pp. 285-293), William H. Riker. Copyright 1953 by The Macmillan Company and used with their permission.

Chandler for Barkley. All this activity was quiet maneuvering, however, not extensively reported in the newspapers; all the public statements were made by other people, not directly using the President's name; and his so-called interference was either in support of sitting Senators or in the interest of party harmony. What Roosevelt did, therefore, was no more than what many of his predecessors had done. It would have been very strange indeed had he not helped his loyal floor leader, Barkley; and it would have been stranger still if he had ignored Pepper, who was one of the few Southern Democrats in favor of the very controversial and—in the President's view—extraordinarily important wage and hour bill, and whose renomination would certainly swing some wavering Southerners to its support.

The first intimation that Roosevelt intended a real break with political precedent came during a vacation at Warm Springs, Georgia, at the end of March. Reporters were quick to notice that he praised Governor Rivers and Representative Weichel without mentioning Senator George who was up for renomination. Another hint was dropped a month later when Jim Farley, still then Postmaster-General and Chairman of the Democratic National Committee, was quoted as saying that Maryland Democrats should defeat Senator Tydings in the primary. Several Maryland politicians, eager to be the President's candidate, promptly scurried to the White House to beg for approval. By the end of May the President's new role in the primaries was clear to journalists, if not to the public generally, and the word "purge" had begun to appear in the headlines. When the Governor of Oregon, a very conservative Democrat, implied that the President favored his renomination, Roosevelt's press secretary issued a sharp denial and a few days later Secretary of the Interior Ickes advised Oregon Democrats to vote for the other, more liberal Democrat in the primary. At the same time Governor Johnson of South Carolina, a New Dealer, emerged from an interview with the President to announce that he would try to get the Democratic senatorial nomination over the incredibly reactionary Senator "Cotton Ed" Smith; and Governor Rivers of Georgia, also after seeing the President, intimated to reporters that he had been urged to run in the primary against Senator George. These were clear enough indications that Roosevelt was trying to defeat those Democratic Senators who were lukewarm about the New Deal.

Then came the first clear evidence of a plan to purge. Harry Hopkins, then the Administrator of the WPA, told a reporter that, if he were voting in the Iowa primary, he would support, not Senator Gillette who was seeking renomination, but Representative Otha Wearin who was seeking promotion. Senator Gillette, and other Democratic Senators who fearfully visualized a similar pronouncement about themselves, were outraged and excited by what they thought was a threat to use WPA money against Democrats. They spent the whole day debating it in the Senate. Faithful Administration Senators, like Barkley and Mrs. Caraway, defended Hopkins, saying that he had been badgered by reporters into an indiscretion; even they did not then conceive of arguing that the Administration ought to campaign publicly against sitting Democratic Senators in the Democratic primaries.

After the excitement aroused by Hopkins' remark, Roosevelt evidently wavered. The next day, coming out of a conference with the President, Representative Eicher of Iowa, announced his support of Wearin; but a few days later at a press conference Roosevelt refused to discuss the Iowa primary and said that Hopkins' comment was off-the-record and ought not to have been published. Roosevelt's wavering reflected the division among his official intimates. While Hopkins, Corcoran, and Ickes were evidently urging aggressive action, Jim Farley seemed to support Gillette; and Henry Wallace, the only Iowan high in the Administration, kept discreetly, even noticeably, silent. Roosevelt, uncertain and unwontedly indecisive, did nothing, Gillette won, and a few days later the two sat down to a hatchet-burying luncheon, in shirtsleeves, so reporters said.

If Roosevelt intended to appeal to the people for support, the Iowa primary was an inauspicious start—ill-prepared, ill-timed, ill-managed, and necessitating at the end an embarrassing reconciliation. Perhaps Roosevelt was piqued by the failure; perhaps he had gone too far to stop—he had, for example, already selected Governor Johnson of South Carolina to oppose Senator "Cotton Ed" Smith; he had already given his blessing to one Lawrence Camp in the Georgia primary against Senator George; and Senator Guffey of Pennsylvania —always loyal, but always too blunt—had already been forced off the Democratic Senatorial Campaign Committee for proposing a purge of all those Democratic Senators who had voted against the Court reform bill. In any event, whether piqued by a messy failure or trapped by events which in his hesitancy he allowed to slip from his control, he told the people in a fireside chat that he intended to intervene in Democratic primaries:

As the head of the Democratic Party . . . charged with the responsibility of carrying out the definitely liberal declaration of principles set
forth in the 1936 Democratic platform, I feel that I have every right to
speak in those few instances where there may be a clear issue between
candidates for a Democratic nomination involving these principles. . . .

Do not misunderstand me. I certainly would not indicate a preference
in a State primary merely because a candidate, otherwise liberal in outlook, had conscientiously differed with me on any single issue . . . [but].
. . . We all know that progress may be blocked by out-spoken reaction-
aries and also by those who say "yes" to a progressive objective, but who
always find some reason to oppose any specific proposal to gain that objective. I call that type of candidate a "yes, but" fellow.

Soon thereafter he started out on a trip through the South to California, presumably to campaign in the Democratic primaries for New
Dealers and against the " 'yes, but' fellows," the ones who had opposed not only the Court bill, but also the wage and hour bill, the administrative reorganization bill, and the public utility holding company death sentence clause. He made four speeches for Senator
Barkley in Kentucky; but after that the "purge" was, as an editor of
Nation complained, allowed "almost to peter out." Instead of campaigning forthrightly for his supporters, he ceased to mention primaries, substituting:

an elaborate code of graduated approval—with candidates designated as
"friend," "old friend," and "dear old friend" according to the degree of
White House enthusiasm for their respective nominations.

In Covington, Kentucky, he had asked Democrats to renominate the
Senate floor leader because:

We in this country operate principally through what we call the party
system. We so operate because we believe that party responsibility
eliminates a large part of the confusion which would result from a complete lack of party leadership.

But by the time he spoke for Senator Thomas in Oklahoma, he had
cheapened the argument from an appeal for executive democratic
government to an appeal to sordid self-interest:

Senator Thomas has been of enormous help to me and to the Administration in keeping me advised as to the needs of your State, and as to how
we, in Washington, could help meet them.

In Colorado and Nevada, where Senators Adams and McCarran, two
who really qualified for the "yes, but" category, were up for renomi-

nation, he ignored their opponents and referred to McCarran as a "friend," albeit the lowest degree of approval.

Back again in the Old South, and encouraged perhaps by the news of Barkley's victory, he was more forthright. At Barnsville, Georgia, he made a full dress speech for Lawrence Camp, the Federal District Attorney whom he had encouraged to run against Senator George. In South Carolina he obliquely supported Governor Johnson who was running against Senator "Cotton Ed" Smith. In Maryland, he made the most powerful and partisan speech of the campaign endorsing Representative Davey Lewis, who was trying to unseat Senator Tydings. Finally in a New York City Congressional district, he strongly supported one James Fay, a deputy collector of internal revenue, against Represestative O'Connor, a Tammany Democrat, chairman of the House Rules Committee, and the man who more than anyone else delayed consideration of the wage and hour bill.

And the result of his campaigning? Senator Barkley won in Kentucky, Senator Caraway, whom he had mildly supported, won in Arkansas, Senator Thomas won in Oklahoma. Three victories. But Senator George won in Georgia, Senator Smith won in South Carolina, Senator Tydings won in Maryland. Three defeats. James Fay won in the New York 16th District. A victory. As many journalists and scholars have pointed out, every sitting Congressman, with the exception of O'Connor, won—which suggests that Roosevelt's campaigning had no significant effect, except perhaps in New York City. Of course, 1938 was a bad year for the New Deal in the fall elections and it may be that he did at least save Barkley and Thomas from defeat. Otherwise, however, he did not accomplish very much, certainly not enough to compensate for the bad feeling he engendered among conservative Democrats.

Why the meagre result?

Perhaps in part Roosevelt failed because of simple lack of preparation. While some of his advisors may have conceived the plan in 1937, Roosevelt himself probably did not decide just what to do until late in the campaign year. How else can one explain his wavering over the Iowa primary? How else can one explain the elaborate trip West, starting out just after the promise made in the fireside chat to "indicate preferences," a trip taking him through eleven states during their primary campaigns, and yet a trip on which he indicated a preference plainly in only three states and hinted at a preference in only two more? Reconstructing the events now, it seems likely that, with his advisors divided, he planned at first merely to have certain recognized intimates speak out, as his son James did in Florida, or as Harry Hopkins did in Iowa, but that he changed his mind after the Iowa fiasco. No doubt it is futile now to pry into long-forgotten thoughts, but one fact is certain: He did not select his candidates in Georgia or Maryland until sometime in May, unfortunately after the junior Senator in each state—both good New Dealers—had agreed to campaign for the men he was trying to purge. Yet one rule upon which most experienced politicians would agree is that, in a primary campaign to unseat a fairly popular officeholder, the aspirant ought to work full-time at his campaign for at least six or nine months before the election. By this standard the purge was ill-planned; the hesitancy on his trip West indicates that the affair was ill-managed. In his own campaigns, Roosevelt was extraordinarily astute; but here he blundered.

The blunder is understandable. He was attempting something entirely new in American politics. Furthermore, he was running counter to the tradition of localism and state sovereignty in American politics. So it is not strange that he blundered in an unexplored land. Consider the blank amazement and unbelief displayed by Hiram Johnson when Hopkins' remark about the Iowa primary was reported to the Senate:

Mr. Johnson. . . . I take it Mr. Hopkins is a resident of Iowa.
Mr. Wheeler. I do not know.
Mr. Johnson. He must be, or he would not think of doing such a thing.
Mr. Wheeler. No, he is not, I am told.
Mr. Johnson. The Senator must be in error. Mr. Hopkins must be a resident of Iowa, or he would not think of doing such a thing.
Mr. Wheeler. Mr. Hopkins, I am informed, votes in New York . . . he is being talked of as a candidate for Governor of the State of New York.

And having considered Johnson's incredulity, consider then how difficult to plan and execute was Roosevelt's self-imposed assignment.

It is a superficial explanation, however, to say that the meagre result of Roosevelt's campaign was due only to blundering. Behind the blundering lies the fact of federalism. What this whole episode demonstrates more than anything else is the resistance of local politicians to national leadership. With their own well-oiled local machines, all the sitting Senators won, whether Roosevelt favored or opposed them. The only place where Roosevelt unseated a Congressman was in his own state of New York; and there he was perforce a local politician himself, the leader of a local faction; so his victory must be attributed as much to his residence as to his national leadership.

12   *How the Farmers Get What They Want*
THEODORE LOWI

In his Farm Message of January 31, President Johnson proposed that Congress establish a bipartisan commission to investigate the concentration of power in the food industry. In the same message the President called for new legislation to strengthen farmer cooperatives, to encourage their expansion through merger and acquisition, and to provide them with further exemptions from the antitrust laws.

This was the beginning of the "Johnson round" in agriculture. It is part of a familiar pattern. An attack on the food industry's market power, coupled with proposals for expanded and stronger farm cooperatives, is obviously not an attack on concentration itself. Rather it is an attack on the intervention of non-agricultural groups into strictly agricultural affairs.

That agricultural affairs should be handled strictly within the agricultural community is a basic political principle established before the turn of the century and maintained since then without serious reexamination. As a result, agriculture has become neither public nor private enterprise. It is a system of self-government in which each leading farm interest controls a segment of agriculture through a delegation of national sovereignty. Agriculture has emerged as a largely self-governing federal estate within the Federal structure of the United States.

From Theodore Lowi, *The Reporter* (May 21, 1964, pp. 34-37), Copyright 1964 by the Fortnightly Publishing Company, Inc., New York.

President Johnson recognized these facts within three weeks of his accession when he summoned a conference of agricultural leaders to formulate a program by which agriculture should be served and regulated. The most recent concession to agriculture's self-government was the wheat-cotton bill. Because cotton supports were too high, the cotton interests wrote a bill providing for a subsidy of six to eight cents a pound to mills in order to keep them competitive with foreign cotton and domestic rayon without touching the price supports. On the other hand, wheat supports were too low because wheat farmers last year in referendum overwhelmingly rejected President Kennedy's plan to provide some Federal regulation along with supports. The wheat section of the new act calls for a program whereby wheat farmers may voluntarily comply with acreage reduction for subsidies of up to seventy cents a bushel but without the Federal supply regulations. The press called this a major legislative victory for Mr. Johnson, but the credit is not his. That the press could see this as a victory for anyone but organized cotton and wheat is a testimonial to the total acceptance by President, press, and public of the principle that private agricultural interests alone govern agriculture and should do so.

The reasons for agriculture's self-government are deep-rooted, and the lessons to be drawn are important to the future of American politics. For a century agriculture has been out of step with American economic development. Occasional fat years have only created unreal expectations, to be undercut by the more typical lean years.

Quite early, farmers discovered the value of politics as a counterweight to industry's growth and concentration. Land-grant and homesteading acts were followed by governmental services in research and education. Continuing distress led to bolder demands. First there were efforts to effect a redistribution of wealth in favor of agriculture. As a debtor class, farmers saw inflation as the solution, and Bryan was their spokesman for cheaper money and cheaper credit. The monopolies, the railroads, the grain merchants and other processors, the banks, and the brokers were to be deprived of power over the market by dissolution or by severe restraints. Next, farmers sought solutions by emulating the business system: the co-operative to restrain domestic trade and international dumping over high tariff walls and to restrain international trade. Yet all these mechanisms either were not enacted or did not live up to expectations.

With the coming of the New Deal and with its help, organized agriculture turned to self-regulation. The system created during the 1930's has endured to this day, and with only a few marginal additions and alterations is accepted almost unanimously by farm leaders. Self-regulation might have taken several forms, the most likely one being a national system of farm-leader representation within a farmers' NRA. Instead, a more complicated system of highly decentralized and highly autonomous subgovernments developed, largely for Constitutional reasons. Agriculture was the most "local" of the manufacturing groups the Federal government was trying to reach. The appearance if not the reality of decentralizing Federal programs through farmer-elected local committees helped avoid strains on the interstate commerce clause of the Constitution. But this avoidance of Constitutional troubles created very special political difficulties.

THE LOCAL COMMITTEES

The Federal Extension Service shows how the system works. It is "co-operative" in that it shares the job of farm improvement with the states, the land-grant colleges, the county governments, and the local associations of farmers. The county agent is actually employed by the local associations. In the formative years, the aid of local chambers of commerce was enlisted, the local association being the "farm bureau" of the chamber. In order to co-ordinate local activities and to make more effective claims for additional outside assistance, these farm bureaus were organized into state farm bureau federations. The American Farm Bureau Federation, formed at the Agriculture College of Cornell University in 1919, was used as a further step toward amalgamation. To this day there is a close relationship between the farm bureaus, the land-grant colleges, and the Extension Service. This transformation of an administrative arrangement into a political system has been repeated in nearly all the agricultural programs during recent decades. The Extension Service exercises few controls from the top. There are cries of "Federal encroachment" at the mere suggestion in Washington that the Department of Agriculture should increase its supervision of the extension programs or co-ordinate them with other Federal activities.

As the financial stakes have grown larger, the pattern of local self-government remains the same. Price support—the "parity program" —is run by the thousands of farmer-elected county committees that function alongside but quite independently of the other local committees. Acreage allotments to bring supply down and prices up are apportioned among the states by the Agricultural Stabilization and Conservation Service. State committees of farmers apportion the allotment among the counties. The farmer-elected county Stabilization and Conservation Committees receive the county allotment.

These committees made the original acreage allotments among individual farmers back in the 1930's; today, they make new allotments, work out adjustments and review complaints regarding allotments, determine whether quotas have been complied with, inspect and approve storage facilities, and perform as the court of original jurisdiction on violations of price-support rules and on eligibility for parity payments. The committees are also vitally important in the campaigns for the two-thirds vote required to fix high price supports. Congress determines the general level of supports, and the Secretary of Agriculture proclaims the national acreage quotas for adjusting the supply to the guaranteed price. But the locally elected committees stand between the farmer and Washington.

Most other agricultural programs have evolved similarly. Each is independent of the others, and any conflicts or overlapping mandates have been treated as nonexistent or beyond the jurisdiction of any one agency. The Soil Conservation Service operates through its independent soil-conservation districts, of which there were 2,936 in 1963, involving ninety-six per cent of the nation's farms. Each district's farmer-elected committee is considered a unit of local government. The Farmer Co-operative Service operates through the member-elected boards of directors of the farm co-ops. In agricultural credit, local self-government is found in even greater complexity. The Farm Credit Administration exists outside the Department of Agriculture and is made up of not one but three separate bodies politic, a triangular system mostly farmer-owned and totally farmer-controlled.

Ten Systems and Policies

The ten principal self-governing systems in agriculture, in fiscal 1962, disposed of $5.6 billion of the total of $6.7 billion in expenditures passing through the Department of Agriculture. During the calendar year 1962, $5.8 billion in loans was handled similarly. This combined amount represents a large portion of the total of Federal activity outside national defense.

Each of the ten systems has become a powerful political instrumentality. The self-governing local units become one important force in a system that administers a program and maintains the autonomy of that program against political forces emanating from other agricultural programs, from antagonistic farm and nonfarm interests, from Congress, from the Secretary of Agriculture, and from the President. To many a farmer, the local outpost of one or another of these systems *is* the government.

The politics within each system is built upon a triangular trading pattern involving the central agency, a Congressional committee or sub-committee, and the local district farmer committees (usually federated in some national or regional organization). Each side of the triangle complements and supports the other two.

The Extension Service, for example, is one side of the triangle completed by the long-tenure "farm bureau" members of the Agriculture Committees in Congress and, at the local level, the American Farm Bureau Federation with its local committees. Further group support is provided by two intimately related groups, the Association of Land Grant Colleges and Universities and the National Association of County Agricultural Agents.

Another such triangle unites the Soil Conservation Service, the Agriculture subcommittee of the House Appropriations Committee, and the local districts organized in the energetic National Association of Soil Conservation Districts. Further support comes from the Soil Conservation Society of America (mainly professionals) and the former Friends of the Land, now the Izaak Walton League of America.

Probably the most complex of the systems embraces the parity program. It connects the Agricultural Stabilization and Conservation Service with the eight (formerly ten) commodity subcommittees of the House Agriculture Committee and the dozens of separately organized groups representing the various commodities. (Examples: National Cotton Council, American Wool Growers Association, American Cranberry Growers Association.) These groups and congressmen draw support from the local price-support committees wherever a particular commodity is grown.

The Farmer Had His Way

These systems have a vigorous capacity to maintain themselves and to resist encroachment. They have such institutional legitimacy that they have become practically insulated from the three central sources of democratic political responsibility. Thus, within the Executive branch, they are autonomous. Secretaries of Agriculture have tried and failed to consolidate or even to co-ordinate related programs. Within Congress, they are sufficiently powerful to be able to exercise an effective veto or create a stalemate. And they are almost totally removed from the view, not to mention the control, of the general public. (Throughout the 1950's, Victor Anfuso of Brooklyn was the only member of the House Agriculture Committee from a non-farm constituency.)

Important cases illustrate their power:

In 1947, Secretary of Agriculture Clinton P. Anderson proposed a consolidation of all soil-conservation, price-support, and FHA programs into one committee system with a direct line from the committees to the Secretary. Bills were prepared providing for consolidation within the price-support committees. Contrary bills provided for consolidation under soil conservation districts. The result: stalemate. In 1948, a leading farm senator proposed consolidation of the programs under the local associations of the Extension Service. Immediately a House farm leader introduced a contrary bill. The result: continuing stalemate.

In Waco, Texas, on October 14, 1952, Presidential candidate Eisenhower said: "I would like to see in every county all Federal farm agencies under the same roof." Pursuant to this promise, Secretary Ezra Taft Benson issued a series of orders during early 1953 attempting to bring about consolidation of local units as well as unification at the top. Finally, amid cries of "sneak attack" and "agricrat," Benson proclaimed that "any work on the further consolidation of county and state offices . . . shall be suspended."

From the very beginning, Secretary Benson sought to abandon rigid price supports and bring actual supports closer to market prices. In 1954, as he was beginning to succeed, Congress enacted a "commodity set-aside" by which $2.5 billion of surplus commodities already held by the government were declared to be a "frozen reserve" for national defense. Since the Secretary's power to cut price supports depends heavily upon the amount of government-owned surplus carried over from previous years, the commodity set-aside was a way of freezing parity as well as reserves. Benson eventually succeeded in reducing supports on the few commodities over which he had authority. But thanks to the set-aside, Congress, between fiscal 1952 and 1957, helped increase the value of commodities held by the government from $1.1 billion to $5.3 billion. What appeared, therefore, to be a real Republican policy shift amounted to no more than giving back with one hand what had been taken away by the other.

President Eisenhower's first budget sought to abolish farm homebuilding and improvement loans by eliminating the budgetary request and by further requesting that the 1949 authorization law be allowed to expire. Congress overrode his request in 1953 and each succeeding year, and the President answered Congress with a year-by-year refusal to implement the farm housing program. In 1956, when the President asked again explicitly for elimination of the program, he was rebuffed. The Housing subcommittee of the House Banking and Currency Committee added to the President's omnibus housing bill a renewal of the farm housing program, plus an authorization for $500 million in loans over a five-year period, and the bill passed with a Congressional mandate to use the funds. They were used thereafter at a rate of about $75 million a year.

On March 16, 1961, President Kennedy produced a "radically different" farm program in a special message to Congress. For the first time in the history of price supports, the bill called for surplus control through quotas placed on bushels, tons, or other units, rather than on acreage. An acreage allotment allows the farmer to produce as much as he can on the reduced acreage in cultivation. For example, in the first ten years or so of acreage control, acreage under cultivation dropped by about four per cent, while actual production rose by fifteen per cent. The Kennedy proposal called for national committees of farmers to be elected to work out the actual program. This more stringent type of control was eliminated from the omnibus bill in the Agriculture Committees of both chambers and there were no attempts to restore them during floor debate. Last-minute efforts by Secretary Orville L. Freeman to up the ante, offering to raise wheat supports from $1.79 to $2.00, were useless. Persistence by the administration led eventually to rejection by wheat farmers in 1963 of all high price supports and acreage controls.

The politics of this rejected referendum is of general significance. Despite all the blandishments and inducements of the administration, the farmer had his way. The local price-support committees usually campaign in these referendums for the Department of Agriculture, but this time they did not. And thousands of small farmers, eligible to vote for the first time, joined with the local leadership to help defeat the referendum. It is not so odd that wheat farmers would reject a proposal that aims to regulate them more strictly than before. What is odd is that only wheat farmers are allowed to decide the matter. It seems that in agriculture, as in many other fields, the regulators are powerless without the consent of the regulated.

Agriculture is the field where the distinction between public and private has been almost completely eliminated, not by public expropriation of private domain but by private expropriation of public domain. For more than a generation, Americans have succeeded in expanding the public sphere without giving thought to the essential democratic question of how each expansion is to be effected. The creation of private governments has profoundly limited the capacity of the public government to govern responsibly and flexibly.

CONGRESS AS AN INSTRUMENT OF GOVERNMENT

Part A. THE FORMULATION OF POLICY

13   *Legislative History of the Securities Act of 1933*
JAMES M. LANDIS

The act naturally had its beginnings in the high financing of the Twenties that was followed by the market crash of 1929. Even before the inauguration of Franklin D. Roosevelt as President of the United States, a spectacularly illuminating investigation of the nature of this financing was being undertaken by the Senate Banking and Currency Committee under the direction of its able counsel, Ferdinand D. Pecora. That Committee spread on the record more than the peccadillos of groups of men involved in the issuance and marketing of securities. It indicted a system as a whole that had failed miserably in imposing those essential fiduciary standards that should govern persons whose function it was to handle other people's money. Investment bankers, brokers and dealers, corporate directors, accountants, all found themselves the object of criticism so severe that the American public lost much of its faith in professions that had theretofore been regarded with a respect that had approached awe. As the criticism mounted, doubts as to the value of the very system of private enterprise was generated, and a wide demand was prevalent for the institution of procedures of governmental control that would in essence have created a capital issues bureaucracy to control not only the manner in which securities could be issued but the very right of any enterprise to tap the capital market.

It is of interest to note that Mr. Roosevelt declined to endorse this

From James M. Landis, *The George Washington Law Review* (28 Geo. Wash. L. Rev. 1959). Reprinted by permission demand. His message to the Congress on March 29, 1933, contains these two paragraphs:

Of course, the Federal Government cannot and should not take any action which might be construed as approving or guaranteeing that newly issued securities are sound in the sense that their value will be maintained or that the properties which they represent will earn profit.

There is, however, an obligation upon us to insist that every issue of new securities to be sold in interstate commerce shall be accompanied by full publicity and information, and that no essentially important element attending the issue shall be concealed from the buying public.

Meanwhile the task of drafting the legislation to carry out this message had been assigned to Houston Thompson, a former member of the Federal Trade Commission, whose draft bill introduced on that very day was totally inconsistent with the President's expressed desires. That bill, which sought to institute a system of registration of securities proposed to be offered, provided "that the Commission [the Federal Trade Commission] may revoke the registration of any security by entering an order to that effect, if upon examination . . . it shall appear . . . (e) that its [sic] or their affairs are in unsound condition or insolvent; or (f) that the enterprise or business of the issuer, or person, or the security is not based upon sound principles, and that the revocation is in the interest of the public welfare."

The Thompson bill introduced by Mr. Rayburn in the House of Representatives and by Senator Robinson (for Senator Ashurst) in the Senate was referred respectively to the House Committee on Interstate and Foreign Commerce and the Senate Committee on Banking and Currency. Mr. Sam Rayburn was Chairman of the former and Senator Duncan U. Fletcher of Florida of the latter. The committees thereupon proceeded to hearings upon the bill.

The hearings before the House committee were brief but sufficient to disclose the unworkability of the Thompson bill. Its draftsmanship was of decidedly inferior quality. It has based itself in large measure on the blue sky* legislation of the states, but went beyond the most

* This name derived from the belief that irresponsible securities dealers would sell shares not only in the Brooklyn Bridge but even the blue sky. Generally state securities laws provided (1) criminal penalties for fraudulent sales and permanent injunctions from future sales in the state; (2) the licensing of sellers of securities subject to revocation, based on the "good repute" of the dealer; and (3) the registration of all securities with full information on the company and the security, in most cases requiring state commission approval before a sale could be made. This generally involved the commission in a judgment of the soundness of the security.—Ed.

severe of these state statutes in lodging extensive powers to control the issuance and sale of securities in the federal government. . . .

The hearings before the House committee on the Thompson bill convinced Mr. Rayburn and his committee that that bill provided no basis for sound federal securities legislation. His deep concern over this matter was communicated to the White House and the White House in turn went to other sources for help.

Professor Felix Frankfurter, now Mr. Justice Frankfurter, had been in close touch with the Roosevelt campaign of 1932. His associations with the President-Elect and particularly the reputed head of his "Brain Trust," Professor Raymond S. Moley, became even more frequent after the election. His wide knowledge of public law, his fertile mind, and his intimacy with the younger generation of lawyers upon whose help he could always count, made him invaluable to the new administration. I happened to have had the good fortune of being closely associated with him both as a student and later as his colleague, having cooperated with him in the production of a book and several articles, none of which, however, dealt with securities legislation. As a recently appointed Professor of Legislation at the Harvard Law School, I had spent considerable of my time and that of my small class in an attempt to explore the nature and variety of the sanctions available to government to bring about conformance with its statutory mandates and in dealing with the nature of standards capable of reasonable enforcement. An understanding of both problems seemed to me essential in order to grasp the elements of legislative draftsmanship. A particularly illuminating field, filled with challenge, had been state blue sky legislation. For the last years my seminar, as well as I, had been exploring this field. Little in the way of scholarly research had characterized that field and it had precipitated few judicial decisions of any consequence. Consequently, when in response to Rayburn's concern, Moley turned to Frankfurter for assistance, he, in turn, asked me to assist him. I can recall well the morning of that request. It was a Thursday in early April and my next classes were scheduled for the following Monday. Frankfurter, however, thought that the job could be done over that week-end. We consequently left on the night train for Washington.

The next morning in Washington we met with Benjamin V. Cohen and Thomas G. Corcoran. Cohen had been summoned by Frankfurter from the ranks of active practitioners. I was told he was a most brilliant man, knowledgeable in the field of securities, and that he possessed a gentle personality. My information was correct. Corcoran I had known intimately since law school days. I knew of his experience with the law firm of Cotton & Franklin in New York City and of his work with that firm in the securities field. Considerably disillusioned after 1929, Corcoran had come to Washington abetted by Frankfurter and was then serving as counsel to the Reconstruction Finance Corporation. It was a strange team—Corcoran ebullient, moving easily with the new forces in the administration; Cohen reserved and almost shy; but both brilliant and indefatigable workers.

After a brief session with Frankfurter, where we determined to take as the base of our work the English Companies Act with which Cohen was very familiar, Cohen, Corcoran and I set to work. Frankfurter had other political duties to attend to. By late Saturday night we had a draft of the bill in reasonable shape. We had to work under certain limitations imposed upon us by the fact of the Thompson bill. Tactically it seemed wise to shape our proposals as "perfecting" amendments to that bill, with the result that our original bill embodied a number of proposals contained in the Thompson bill that were subsequently happily discarded. The core of the Securities Act of 1933 is, however, to be found in that hurried draft of ours.

Our draft remained true to the conception voiced by the President in his message of March 29, 1933 to the Congress, namely that its requirements should be limited to full and fair disclosure of the nature of the security being offered and that there should be no authority to pass upon the investment quality of the security. This, of course, is the theory of the English Companies Act, but to the sanctions of that act we added the right of the Commission to suspend the registration of any security if inadequate compliance with the stated requirements for disclosure of misrepresentations of fact were found to exist in its registration statement. . . .

On Sunday, Frankfurter informed us that Rayburn had called a special meeting of his Committee for Monday to consider our draft. I arranged to put off my classes for a day, trusting to be able to take Monday's night train back to Cambridge. . . .

In addition to the members of the House Committee, there were present at this private hearing Frankfurter, Thompson, Cohen, Beaman, Perley and myself. Middleton Beaman had been for many years a chief legislative draftsman for the House of Representatives. Members of both political parties trusted him, and rightly so, for his complete impartiality and his competence. His function, as he always saw it, was to put into effective statutory language the ideas, whatever they might be, of the sponsors of such legislation as might be referred to him. Allan H. Perley, who later succeeded him, was only slightly less able than Beaman.

Frankfurter took the lead in the exposition of our draft. It was a brilliant performance. Questions of detail were referred by him to Cohen and to me, but he handled the main structure of the bill magnificently as well as the relationship of this bill in the nature of a "perfecting" amendment to the Thompson bill. The session, punctuated by questioning from members of the Committee, continued throughout the morning. We adjourned for lunch and resumed in the afternoon. It was difficult for me to assess the effect of our draft upon the Committee, particularly on Rayburn, whom I had never seen before. About five o'clock the meeting ended and the Committee held a brief executive session from which every non-member was excluded except Frankfurter. At its close, Rayburn and Frankfurter came out to talk to Cohen and myself, and Rayburn asked us to continue to work with the Committee and with Beaman's office as consultants to perfect our draft. Upon Frankfurter's assurance that my classes at Cambridge could be covered, I agreed to do so. Cohen also was willing to continue. That night Frankfurter, I believe, left for Cambridge. Cohen and I stayed on, for what I believed would be only another few days. It became almost two months.

Middleton Beaman is a difficult man to describe. I had thought I knew something of legislative draftsmanship until I met him. The next days were spent in continuous conference with him and Perley at his offices deep in the bowels of the old House Office Building. For days Beaman would not allow us to draft a line. He insisted instead on exploring the implications of the bill to find exactly what we had or did not have in mind. He probed always for the extent and nature of these hiatuses that any proposed important legislation necessarily possesses. It was exasperating to both Cohen and myself. We would meet Corcoran in the evenings, inasmuch as his duties prevented him from giving his full time to this project, and give vent to our suspicions that this delay bore symptoms of sinister Wall Street plotting. We were wrong. It was these discussions that first evolved the exact scope that we wanted the Securities Act to cover. . . .

The House committee had created a subcommittee to deal with this legislation, consisting of five members, three of whom were Democrats and two Republicans. Its chairman was Sam Rayburn. It had been agreed between them that no publicity of any nature would be given to our work until a draft satisfactory to the subcommittee was reported out to the full committee. That agreement was faithfully kept until almost the very last, despite the fact that Wall Street was aware that the Thompson bill had been discarded and that we were preparing a new draft. In addition to the new print of our original draft, five successive confidential committee drafts were printed and circulated among the subcommittee members. None of them "leaked," with the exception noted below, although there was considerable speculation and concern about the nature of our work in the *Wall Street Journal* and other financial columns, particularly in the light of the dismay, not to say terror, that the Thompson bill had aroused. It amuses me in retrospect to recall that Cohen and I during those days had a room on the seventh floor of the Carleton Hotel. Just above us was J. P. Morgan, Jr., and his staff, who had been summoned to testify in the Pecora hearings. We frequently met in the elevator in the morning or in the evening. We naturally recognized him, but we passed unnoticed, happy that our burrowing into the structure of that empire had no noticeable reverberations above.

Four revisions of our draft were completed before we were ready to meet with the subcommittee. Members of that subcommittee had, however, dropped in frequently in their individual capacity to make a suggestion or to inquire as to the meaning of a particular section. The number of exempted securities had been expanded. Municipal bonds, which we sought to include in our original draft, were made exempt for obvious political reasons. Securities of building and loan associations, savings and loan associations, and homestead associations were also excluded for similar reasons. Securities of common carriers issued subject to the provisions of section 20a of the Interstate Commerce Act were exempted to the theory that otherwise there would be a dual jurisdiction by the Federal Trade Commission and the Interstate Commerce Commission over these securities. Rayburn insisted on their exclusion despite our contention that the Interstate Commerce Commission exercised no controls over the manner in which railroad securities authorized under section 20a of the Interstate Commerce Act could be sold.

Two sessions of the subcommittee were held and further changes made, but none of major consequence other than the reduction of the statute of limitations from six to two years.

When the bill was ready to be reported to the full committee a somewhat extraordinary circumstance occurred. Wall Street's concern over our work and its inability to see it in its formative stages has already been noted. Some friends of Moley, however, stirred him up to such a degree by misrepresenting to him the character of our work as well as our motives to the point that he insisted with Rayburn that a select group of New York lawyers versed in security matters should be given a copy of the bill and have an opportunity to express their views on it to the subcommittee. Rayburn was loath to agree to this procedure but finally acquiesced in it upon the condition that Cohen and I should be entitled to be present and make such comments as we might choose in defense of our handiwork.

This meeting occurred on a Saturday morning. John Foster Dulles, A. I. Henderson, and Arthur H. Dean constituted the group of New York lawyers.[1] Dulles started the attack. His preparation, however, had not been adequate. Allegations he made as to the import of the bill were incapable, as we pointed out, of substantiation. Rayburn, who is an expert in judging experts, exhibited considerable annoyance at these accusations, not merely on our account, but at Dulles' allegations that Rayburn was sponsoring legislation that would undermine our financial system. Rayburn insisted that all that was being demanded was that the system should live up to its pretensions.[2] Henderson and Dean were far better acquainted with the details of the bill. Their criticism went primarily to certain technical features and much of it had merit. The subcommittee adjourned shortly after noon with the understanding that Henderson and Dean would meet with Cohen and myself that afternoon and consider their

[1] They represented the Wall Street law firms of Sullivan & Cromwell; and Cravath, DeGersdorf, Swaine and Wood, firms active in security matters of large moment.

[2] Similar allegations were not uncommon. A memorandum circulated by the Investment Bankers Association on the bill as passed by the House, dated May 6, 1933, stated that its "practical results . . . will be to suspend the underwriting of distribution of many capital issues by responsible persons. . . . The bill as a whole might be exceptionally deflationary in its effect because it affords unreasonable interference with honest business. . . . The Act goes beyond publicity and, despite its protestations, would encourage the public to believe that the Government had accepted the duty of passing officially upon the safety of investments." Admittedly the Securities Act of 1933 in its original form did hamper the normal flow of capital into enterprise, a check which was not overcome until the 1934 amendments were enacted. That check, however, in my opinion was due less to the provisions of the original act than to their misinterpretation, deliberate to a great degree, by the widely publicized utterances of persons prominent in the financial world together with their lawyers.

suggestions in detail. Rayburn led us to understand that whatever we accepted need not go back to the committee for formal approval but could be incorporated in the bill as submitted to the full committee. We spent a long, hot afternoon with Henderson and Dean, ending with a number of technical changes particularly in the schedules to the bill that had not had a thorough going over by the subcommittee.

The hearing before the full committee was public. Little basic opposition to the bill developed publicly. The changes made by the full committee were few. Two were, however, important. The first added to the list of exempted securities, which already included those issued by national banks, the securities of state and territorial banks if supervised by their respective governmental banking officials. The second expanded and also contracted the list of exempt transactions by exempting transactions by an issuer with or through an underwriter only so long as they did not involve a public offering. Underwriters could consequently participate in private offerings without the need for registration, but issuers could not make a public offering of their securities even though no underwriting might be involved.

The report of the House committee, drafted by us, is an analysis of the bill. . . .

In the House the bill went under a special rule because of its complexities and the danger that an unstudied amendment, apparently fair on its face, might unbalance the careful articulation of its various sections. This rule permitted the consideration of amendments only if they had the approval of the committee chairman. With Cohen at his side, Rayburn had complete control of the situation. The bill passed with scarcely a murmur of dissent.

In the Senate an entirely different story was unfolding. The Senate had nothing but the Thompson bill to work on. Moreover, the Senate Committee on Banking and Currency was busy with its investigation of securities transactions and securities markets. Pecora and his staff were occupied with this investigation and had no time to devote to other matters. Two lawyers formerly active with Thompson were attached to the Senate Committee but they had admittedly neither the time to devote to it nor the experience that would allow them to be regarded as experts. The Senate legislative drafting service operates on different lines than that of the House. No one on its staff had the same authority and prestige as Beaman had on the House side and, furthermore, its services could be availed of by any Senator with the result that it did not have the time to spare for another major job.[3] It became apparent fairly early that on the Senate side the bill would bumble along and that our hope for the side-tracking of that bill would have to rest upon an agreement in conference that the House bill would be the basis for the final draft.

In the Senate, however, one major development had taken place. Senator Hiram Johnson of California had become interested in the debacle of the billions of foreign governmental securities that had been sold to the American public, primarily those issued by Latin American governments. They had been hawked to investors in the Twenties by many of the larger New York investment banking firms. Not only were most of these securities in default but the circumstances attending their issuance and sale reflected seriously upon the integrity of these underwriting houses. Senator Johnson naturally had a sympathy with those provisions of the proposed securities legislation that would subject foreign governmental issues in the future to controls of a type roughly comparable to those dealing with private offerings. But he also wanted to do something for the outstanding bondholders in the hope that their investments might to some degree be recouped. The existing intrusion of various protective committees had developed abuses almost as bad as those that surrounded the original issuance of these securities. With this in mind, he introduced into the Senate a bill to create a Corporation of Foreign Bondholders, whose directors would be appointed by the Federal Trade Commission and whose initial financing would come from the Reconstruction Finance Corporation. The directors would act as representatives of these defaulted bondholders in negotiating with the foreign governments involved and see that the flow of any funds that might be made available, should go to the defaulted bondholders. Admirable as Senator Johnson's motives were, his proposal immediately ran afoul of the State Department. That Department had a natural aversion to the creation of any independent governmental agency empowered to deal directly with foreign governments. Such an agency was only too likely to pursue negotiations and take attitudes with our Latin American friends in direct conflict with those that the State Department was evolving in the development of its new Good Neighbor Policy. The State Department in lieu of the proposed Corporation of Foreign Bondholders, wanted to see the

[3] In the House only chairmen of committees could generally command the services of its legislative drafting staff.

creation of a responsible non-governmental group to handle these problems so that the United States as a government would not have to take inconsistent positions at the same time and to the same nation.

President Roosevelt stood in the midst of this conflict. Both policies were in a sense integral to his program but both could not be satisfied at the same time. Senator Johnson's cause was a popular and worthy one and in line with the general trend of the New Deal. On the other hand, his new Securetary of State, Cordell Hull, was not a person to offend with impunity. To place him and his Department in potential conflict with another agency of the government might in the long run be disastrous. Proponents of both sides of this issue sought the aid and assistance of the President, and both sides were given that aid and assistance but not quite at the same time. On one day the President would be quoted, probably correctly, in favor of Senator Johnson's proposal. On the next, he would be found in the State Department's camp. Senator Johnson, however, somehow succeeded in getting his bill tacked on as an amendment to the Senate's securities bill as a new Title II. He was backed up in all probability by many Senators who were willing to vote for it on the theory that its ultimate fate would be determined by the House and Senate Conference Committee which would have to reconcile the differences between the two bills.

The rules of a Conference Committee are apparently not unlike those rules that govern collective bargaining negotiations. If they exist, and documentary evidence to that effect is to be found in *Hine's Precedents*, they are observed as much in breach as in conformance. In theory the Conference Committee is supposed to reach some sort of a mean between the positions taken by the two Houses and should abjure the introduction of new matter. In fact, new matter, either consisting of new ideas or of extensive emendations to what the two Houses may have passed without too thorough a consideration, again and again finds its way into their reports and is adopted without opposition by both Houses. In theory also, the House and the Senate members of the committee each vote as a unit; in fact, the weakening of any member on either side tends to bring about agreement. The atmosphere of a Conference Committee is tense where the committee is concerned with legislation that is other than routine. Its members are always members of the committees who have most actively sponsored the legislation in their respective chambers and have consequently developed strong predilections for the points of view that their hard won bills represent.

It was in an atmosphere such as this that the Conference Committee met on a Monday morning in May. Senator Fletcher was the chairman of the Senate group and Sam Rayburn headed the House delegation. Cohen and I were present, and Beaman and Perley were still with us. The two Senate advisers also were present at most of the sessions. The Senate, however, was most ably represented by a former student in my seminar in legislation, then attached to the Senate drafting service and later to become a chairman of the Securities and Exchange Commission, namely Ganson Purcell. On the Senate side, there were such distinguished names as Carter Glass of Virginia, James Couzens of Michigan and Hiram Johnson of California.[4] Senator Fletcher of Florida also commanded considerable prestige for his conduct of the Pecora investigations and his unwavering support of his counsel amid a number of trying circumstances. The House, on the other hand, had no such distinguished personalities except for Sam Rayburn, although each of its members was far better acquainted with the subject matter at hand than the representatives of the Senate.

Jockeying occurred at the beginning as to the procedures that should be adopted. In its midst Senator Glass, who had been rapidly scanning the House bill, broke out into a tirade to the effect that he was the proponent of legislation dealing with banks and their relationship to the sale of securities and that he wanted no interference with his handling of these issues.[5] We pointed out to him that the House bill had carefully excluded from its operation all securities issued by banks, whether state or federal, as contrasted with the Senate bill which exempted only the securities issued by national banks, and also that nothing in the House bill in any way conflicted with the proposals contained in his bill to divorce banks from their security affiliates. He growled, thumbed the bill for any further reference to banks, found none, and shortly thereafter left the committee never to reappear.

Senator Fletcher, with the courteousness that always characterized him, suggested to Rayburn that he should accept the chairmanship

[4] Senator Robert Wagner of New York was also a member of this Conference Committee. Although he signed its final report I cannot recall his appearance at any of the sessions. He was, of course, busily occupied at the time with other phases of the "Recovery Program."

[5] This bill introduced by Senator Glass became the Banking Act of 1933. . . .

of the committee at least for the first meeting. Rayburn agreed and shortly thereafter suggested that the first business was to come to a determination of which bill should become the basic working draft for the committee.[6] Rayburn quietly asked Senator Fletcher if he did not desire to make a motion on this matter. The Senator replied by moving that the Senate bill should be made the working draft. Rayburn took a vote on this motion and, finding that all the Senators voted for the motion and all the members of the House voted against the motion, applied the unit rule and declared that *since the vote was a tie the motion failed of adoption and consequently the House bill would become the basic draft.** That was the last we heard of the unit rule, and the last of Title I of the Senate bill except for an occasional reference to its provisions as a basis for comparison.

Work moved reasonably smoothly thereafter and Title I was completed by Friday. Senator Fletcher never requested to alternate the chairmanship and, absent any request from him, Rayburn continued to guide the proceedings. The committee met daily. Its sessions carried on throughout the mornings, the afternoons being occupied by sessions of the full House and Senate. The representatives of the House were assiduous in their attendance, the Senate members less so. The tenseness of the first day's session became relieved as Rayburn made it plain that any suggestion of any Senator would receive the most careful consideration. A goodly number of suggestions came from Senator Townsend of Delaware, a Republican, who was in close touch with the financial world but who under no circumstances would take their suggestions as commands or as ideas to hold on to in the face of a compelling argument to the contrary. In fact, friendship and mutual respect under Rayburn's guidance developed friendships not only among the members but between the members and the staff.

Cohen, Beaman, Perley, and I took the opportunity these days gave us to improve further the House bill. The Investment Bankers

[6] The two persons attached as experts to the Senate Committee had anticipated that this question would arise. Their loyalties being to the Senate, they had prepared and had printed a "Confidential Conference Committee Print" based on the Senate bill and embodying portions of the House bill that they believed might be sufficient to bring about acquiescence on the part of the House representatives. The result was an unbelievable patchwork. Their attempt to get this draft circulated in the Conference Committee was rudely but firmly brushed off by Rayburn. . . .

* Emphasis added.—Ed.

Association had suggested a series of amendments to the House bill, all of which had to be scanned carefully and most of which were discarded. The Federal Trade Commission submitted a carefully detailed memorandum, which I later learned was prepared by Baldwin B. Bane, later to become the first chief of its Division of Securities, commending the House bill despite the fact that the Commission's Chief Counsel, Robert E. Healey, later to become one of the original members of the Securities and Exchange Commission, had favored and still favored the Thompson bill. Numerous other memoranda were filed with the committee or with the individual members. Requests were also made through them for consultation with the staff by lawyers and others, to which it was difficult not to accede.

Four drafts of the bill found their way into print before the final draft was accepted. There were numerous changes made, of which the significant ones are noted in the Statement of the House Managers contained in the Conference Report as submitted to the House. . . .

The Conference Report also deliberately contained language commenting upon the meaning of certain of the most contentious provisions of the bill in the hope that that language as an expression of the "intent" of Congress would control the administrative and judicial interpretation of the act. This is particularly true with respect to the nature of the fiduciary obligations assumed by officers and directors of a registrant. It seemed impossible to define in statutory language the extent to which a fiduciary might lawfully delegate his duties to others. In lieu of such an effort, resort was made to general language in the report to indicate that a goodly measure of delegation was justifiable, particularly insofar as corporate directors are concerned.

The bitterest struggle between the House and Senate members of the Conference Committee concerned the civil liability that should be imposed upon the officers and directors of the registrant. The Senate bill imposed a liability akin to that of insurer's liability with respect to the accuracy of the statements made by them in the registration statement. The House bill, on the other hand, held his liability to the standard of due care, recognizing that the due care involved was that of a fiduciary. The victory of the House representatives on this issue was important. A contrary result would obviously have imposed an unjust and insurmountable burden on those who have the responsibility for the conduct of corporate enterprise.

With the conclusion of the conference work on Title I, the committee on Saturday morning turned to the problem of Title II—the Corporation of Foreign Bondholders Act. For some days the question of what to do with Title II had bothered Rayburn. It had also worried Cohen and myself who wished no part of the controversy between Senator Johnson and the State Department but were worried by the fear that that controversy might imperil the Title I legislation. Rayburn, who was quite willing to follow any suggestion that the President might make, had asked Senator Johnson to get a definitive answer one way or the other upon the question. Saturday morning no such answer had yet been received and Rayburn was in a quandary as to what to do. After some discussion Senator Johnson suggested to Rayburn that he should telephone the President directly and see if he could get an answer to the problem. Rayburn requested me to accompany him to an adjoining room presumably on the theory that I might be helpful in answering such technical questions as might arise. I listened in on the conversation. The sum and substance of it was that the President had no idea as to what to do and ended up by telling Rayburn to do whatever he thought best.

This left Rayburn in exactly the same position in which he had been all week. This was when I thought of adding to Title II the provision that that title should take effect only if, and when the President determined that it should do so in the public interest and issued a declaration to the effect. Rayburn recognized that, if Johnson would accept this provision, it would put the problem squarely back in the lap of the President and make possible the immediate passage of both Title I and Title II. I hastily drafted the provision and we returned to the committee room. I explained the provision to Senator Johnson and the committee. Beaman started to question the constitutionality of the provision as being an unconstitutional delegation of legislative power to the President. Although I had my doubts as to its validity and still retain them, I argued in behalf of its constitutionality. Cohen joined me, and Beaman, realizing the quandary in which the President had put Rayburn, ceased to advance any further objections. We turned hopefully to Senator Johnson to get his agreement. To our amazement he accepted it without further argument. The Conference Committee's labors thus came to an end. There remained only the passage of the bill.

. . . All of the Republican representatives of the House had signed the Conference Report. None of the Republican Senators had done so, although they voiced no disagreement to the report. It passed both Houses with no substantial opposition and on May 27, 1933, became a law. . . .

14   *The Day We Didn't Go to War*
CHALMERS M. ROBERTS

Saturday, April 3, 1954, was a raw, windy day in Washington, but the weather didn't prevent a hundred Americans from milling around the Jefferson Memorial to see the cherry blossoms—twenty thousand of them from watching the crowning of the 1954 Cherry Blossom Queen.

President Eisenhower drove off to his Maryland mountain retreat called Camp David. There he worked on his coming Monday speech, designed, so the White House said, to quiet America's fears of Russia, the H-bomb, domestic Communists, a depression. But that Saturday morning eight members of Congress, five Senators and three Representatives, got the scare of their lives. They had been called to a secret conference with John Foster Dulles. They entered one of the State Department's fifth-floor conference rooms to find not only Dulles but Admiral Arthur W. Radford, chairman of the Joint Chiefs of Staff, Under Secretary of Defense Roger Kyes, Navy Secretary Robert B. Anderson, and Thruston B. Morton, Dulles's assistant for Congressional Relations. A large map of the world hung behind Dulles's seat, and Radford stood by with several others. "The President has asked me to call this meeting," Dulles began.

URGENCY AND A PLAN

The atmosphere became serious at once. What was wanted, Dulles said, was a joint resolution by Congress to permit the President to

From Chalmers M. Roberts, *The Reporter* (September 14, 1954, pp. 31-35). Copyright 1954 by the Fortnightly Publishing Company, Inc., New York.

use air and naval power in Indo-China. Dulles hinted that perhaps the mere passage of such a resolution would in itself make its use unnecessary. But the President had asked for its consideration, and, Dulles added, Mr. Eisenhower felt that it was indispensable at this juncture that the leaders of Congress feel as the Administration did on the Indo-China crisis.

Then Radford took over. He said the Administration was deeply concerned over the rapidly deteriorating situation. He used a map of the Pacific to point out the importance of Indo-China. He spoke about the French Union forces then already under siege for three weeks in the fortress of Dienbienphu.

The admiral explained the urgency of American action by declaring that he was not even sure, because of poor communications, whether, in fact, Dienbienphu was still holding out. (The fortress held out for five weeks more.)

Dulles backed up Radford. If Indo-China fell and if its fall led to the loss of all of Southeast Asia, he declared, then the United States might eventually be forced back to Hawaii, as it was before the Second World War. And Dulles was not complimentary about the French. He said he feared they might use some disguised means of getting out of Indo-China if they did not receive help soon.

The eight legislators were silent: Senator Majority Leader Knowland and his G.O.P. colleague Eugene Millikin, Senator Minority Leader Lyndon B. Johnson and his Democratic colleagues Richard B. Russell and Earle C. Clements, House G.O.P. Speaker Joseph Martin and two Democratic House leaders, John W. McCormack and J. Percy Priest.

What to do? Radford offered the plan he had in mind once Congress passed the joint resolution.

Some two hundred planes from the thirty-one-thousand-ton U.S. Navy carriers *Essex* and *Boxer*, then in the South China Sea ostensibly for "training," plus land-based U.S. Air Force planes from bases a thousand miles away in the Philippines, would be used for a single strike to save Dienbienphu.

The legislators stirred, and the questions began.

Radford was asked whether such action would be war. He replied that we would be in the war.

If the strike did not succeed in relieving the fortress, would we follow up? "Yes," said the chairman of the Joint Chiefs of Staff.

Would land forces then also have to be used? Radford did not give a definite answer.

In the early part of the questioning, Knowland showed enthusiasm for the venture, consistent with his public statements that something must be done or Southeast Asia would be lost.

But as the questions kept flowing, largely from Democrats, Knowland lapsed into silence.

Clements asked Radford the first of the two key questions: "Does this plan have the approval of the other members of the Joint Chiefs of Staff?"

"No," replied Radford.

"How many of the three agree with you?"

"None."

"How do you account for that?"

"I have spent more time in the Far East than any of them and I understand the situation better."

Lyndon Johnson put the other key question in the form of a little speech. He said that Knowland had been saying publicly that in Korea up to ninety per cent of the men and the money came from the United States. The United States had become sold on the idea that that was bad. Hence in any operation in Indo-China we ought to know first who would put up the men. And so he asked Dulles whether he had consulted nations who might be our allies in intervention.

Dulles said he had not.

The Secretary was asked why he didn't go to the United Nations as in the Korean case. He replied that it would take too long, that this was an immediate problem.

There were other questions. Would Red China and the Soviet Union come into the war if the United States took military action? The China question appears to have been sidestepped, though Dulles said he felt the Soviets could handle the Chinese and the United States did not think that Moscow wanted a general war now. Further, he added, if the Communists feel that we mean business, they won't go "any further down there," pointing to the map of Southeast Asia.

John W. McCormack, the House Minority Leader, couldn't resist temptation. He was surprised, he said, that Dulles would look to the "party of treason," as the Democrats had been called by Joe McCarthy in his Lincoln's Birthday speech under G.O.P. auspices, to take the lead in a situation that might end up in a general shooting war. Dulles did not reply.

In the end, all eight members of Congress, Republicans and Democrats alike, were agreed that Dulles had better first go shopping for allies. Some people who should know say that Dulles was carrying, but did not produce, a draft of the joint resolution the President wanted Congress to consider.

The whole meeting had lasted two hours and ten minutes. As they left, the Hill delegation told waiting reporters they had been briefed on Indo-China. Nothing more.

This approach to Congress by Dulles and Radford on behalf of the President was the beginning of three weeks of intensive effort by the Administration to head off disaster in Indo-China. Some of those at the meeting came away with the feeling that if they had agreed that Saturday to the resolution, planes would have been winging toward Dienbienphu without waiting for a vote of Congress—or without a word in advance to the American people.

For some months now, I have tried to put together the bits and pieces of the American part in the Indo-China debacle. But before relating the sequel, it is necessary here to go back to two events that underlay the meeting just described—though neither of them was mentioned at that meeting.

On March 20, just two weeks earlier, General Paul Ely, then French Chief of Staff and later commander in Indo-China, had arrived in Washington from the Far East to tell the President, Dulles, Radford, and others that unless the United States intervened, Indo-China would be lost. This was a shock of earthquake proportions to leaders who had been taken in by their own talk of the Navarre Plan to win the war.

In his meetings at the Pentagon, Ely was flabbergasted to find that Radford proposed American intervention without being asked. Ely said he would have to consult his government. He carried back to Paris the word that when France gave the signal, the United States would respond.

The second event of importance is the most difficult to determine accurately. But it is clear that Ely's remarks started a mighty struggle within the National Security Council, that inner core of government where our most vital decisions are worked out for the President's final O.K. The argument advanced by Radford and supported by Vice-President Nixon and by Dulles was that Indochina must not be allowed to fall into Communist hands lest such a fate set in motion a falling row of dominoes.

Eisenhower himself used the "row-of-dominoes" phrase at a press conference on April 7. On April 15, Radford said in a speech that Indo-China's loss "would be the prelude to the loss of all Southeast Asia and a threat to a far wider area." On April 16 Nixon, in his well-publicized "off-the-record" talk to the newspaper editors' convention, said that if the United States could not otherwise prevent the loss of Indo-China, then the Administration must face the situation and dispatch troops. And the President in his press conference of March 24 had declared that Southeast Asia was of the "most transcendent importance." All these remarks reflected a basic policy decision.

It is my understanding, although I cannot produce the top secret NSC [National Security Council] paper to prove it, that some time between Ely's arrival on March 20 and the Dulles-Radford approach to the Congressional leaders on April 3, the NSC had taken a firm position that the United States could not afford the loss of Indo-China to the Communists, and that if it were necessary to prevent that loss, the United States would intervene in the war—*provided* the intervention was an allied venture and *provided* the French would give Indo-China a real grant of independence so as to eliminate the colonialism issue. The decision may have been taken at the March 25 meeting. It is also my understanding that this NSC paper has on it the approving initials "D.D.E."

On March 29, Dulles, in a New York speech, had called for "united action" even though it might involve "serious risks," and declared that Red China was backing aggression in Indo-China with the goal of controlling all of Southeast Asia. He had added that the United States felt that "that possibility should not be passively acceped but should be met by united action."

The newspapers were still full of reactions to this speech when the Congressional leaders, at the April 3 secret meeting with Dulles and Radford, insisted that Dulles should line up allies for "united action" before trying to get a joint resolution of Congress that would commit the nation to war.

The Secretary lost no time. Within a week Dulles talked with diplomatic representatives in Washington of Britain, France, Australia, New Zealand, the Philippines, Thailand, and the three Associated States of Indo-China—Vietnam, Laos, and Cambodia.

There was no doubt in the minds of many of these diplomats that Dulles was discussing military action involving carriers and planes. Dulles was seeking a statement or declaration of intent designed to be issued by all the nations at the time of the U.S. military action, to explain to the world what we were doing and why, and to warn the Chinese Communists against entering the war as they had done in Korea.

In these talks Dulles ran into one rock of opposition—Britain. Messages flashing back and forth between Washington and London failed to crack the rock. Finally Dulles offered to come and talk the plan over personally with Prime Minister Churchill and Foreign Secretary Anthony Eden. On April 10, just a week after the Congressional meeting, Dulles flew off to London and later went on to Paris.

Whether Dulles told the British about either the NSC decision or about his talks with the Congressional leaders I do not know. But he didn't need to. The British had learned of the Congressional meeting within a couple of days after it happened. When Dulles reached London they were fully aware of the seriousness of his mission.

The London talks had two effects. Dulles had to shelve the idea of immediate intervention. He came up instead with a proposal for creating a Southeast Asia Treaty Organization (SEATO). Dulles felt this was the "united front" he wanted and that it would lead to "united action." He thought that some sort of *ad hoc* organization should be set up at once without waiting for formal treaty organization, and to this, he seems to have felt, Churchill and Eden agreed.

Just what the British did agree to is not clear, apparently not even to them. Dulles, it appears, had no formal SEATO proposal down on paper, while the British did have some ideas in writing. Eden feels that he made it plain that nothing could be done until after the Geneva Conference, which was due to begin in two weeks. But he apparently made some remark about "going on thinking about it" in the meantime.

At any rate, on his return to Washington Dulles immediately called a SEATO drafting meeting for April 20. The British Ambassador (who at this point had just read the Nixon off-the-record speech in the newspaper) cabled London for instructions and was told not to attend any such meeting. To cover up, the meeting was turned into one on Korea, the other topic for the Geneva Conference. Out of this confusion grew a thinly veiled hostility between Dulles and Eden that exists to this day. Dulles felt that Eden had switched his position and suspects that Eden did so after strong words reached London from Prime Minister Nehru in New Delhi.

A few days later, Dulles flew back to Paris, ostensibly for the NATO meeting with Eden, France's Georges Bidault, and others during the week-end just before the Geneva Conference opened.

On Friday, April 23, Bidault showed Dulles a telegram from General Henri-Eugene Navarre, then the Indo-China commander, saying that only a massive air attack could save Dienbienphu, by now under siege for six weeks. Dulles said the United States could not intervene.

But on Saturday Admiral Radford arrived and met with Dulles. Then Dulles and Radford saw Eden. Dulles told Eden that the French were asking for military help at once. An allied air strike at the Vietminh positions around Dienbienphu was discussed. The discussion centered on using the same two U. S. Navy carriers and Philippine-based Air Force planes Radford had talked about to the Congressional leaders.

Radford, it appears, did most of the talking. But Dulles said that if the allies agreed, the President was prepared to go to Congress on the following Monday, April 26 (the day the Geneva Conference was to open) and ask for a joint resolution authorizing such action. Assuming quick passage by Congress, the strike could take place on April 28. Under Secretary of State Walter Bedell Smith, an advocate of intervention, gave the same proposal to French Ambassador Henri Bonnet in Washington the same day.

The State Department had prepared a declaration of intentions, an outgrowth of the earlier proposals in Washington, to be signed on Monday or Tuesday by the Washington ambassadors of the allied nations willing to back the venture in words. As it happened, there were no available British or Australian carriers and the French already were fully occupied. Hence the strike would be by American planes alone, presented to the world as a "united action" by means of the declaration of intentions.

Eden, on hearing all these details from Dulles and Radford, said that this was a most serious proposition, amounting to war, and that he wanted to hear it direct from the French. Eden and Dulles thereupon conferred with Bidault, who confirmed the fact that France was indeed calling desperately for help—though no formal French request was ever put forward in writing.

Eden began to feel like Horatius at the bridge. Here, on the eve of a conference that might lead to a negotiated end of the seven-year-old Indo-China war, the United States, at the highly informal request of a weak and panicky French Government, was proposing military action that might very well lead to a general war in Asia if not to a third world war.

DULLE'S RETREAT

Eden said forcefully that he could not agree to any such scheme of intervention, that he personally opposed it. He added his conviction that within forty-eight hours after an air strike, ground troops would be called for, as had been the case at the beginning of the Korean War.

But, added Eden, he alone could not make any such formal decision on behalf of Her Majesty's Government. He would fly to London at once and put the matter before a Cabinet meeting. So far as I can determine, neither Dulles or Bidault tried to prevent this step.

Shortly after Eden flew off that Saturday afternoon, Dulles sat down in the American Embassy in Paris with his chief advisers, Messrs. MacArthur, Merchant, Bowie, and McCardle, and Ambassador Dillon. They composed a letter to Bidault.

In this letter, Dulles told Bidault the United States could not intervene without action by Congress because to do so was beyond the President's Constitutional powers and because we had made it plain that any action we might take could only be part of a "united action." Further, Dulles added, the American military leaders felt it was too late to save Dienbienphu.

American intervention collapsed on that Saturday, April 24. On Sunday Eden arrived in Geneva with word of the "No" from the specially convened British Cabinet meeting. And on Monday, the day the Geneva Conference began, Eisenhower said in a speech that what was being sought at Geneva was a "*modus vivendi*" with the Communists.

All these events were unknown to the general public at the time. However, on Sunday the New York *Times* printed a story (written in Paris under a Geneva dateline) that the U.S. had turned down a French request for intervention on the grounds Dulles had cited to Bidault. And on Tuesday Churchill announced to a cheering House of Commons that the British government was "not prepared to give any undertakings about United Kingdom military action in Indo-

China in advance of the results of Geneva" and that "we have not entered into any new political or military commitments."

Thus the Geneva Conference opened in a mood of deepest American gloom. Eden felt that he had warded off disaster and that now there was a chance to negotiate a peace. The Communists, whatever they may have learned of the behind-the-scenes details here recounted, knew that Britain had turned down some sort of American plan of intervention. And with the military tide in Indo-China flowing so rapidly in their favor, they proceeded to stall.

In the end, of course, a kind of peace was made. On June 23, nearly four weeks before the peace, Eden said in the House of Commons that the British Government had "been reproached in some unofficial quarters for their failure to support armed intervention to try to save Dienbienphu. It is quite true that we were at no time willing to support such action . . ."

This mixture of improvisation and panic is the story of how close the United States came to entering the Indo-China war. Would Congress have approved intervention if the President had dared to ask it? This point is worth a final word.

On returning from Geneva in mid-May, I asked that question of numerous Senators and Representatives. Their replies made clear that Congress would, in the end, have done what Eisenhower asked, provided he had asked for it forcefully and explained the facts and their relation to the national interest of the United States.

Whether action or inaction better served the American interest at that late stage of Indo-China war is for the historian, not for the reporter, to say. But the fact emerges that President Eisenhower never did lay the intervention question on the line. In spite of the NSC decision, April 3, 1954, was the day we *didn't* go to war.

15   *A Law is Passed — The Atomic Energy Act of 1946*
BYRON MILLER

An unusually clear example of the role which democratic
processes can play in the framing of legislation is presented by the
history of the law controlling atomic energy within the United States.
Several unique factors combined to deprive the legislator of his com-
fortable patterns for reaching policy decisions. He was not dealing
with a recast of conventional controversy, a labor versus management
or debt reduction versus public spending issue, on which his attitudes
had long been fixed, his speeches ready at tongue, the public reception and opposition tactics already known. He could not judge by the
people lined up on one or the other side, for traditional alignments
were criss-crossed. Even commercial special interest groups were
largely silent. In short, for most senators and many representatives,
atomic energy legislation required an almost pure exercise of judgment. The very same factors also operated to induce a surprisingly
wide expression of opinion by the public.

The response of the Congress to this unparalleled necessity for
original judgment was not one of imaginative suggestion. Rather, the
reaction of many legislators was to escape the entire problem, one
senator openly expressing a wish to dump all atomic energy knowledge into the ocean. Most, however, felt lost in a morass of technol-
ogy, an attitude which appeared to survive the educational hearings.
Hence the debates both in and out of Congress all too often exhibited
a stubborn tendency to pose choices in terms of conventional oppo-
sites which bore little relation to the issues being decided.

The factors responsible for this atypical legislative history can be
grouped roughly as follows:

(1) *The Atomic Bomb.* The military and political significance of

From Byron S. Miller, *University of Chicago Law Review* (Summer 1948,
Vol. 15, No. 4). Copyright 1948 by the University of Chicago.

the A-bomb and the political, social, and economic significance of its civilian counterpart, atomic energy, were problems enough; but they were almost eclipsed by the engulfing emotions of fear and awe which then surrounded the subject. The compelling demand for international control was an additional element with a very practical relation to domestic legislation. Each of these factors constituted unique legislative considerations. And the element of fear was not confined to problems bred by the bomb from which it had sprung; rather it diffused through the entire legislative atmosphere in the illogical fashion of a primitive emotion.

(2) *The Newness of the Problem.* Multiplying the problems raised by the special incidents of atomic energy was the total absence of any convenient framework into which the legislative problem could be fitted. The door was open for all manner of entrants into the legislative contest. Fortunately, the universal interest in the subject opened publicity avenues to a degree rarely available to private citizens seeking to make their positions and reasons known.

(3) *The Political Activity of the Scientists.* Into the idea vacuum created by the fear, the stupendous prophecies of atomic energy uses, and the unfamiliarity of the problems presented marched an array of political unknowns, the scientists. These Men Who Made the Bomb personified the factors which had unsettled the legislators. They were awesome creatures indeed to have built the bomb, men of limitless capacity to have harnessed such a colossal new source of energy, and men almost from a different planet, politically speaking. Before the bomb, physical scientists had almost uniformly been silent on public affairs, apparently preferring the precision and predictability of natural forces to the inexact conflicts and compromises of the social world. Yet here they were, mostly young, forceful, and hopeful men and women dealing with old and tired legislators of few ideals, earnest and sure of their subject in contrast to Congressional fear and uncertainty. Matching their energy and capacity to the opportunity, the scientists soon became a major factor in the formulation of atomic energy legislation.

(4) *The Postwar Attitude toward the Armed Forces.* In the wake of victory our armed forces enjoyed a prestige and political strength in Congress then unprecedented in American history. In those quarters, at least, the capacity of the military to control atomic energy in peacetime was demonstrated beyond doubt by their victory in the war. At the same time most veterans, particularly enlisted men, had developed an opposite attitude toward supervisors—the "brass hats" —at least so far as non-military activities were concerned. The general public exhibited attitudes in the full range between these two; but perhaps the larger portion was more readily affected by stories of specific abuses than by the generality of victory. The result may be ungrateful, even illogical; but there can be no disputing the popularity of Mauldin and similar cartoonists.

Each of these factors contributed to make the Congress and the executive branch more susceptible to the wishes of the public than is usually the case. The result was a law unprecedented in scope, in technique, and in constructive potentialities. That the ultimate enactment was of such a high standard is a tribute to our means of communication and our human resources—in other words, to our democratic system. This victory was made possible by articulate public opinion; yet the same freedom of expression in the hands of less well-meaning individuals and legislators came uncomfortably close to defeating the will of the overwhelming majority, as the following history indicates.

I. Early Developments: the May-Johnson Bill

Until August 5, 1945, when the first atomic bomb was dropped on Hiroshima, neither Congress nor the public knew that an instrument of such vast destructive possibilities was even contemplated. Only the scientists, the military leadership of the Manhattan Project, and the very highest echelon of the Administration knew of the work and of its almost limitless consequences should a bomb be successfully produced. Thus, the secrecy surrounding the project gave these two groups, the scientists and the military, an enormous head start over the rest of the country (and the world) in anticipating the problems created by the release of atomic energy and in developing techniques for meeting these problems.

As early as 1943 the scientists began writing and circulating papers covering such topics as the destructive capacity of the bomb, possible national and international political consequences of its use, and possible peacetime uses of atomic energy. Accounts are available elsewhere of the psychological conflicts which many scientists underwent in trying to live with the knowledge that their goal was the production of a weapon endangering civilization itself. By the end of 1944, however, they had settled upon the need for quick dissemination throughout the world of the few basic facts which would permit an unprepared public to understand the new problems presented by atomic energy. In February 1945 the formation of an organization of atomic scientists was considered but security rules of course precluded action at the time. Finally, the preliminary work of the scientists was gathered together by the Committee on Social and Political Implications, headed by Professor James Franck; this work was incorporated into a special report sent to Secretary of War Stimson on June 11, 1945.

Meanwhile the military leadership had also become active. Shortly after President Roosevelt's death, President Truman was first informed of the atomic project. In May, 1945, with the latter's approval, Secretary Stimson set up the Interim Committee to advise the President on the use of the bomb and to recommend legislation that would insure the most advantageous use of this new discovery. The legislative assignment, however, was kept a tight secret.[1] Both the scientists and the Interim Committee considered at lengh the best way to use the bomb, an effort which culminated in its actual use at Hiroshima and Nagasaki.

Despite contrary assurances from the War Department, no adequate informational measures had been prepared to enable the public to form an intelligent understanding of the significance of the atomic bomb. First reports about the bomb created mental chaos; the few carefully prepared articles were no match for the fanciful speculations put forth by writers, broadcasters, and speakers all over the country. The scientists attempted to fill the information void, but without preparation, without experience in the workings of our mass communications system, and without adequate resources or freedom to reach the bulk of the people before misleading, even harmful, first impressions had been formed. Indeed, it is hard to conceive how any system short of mass censorship during distribution of prepared material could possibly have transmitted the story of the atomic bomb without creating the very first impressions which have since caused so much harm—the notion of "secrets"; the confident expectation of a defense against the bomb; and the assumption that other nations will be incapable of atomic warfare for almost a generation.

The May-Johnson Bill. During these months legislation was being drafted under the supervision of the Interim Committee, behind locked doors and subject to severe security precautions, by General Royall, then Special Assistant to the Undersecretary of War, and William L. Marbury, a well-known private attorney. There is some

[1] Various scientists were told no legislation was yet being contemplated.

indication that this secrecy was continued even after Hiroshima; hence the scientists were caught unawares when President Truman sent a special message to Congress on October 3, followed the same day by introduction of the Interim Committee bill in the House by Representative May and in the Senate by Senator Johnson—the May-Johnson bill. There can be no question that the bill reached Congress in unorthodox fashion, since it was not cleared through the Bureau of the Budget, or by the bureau with other departments and agencies as is customary.

The May-Johnson bill was widely denounced as a drive for military control of atomic energy in time of peace, though the bill was sponsored expressly for the purpose of substituting civilian control for War Department supervision. The accusation derives not from explicit grant of authority to the military but from a series of provisions which readily lent themselves to military domination. . . .

The May-Johnson bill was detained at the presiding officer's table in the Senate because of a jurisdictional dispute; in the House, however it moved smoothly and efficiently into the guiding hands of Andrew Jackson May, chairman of the military affairs committee. While the Senate wrangled over referral to the foreign affairs, military affairs, or a proposed new atomic energy committee, Mr. May opened and closed public hearings on October 9, 1945, and rushed executive committee sessions designed to report the bill out promptly.

Opposition Develops. From the standpoint of the May-Johnson bill's backers such haste was well advised. No sooner was the bill introduced than there rose from atomic scientists throughout the nation an avalanche of outraged criticism that could only have been spontaneous and deeply felt. During the operations of the Manhattan Project in wartime, there had gradually developed a cleavage between most of the scientists and their military supervisors. Without here repeating the many incidents which explain the unenthusiastic attitude of most scientists toward military supervision, it may be sufficient to cite the conclusion of one of the key men in the Project that the military "delayed the bomb by 18 months."

Local organizations of scientists had been formed at each of the principal sites shortly after Hiroshima. Educational efforts directed toward helping the public attain an intelligent understanding of the physical facts of atomic energy and some of their political, social, and economic consequences were under way when the May-Johnson bill suddenly appeared on the scene. Immediately, a major share of the scientists' energies was thrown into a fight for more careful consideration of the bill. Led by such outstanding men as Drs. Condon, Szilard, and Urey, they descended upon Washington insisting that a single day's hearings limited to favorable witnesses was a shocking abuse of legislative discretion in dealing with such a momentous and largely uncomprehended subject. When their request for further hearing was initially refused, they met informally with a large caucus of congressmen, then used the hearings of a Senate subcommittee considering science legislation as a sounding board for airing the defects of the May-Johnson bill. Simultaneously, they were calling on prominent private citizens, editors and publishers, on leading figures in the Administration, and on influential senators and representatives. Their efforts so moved Mr. May that he reopened hearings—for a single day. A few witnesses testified against the bill, a few more for the bill, and the committee resumed executive sessions, with General Royall in daily attendance. The bill was reported out with a few amendments, only one of consequence, on November 5. Two Democrats filed dissenting views; nine Republicans voted solidly against government control.

Fortunately for the scientists not all officials in a position to affect the legislation had the stolid single-mindedness of Mr. May. In late October the President began to have misgivings about some aspects of the bill. Indeed, his approval had been given in reliance upon the endorsements of the War Department and the few scientific leaders who served on or with the Interim Committee. He had no notion that scientists would have any serious objection to the proposed law. His concern was echoed by men then occupying key posts under him, such as Budget Director Smith, Secretary Ickes, and Secretary Wallace. In the House of Representatives, Helen Douglas and others had voiced their apprehension so that Speaker Rayburn was of no mind to let the May-Johnson bill come to the floor until the air had cleared. Newspapers, magazines, and broadcasters throughout the country were charging that the bill was being railroaded through without giving the public a chance to form an opinion on the issues.

The Senate Special Committee. Meanwhile the Senate continued in its disagreement as to committee jurisdiction over atomic energy legislation. The logjam was broken in late October when, after a regular session between the President and Democratic legislative leaders, the Senate voted to establish a Special Committee on Atomic Energy. Following custom, though not without opposition, the sponsor of the resolution creating the committee became its chairman—freshman Senator Brien McMahon. As if to make sure that McMahon was kept in his place, the other ten positions on the committee were awarded to Senator Connally, chairman of the Foreign Affairs Committee, Senator Vandenberg, ranking Republican on the same committee, Senator Johnson, sponsor of the May-Johnson bill and ranking Democrat on the Military Affairs Committee, such conservative stalwarts as Senators Tydings, Byrd, Millikin, Russell, and Austin, and freshmen Senators Hickenlooper and (ex-Admiral) Hart.

The legislative strategy soon emerged. The House bill was to be kept off the floor until the new Senate committee had had an opportunity to study the entire field of atomic energy and to prepare alternative legislation. The heat was off; there was time for the scientists, the public, and the government to settle down to the more difficult task of developing constructive suggestions for the content of atomic energy legislation.

The President's concern over the reception accorded the May-Johnson bill has already been mentioned. Even as he was conferring with legislative leaders, his principal assistant, John W. Snyder, then Director of the Office of War Mobilization and Reconversion (OWMR), came to him with an analysis of the defects of the May-Johnson bill and a preliminary outline of the requirements of a good bill. These suggestions were developed after extensive discussion with the high-ranking scientists who were leading the opposition to the May-Johnson bill and were prepared by James R. Newman, head of OWMR's science division, with the author's assistance. The President was so impressed with these suggestions that he forthwith designated OWMR to act for the Administration in connection with atomic energy legislation. Mr. Newman was shortly appointed special counsel to the Senate Special Committee on Atomic Energy, and Dr. Condon, by then the new Director of the National Bureau of Standards, was named Scientific Advisor to the committee.

Through November and most of December the Senate committee busied itself with the task of learning about the physics, production and potential uses of atomic energy and the military significance of the atomic bomb. Since an examination of the criticisms of the May-Johnson bill had shown that modification by amendment was not feasible because of the many basic changes needed, the drafting of an alternative bill was begun by Mr. Newman and the author under the joint guidance of Senator McMahon and the Administration, and in consultation with the scientists and other agencies of the government. The draft was completed as the general hearings of the Senate committee were nearing conclusion and was introduced by Senator McMahon just before the Christmas recess. The Committee agreed to consider specific legislation when it resumed hearings in January, using the McMahon bill, the May-Johnson bill, and a bill submitted by Senator Ball as the bases of discussion.

II. A Bill Emerges from the Senate Committee

Even as the press was daily reporting the testimony of expert witnesses filling in the general facts about atomic energy and as the McMahon bill was quietly being drafted, the protagonists in the May-Johnson bill controversy were preparing to do battle in the new arena —the Senate Special Committee on Atomic Energy.

The isolated site organizations of scientists were consolidated into a single Federation of Atomic Scientists. A simple word change substituting "American" for "Atomic" sufficed to cover the inclusion of other scientific groups not strictly in the atomic energy field. A small office with a lone secretary was opened in Washington, accessible only by ascent of some four flights of steps. Many of the nation-wide civic, labor, and religious groups banded together to form the National Committee on Atomic Information, devoted solely to the educational task of disseminating the basic physical and political facts about atomic energy, the Committee sharing the Federation's lofty perch. The scientists themselves, unable to afford paid representatives in the nation's capital, inaugurated a relay system whereby a member from each site took a two-week leave of absence, spent it in Washington, and returned only to be replaced by an associate for a similar two-week period. In Washington they worked till all hours of the night, meeting with members of all three branches of the government and influential organizations and individuals, writing speeches and articles, and learning as best they could the political ins and outs in the seat of government. For the most part they avoided political bias. Perhaps their rare combination of a non-partisan attitude and an unflagging devotion to a goal of no conceivable personal benefit explains some of the readiness of political leaders to listen to them. The organizations which had joined in creating the Atomic Information Service merged their legislative activities into the Emergency Conference for the Civilian Control of Atomic Energy sparked by the tireless Rachel Bell. And, to complete the girding for battle, groups of prominent individuals nationally and locally were formed into Emergency Committees for the Civilian Control of Atomic Energy. The national committee roster included, among others, Bishop Oxnam, Beardsley Ruml, William Donovan, Palmer Hoyt, Arthur Whiteside, Percival Brundage, Donald Nelson, Cass Canfield, Harry Emerson Fosdick, Sumner Welles, and John Hay Whitney.

Across the ideological gulf the proponents of military control were not napping. Working quietly, mostly through service officers, they brought their wartime prestige and their hard-earned knowledge of the workings of Congress to bear on the more responsive members of both houses. Even a character assassination here and there was not beneath them. Theirs was a double strategy; preferred was the passage of a bill firmly establishing military control in peacetime, but the alternative of no legislation was almost equivalent since the military would have remained in control.

Thus the lines were forming for the most difficult open contest in the Senate with each development exposed to the eyes of the public, unlike the quick trick tried in the House.

The McMahon Bill. . . . The Senate committee spent four weeks hearing witnesses testifying exclusively with respect to legislation for the domestic control of atomic energy. In the course of these hearings the President sent a special letter to Senator McMahon outlining the Administration's views on the principal ingredients of desirable atomic energy legislation. With a minor exception, his recommendations paralleled the McMahon bill, thus bringing into the open his change of heart on the May-Johnson bill.

The hearings concluded, the Committee embarked upon a schedule of executive sessions almost unprecedented in legislative annals. For six weeks practically the full membership of the Committee met in almost daily session, combing over the legislative proposals before them. The Committee's first response to the weight of favorable testimony on the McMahon bill came when, after a preliminary skirmish, it voted to use the bill as a working guide. Section by section, the Committee went through the bill three separate times, emerging with a true group product, a bill which, while still bearing a resemblance to the original McMahon bill, nevertheless contained changes in almost every line. Several sections were completely re-written, others substantially overhauled, a few settled by more or less artful compromise. The result was a superior piece of legislation, a testimonial to the latent capacities of free discussion. True, a few provisions are subject to pointed criticism, but rarely has a legislative body making its own decisions emerged with a bill reflecting as high a caliber of statesmanship as did the Senate Special Committee in reporting out its modified form of S. 1717.

The Committee Product. A full analysis of the Committee's change would not here be appropriate. Some of its evident improvements were: 1) the creation of the post of General Manager, to be appointed by the President and to service the Commission in supervising the four Divisions and other organizational units; 2) the revision of the patents section to provide explicitly that certain inventions were not patentable and to make the availability of utilization patents discretionary rather than automatic; and 3) the addition of section expressly providing that international agreements were to supersede any inconsistent provision of the domestic control law.

Two other provisions, however, received the bulk of the Committee's attention and supplied the fuel for the major controversies within and without the Senate unit. These were the sections dealing first, with the relation between the military departments and civilian Atomic Energy Commission and second, with the determination of appropriate secrecy measures. Though the questions were logically distinct, they were the beaches upon which the civilian and military control proponents engaged, and while the black sand of one issue was distinguishable from the white sand of the other, the heat of the conflict fused them into a single mass of deep disagreement on the special capacity of the military to preserve the national security.

From the time of the President's first offhand statements about preserving our monopoly of the "secrets" of the atomic bomb, the majority of the public, as shown by public opinion polls, accepted the simple notion of "secrets," perhaps subconsciously hoping that preserving these "secrets" would protect us against all danger of atomic warfare. Though later polls showed that most people accepted the intellectual proposition that we could not retain our monopoly, nevertheless their emotional dependence on the concept of "secrets" was probably not seriously affected by the logical inconsistency of such a position.

In this respect members of Congress followed the public pattern. From the early questioning of witnesses on the general subject of atomic energy, there was no question but that the law would contain some provision to preserve the "secrets." Indeed, an early propaganda coup was scored when the words "security" and "secrecy" became interchangeable in this field. Hence, from the outset, few scientists publicly advocated a policy of complete declassification, although many were apprehensive of the evils that had been and could continue to be committed in the name of secrecy.

Assuming, then, that secrecy was not only desirable but vitally linked up with our national security, it was not surprising that one of the principal foci in the civilian versus military control dispute became: "Who could better keep the secrets?" Disclosure of the Canadian espionage story in December and ensuing months, succeeded by dark hints from J. Parnell Thomas of the Un-American Activities Committee that secrets were leaking to other nations from Oak Ridge, were not calculated to let the public forget the issue. Curiously, these stories were urged as proving military control alone could preserve the secrets even though Oak Ridge was still under military control.

Meeting the issue on the same level, the scientists responded with two arguments: first, that only a scientist could know a "secret" from a paragraph of jargon; and second, in many instances War Department secrecy rules had hampered the development of the bomb. Indeed on one occasion it appeared that a whole laboratory might have exploded if one group had not illicitly transmitted information unknown to the group in the endangered lab.

Though the public debate proceeded largely on this level, a few members of the Senate committee had realized that secrecy did not depend on the color of the Commission's coats. More serious to them was Secretary Patterson's objection to the original McMahon bill, that it contained inadequate provision for participation in atomic energy control and development by the regular military departments. Their first plan was to give to the Army Chief of Staff a veto power over acts of the civilian Commission. This "compromise" was discarded when the then Chief of Staff, General Eisenhower, showed no great enthusiasm for the power. Next, they developed the so-called "Vandenberg amendment." This proposed to create a Military Liaison Committee consisting of representatives of the War and Navy Departments with power to advise and consult with the Commission on all matters *it* deemed to affect security, to know of all matters within the Commission and, where it felt any action or proposed action was "inimical to the common defense and security," to appeal the question to the President whose decision would be final. Senator McMahon opposed the amendment, urging instead a compromise as to membership on the Commission. Put to a vote, he was defeated 6 to 1, four committee members being absent. His request for postponement of consideration until the full committee was present was granted, the vote then becoming 10 to 1.

Disclosure of the amendment was the signal for a direct offensive by the scientists, the conference of organizations, the emergency committee of prominent individuals, and the many friends of civilian control in the communications fields and elsewhere. This time the public relations advantage rested with their side. The substance of the amendment was proposed by several other senators; Vandenberg's principal contribution was his suggestion of the final wording. Because it was dubbed the "Vandenberg amendment," however, instead of some shorthand reference, the amendment's fate almost as a matter of senatorial courtesy came to rest with Vandenberg. This was most desirable because he was more responsive to public opinion than some of the other sponsors and it was an election year for him—he could not then know that the November 1946 election was to be a Republican landslide. While the clamor against the amendment steadily mounted (including some influential protests from Vandenberg's home town), the Administration also became concerned. For one thing the proposed amendment by-passed the Secretaries of War and Navy, a result not exactly palatable to them. Shortly, Vandenberg himself indicated a willingness to accept modification. The solution lay in the familiar lawyer's legerdemain of accomplishing fundamental changes in meaning while altering as few words as possible. By limiting the scope of the Liaison Committee's functions to military applications and by restoring regular channels within the military departments, the amended amendment ceased to create an autonomous and powerful military committee and replaced it with an orderly liaison within traditional military department jurisdiction and channels. Vandenberg's acceptance of the changes was readily approved by the Senate committee.

Just as the military control debate merged into the secrecy question, so the fight over the Vandenberg amendment affected the committee's attitude when it reaches the section dealing with control of information. There, for the first time, Vandenberg, Hickenlooper, and others sought advice from leading scientists in close touch with the scientists' organizations and made a determined effort to produce a section which would preserve the maximum secrecy consistent with dissemination of enough data not to hamper research. In this instance the basic problems confronting the scientists flowed from the Espionage Act which the committee not unexpectedly was unwilling to touch. The final section, while indulging Senator Austin's penchant for inserting the phrase "to assure the common defense and security," provided explicitly that the Commission should weigh against the policy of security through secrecy first, the importance of freedom of communication in assuring the progress of research and second, the desirability of eliminating restrictions when adequate international controls were established.

With these and lesser modifications, the Senate committee unanimously approved their bill on April 19, 1946. Unanimity in a committee of such conservative composition on a bill authorizing unprecedented government controls was no minor or accidental achievement, as the ensuing history indicates. After an agonizing delay, the reasons for which have never become clear, Senator McMahon seized the opportunity on a peaceful Saturday afternoon to bring the committee bill up for consideration on the Senate floor. The Senate approved the bill unanimously on that day, June 1, 1946.

III. FINAL PASSAGE

The jubilance of the proponents of civilian control over Senate approval soon faded as they analyzed the membership of the House Military Affairs Committee, to which the bill was then referred. Of this 27-member committee, 9 of the Republicans had already gone on record as opposed to government control in voting against the May-Johnson bill. Chairman May, whose "own" bill had been stopped by advocates of the measure now resting on his desk, was hardly likely to press for prompt action in perhaps the last month of the legislative session. A half-dozen of the Democrats had consistently sided with May on pro-military measures. Then, with ironic timeliness, invitations to witness the gigantic atomic demonstrations at Bikini drew off a number of committee members, one of these being Representative Holifield who almost alone had fought the May-Johnson bill in committee.

After a week's delay Chairman May announced public hearings would be held. Two witnesses were invited—Secretary of War Patterson and Assistant Navy Secretary Kenney. Examination of the witnesses by committee members demonstrated beyond doubt the committee's preoccupation with the military use of atomic energy and their unquestioning assumption that only the military departments were qualified to act in the interests of national security. This testimony concluded, the House unit embarked upon section-by-section consideration of S. 1717 in executive session.

The amendment pattern was soon apparent. Chairman May supported three militarizing amendments, one to permit military men to serve in any position, another requiring at least one member of the Commission to be from the armed forces, and a third requiring the Director of Military Applications to be a military officer. These revisions approved, he then fought off a host of disabling amendments proposed by the dissident Republican members, allowing only an occasional one to slip into the bill.

By the end of June, though the amendment process was substantially finished, the bill encountered such parliamentary obstacles that its chances of stillbirth rose alarmingly. House rules designate a majority of the committee's roster as a quorum and require a quorum for formal action if the point is raised. Several members of the committee were off to Bikini, others were ill or out of town, leaving it within the power of eight or nine members acting in concert to prevent a quorum. The same Republican group then followed the practice of coming to meetings, counting noses, and, if a quorum were present, taking turns leaving the committee room. This process continued for several days despite powerful objections from the public,[2] from the Administration, and from the Speaker of the House. Whether these pressures were enough to have ultimately been successful is purely speculative, because at this point fortune intervened from another quarter. The Senate committee investigating the national defense program chose this moment to release its first tentaive stories on the May-Garsson munitions undertakings. Though Chairman May did not then appear to be much involved, he must have had some foreboding of what was to follow, because almost immediately thereafter he forced the bill out of committee with that uncanny strength which committee chairmen so often display.

This was July 10. The scene shifted to the Rules Committee, where J. Parnell Thomas[3] sought openly to kill the bill on the ground that

---

[2] The Emergency Committee for the Civilian Control of Atomic Energy published two full-page ads in the Washington Post in this period. Their emphasis, as was that of the bill's proponents in the House, was upon the eminence of the men supporting the Senate bill—the Senate Committee, Eisenhower, Baruch, et al. Judging from the attention given these advertisements in later floor debate, they evoked a response which more than justified their expense.

[3] Rep. Thomas was a member of both the Military Affairs and the Un-American Activities Committees.

continued control by the War Department was essential to the nation's safety, urging the conclusion of his Un-American Activities Committee that secrets were leaking to other nations from Oak Ridge. His contention was being supported by some War Department quarters even then, as appears from two concurrent incidents. The Oak Ridge security officer stated over the telephone that the Thomas Committee was inaccurate in quoting him as saying "the peace and security of the United States is definitely in danger." Yet he was somehow unable to obtain clearance to reduce his denial to writing for submission to Congress. Furthermore, as has only recently been revealed, a "high officer in the Manhattan Project" sent a special message to Thomas about this time urging him to order the FBI file on the Senate committee's scientific adviser (Dr. Condon) because some indications of disloyalty might be obtained from it. Thomas' effort failed and by July 16, under Chairman Sabath's guidance, the Rules Committee had approved by a narrow margin a rule permitting prompt consideration of the bill on the floor of the House.

The Administration in working for the passage of the Senate bill was now faced with a difficult tactical situation. In floor debate a bill is always managed by the chairman of the committee from which it emanates—here Mr. May. Opposition time is controlled by the ranking minority member—in this case Dewey Short, who was completely against the bill. Confronted with these obstacles, the Administration depended on Ewing Thomason, next ranking Democrat on the committee, who was personally convinced of the wisdom of the Senate bill. From the outset Thomason set his sights on one goal—House passage of some bill under the number S. 1717, regardless of content or amendments, just so that a bill would go into a conference committee of both houses. Valiantly, he fought against efforts to cripple the legislation: amendments establishing the death penalty for violation of secrecy restrictions; requiring FBI approval of the "character and associations" of all employees and contractors; and replacing patent controls with provisions permitting private patent rights regardless of secrecy requirements. Each of these he lost, but in the final test, a motion to recommit the bill to committee, he won by scant 50 out of 342 votes, and the bill moved into conference.

The House conferees were Democrats May, Thomason, and Durham and Republicans Clason and Thomas. Senate conferees were Democrats McMahon, Johnson, and Russell and Republicans Vandenberg and Millikin. In conference the members of each house vote as a unit; hence the vote of the Senate members cannot overrule the House members or vice versa. The problems in the conference committee were twofold: 1) To what extent would the Senate members now "give in" to House amendments which more closely fitted their normal conservatism? 2) Could a civilian control bill secure the approval of the House delegation if May voted with the Republicans?

In conference committee the Senate delegation soon displayed an impressive unanimity in both substance and tactic. In general, all minor House amendments not inconsistent with the structure of the bill were accepted with few modifications. Two basic issues remained —the role of the military and the patents section. Here, the strength of inner conviction flowing from full consideration and careful decision demonstrated itself. The Senate delegation sustained their own decisions on these points by sheer force of superior knowledge and genuine belief.

Of the two, the patents questions afforded the greater likelihood of departure from the Senate bill. The American Bar Association, the National Association of Manufacturers, a number of Hearst papers, and a National Patent Council had unloosed a violent attack on the Senate patents action *after* the bill had passed the Senate. The chairman of the House Patents Committee had taken the floor to denounce the Senate proposal as the end of the American patent system. A former Assistant Commissioner of Patents, whose current employment by RCA was not revealed by the record, had testified that the Senate provision was modeled after the Russian system. Against a background of Congressional unwillingness to modify the patent system over many years,[4] the intensity of the attack was indeed likely to occasion some or many concessions from the Senate delegation.

To the particular credit of Senator Millikin, a self-designated conservative, the Senate version emerged untouched. After a careful study of the objections raised in the House, he concluded that the Senate section alone could both preserve the secrecy sought by other sections of the bill and serve the public interest in a field developed entirely at taxpayers' expense. After hearing this one-and-a-half-hour speech on the subject in the conference committee, the Senate delegation voted unanimously to substitute the Senate patents sec-

---

[4] Despite a succession of similar recommendations from presidential commissions and legislative committees, the Senate provision contained almost the first limitations in the last hundred years on patentable inventions and on the freedom of patentees in granting or denying licences.

tion and May voted with the Democrats to give the House conferee's concurrence by a 3 to 2 vote.

The military amendments present a different problem because here May's sympathies were clearly with the House Republicans. In this area, Senator Vandenberg bore the brunt of persuasion. Upholding his revised military liaison committee amendment as a fair adjustment of the civilian versus military control issue, he dominated the conference committee discussions. He conceded the requirement that the Director of the Military Applications Division be an active officer, and strove to eliminate both the requirement that at least one member of the commission also be an officer and the clause exempting all commission posts from the 1870 prohibition against military officers in civilian positions. At this point, May was suddenly afflicted with a severe heart attack. His condition not only prevented his testifying before the Senate committee investigating his transactions with the Garssons; it kept him as well from the crucial sessions of the conference committee. In a story-book scene and with a voice implying he was on his death-bed, May finally whispered his acceptance of Vandenberg's proposal. The conference bill was complete, though J. Parnell Thomas in an unusual move refused to sign the report.

Back again on the floor of the House in the closing days of the session, the conference bill drew the same violent opposition which had met the House committee report. Thomas spoke angrily; Patents Chairman Latham denounced the conference bill; others sprang up to attack the bill as dangerous and socialistic. In last-minute desperation the opposition even spread the rumor on the floor of the House that steel was now fissionable; hence the steel industry would be nationalized under the bill. The break came when Clason, the other dissenting House conferee, announced his decision to vote for the bill. In a few moments the conference report was approved by voice vote in the House. Approved by the Senate the same afternoon, it was sent to the President for signature. On August 1, the Atomic Energy Act of 1946 became law.

Conclusion

This review of the history of one of the more significant laws of our time permits a few deductions not peculiar to this legislation. Like all laws receiving wide public consideration, the Atomic Energy Act in its history illustrates: 1) the tendency toward over-simplification of the issues with resultant confusion and concealment of the value judgments actually involved; 2) the effect which the nature of the issue and organized efforts can have upon alignments for and against; and 3) the essentially inconclusive nature of all legislation.

The Issues. In the public eye the principal decision lay in choosing between military and civilian control. . . .

. . . the real "control" question involved decisions as to both the amount and direction of the discretion to be given to those in control and the genuineness of the administrative structure, regardless of who might ultimately be appointed. Was it wiser to give sweeping power with almost absolute discretion to the administering body or to determine initial policy as to research, production, peacetime uses, secrecy, etc., and refine the grants of power to match these decisions? What types of exclusive public ownership, what safeguards for private research, what emphasis upon peacetime uses should the law specifically establish? Would responsibility be effectively lodged in a large part-time commission with outside interests working through a full-time administrator with independent powers? Or would responsibility better match authority in a small full-time commission working through an administrator whose role was primarily executory? These were the "control" issues. Yet no special political astuteness is needed to realize how drab and colorless these questions would have appeared in public debate. No wonder both sides sought support within the framework of the simpler symbols of military versus civilian control. . . .[5]

The Alignments. Political parties have long ceased to be the sole mechanism for organized expression on public issues between elections, if indeed they ever were. Private organizations in bewildering variety supply forums for debate on public questions, take positions, and seek simultaneously to influence and represent the thinking of their members. Business, trade, and farm groups; labor, religious, and civic groups, social, book, and family clubs—all are more or less responsible on matters of public policy.

Over a period of years the more politically active organizations have developed fairly clear policy stands; on a host of conventional

[5] In a very real sense the debate in oversimplified terms contributed to the content of the final bill. Most of the bill's policy conclusions on freedom of research, emphasis on development of peacetime uses, use of traditional methods to preserve secrecy, protection of the public interest in non-military benefits, and leeway for international control followed from subordinate arguments, invoked in favor of civilian control. The simplicity of the issue made public discussion possible; the discussion itself shaped the actual legislative decisions.

controversies their positions can readily be anticipated. Sometimes these positions are described as "liberal" or "conservative"; and repeated organizational alignments have tended to give the groupings themselves liberal or conservative labels.

Mere novelty of an issue is not alone sufficient to break down these habits of alignment, as responses to many of the New Deal innovations demonstrated. The atomic energy controversy, however, supplied proof that established groupings may be redistributed. The issue itself was of course a major factor; but the issue alone would not have broken the momentum if many individuals, scientists and others, had not actively worked toward this objective. The results were roughly as follows:

(1) Organizations such as the Veterans of Foreign Wars, the Farm Bureau, and the General Federation of Women's Clubs joined the League of Women Voters and the Congress of Industrial Organization in supporting civilian control;

(2) The National Association of Manufacturers, the American Bar Association, and similar property-emphasis groups were largely silent until after the Senate had approved its committee's bill; and

(3) A few large corporations worked actively but quietly with the unauthorized military spokesmen who lobbied for military control.
. . .

Part B. INQUIRY AS AN INSTRUMENT
OF GOVERNMENT

16   *Congressional Oversight of Administration:*
      The Power of the Purse
      ARTHUR MACMAHON

Legislative oversight of administration is a familiar and well-grounded assumption of responsible government. Accepted, too, is the corollary that the need for such oversight increases with executive initiative in policy and the delegation of discretion under the broad terms of statutes. . . .

Congress shows novel zest for staffs of its own. In various ways, it seeks to attach strings to action. How far can this double tendency be pushed under the presidential form of government without creating ambiguities of administrative responsibility? There is a related and deeper difficulty. Can a legislative body—the institutional virtue of which lies in the recentralized choice and diffused responsiveness of its individual members—act on details otherwise than through small groups within itself which, by their special biases, may distort the application of public policy and even destroy its integrity? Public policy must be fused from the localisms inherent in popular representative bodies; it must then be carried out with as much wholeness as possible. Mighty issues appear in the present assertiveness of Congress. Welcome as are the stirrings from the lethargy of its own institutional tradition, its restlessness holds at least as much portent as promise.

From Arthur W. Macmahon, *Political Science Quarterly* (March 1943, Vol. LXIII, No. 2, pp. 161-190; June 1943, Vol. LXIII, No. 3, pp. 380-414). Reprinted by permission of the Editors of *Political Science Quarterly*.

185

I

There has been a significant change of emphasis in the Congressional attitude toward administrative discretion and its control. Originally, legislative suspicion and reluctance were reflected in the detailed character of statute law. But, especially in dealing with the flux of economic relations, leeway for administrative determinations was inevitable. . . . The weight is no longer on the initial insertion of statutory detail or upon judicial review. Rather, the legislative body itself seeks to be continuously a participant in guiding administrative conduct and the exercise of discretion. The cords that Congress now seeks to attach to administrative action are not merely the pre-dawn "leading-strings of statutes" of which Woodrow Wilson wrote in *Congressional Government*. The novel feature of the attempted relationship is its immediacy.

The shift of emphasis just described affects one's perspective on the purposes of legislative oversight of administration. In the theory of the matter, four types of objective have been recognized. First, the objective of legislative oversight may be to check dishonesty or waste. Especially is this important when the stream of supervision within the administrative system is poisoned near its source. Apart from checking malfeasance, moreover, legislators have opportunities to see the results of governmental programs; at times they can serve administration almost as a supplementary inspectorate. Second, the objective of legislative oversight may be to guard against unsympathetic or perhaps merely over-zealous attitudes among officials which produce harsh or callous administration. Third, the ideal of legislative oversight has assumed that the non-special minds of legislators, brought to bear upon the administrative routines, may challenge the means in terms of a broad and realistic sense of ends. It may freshen inventiveness as to the means themselves; at least it may rebuke stupidity. Fourth, the objective of legislative oversight may be to see that there is compliance with the legislative intent as embodied in law. This is the face of the theory that is highlighted by the events of the hour.

Within the notion of enforcing compliance with legislative intent a shift is discernible. Formerly compliance meant legality and this was enforced by methods which were essentially external to Congress: the courts, the General Accounting Office as a vast routinized bureau, the Department of Justice, the Treasury controls, and the departmental fiscal offices. Now the legislative intent that is conceived is one of incompletely resolved policy. Without withdrawing power, the Congress seeks in sundry ways to claim what it gave; it asserts the right of continuous intervention.

It is worth pausing to review in baldest fashion some of the methods by which continuous intervention is now essayed. Clues may be drawn from measures or proposals in Congress since January 1943. (1) The amendment of statutes is a method of oversight; as Dr. Elias Huzar has very cogently shown, there is no sharp borderline between legislation and supervision. Recently amendments to wartime laws have been provoked by particular incidents and have cracked like warning whips. (2) Meanwhile Congressional investigations multiply. There is no novelty in this safeguard of free government, but some persons are agitating for a unification of inquiries into the conduct of the war. The thought now is less the convenience of administrators harassed by multiple hearings than the possibility of creating a single instrument of potent influence. (3) The standing legislative committees summon administrators to explain and justify decisions, past and pending. A special House committee investigates the extent to which administrative directives have been inconsistent with law, or arbitrary. Some members of Congress are urging that the standing committees should be permanently empowered to watch and perhaps censor the exercise of administrative discretion in their respective fields of jurisdiction. Others, however, propose more inclusive organs for the exercise of continuous scrutiny. (4) Related in spirit, being a likely opening for intervention in administration, is the preposterous but formidable move to broaden senatorial confirmation of appointments. (5) Meanwhile Congress begins to talk of staffing, but with many shades of opinion about its nature and nexus: whether the personnel should be permanent or transitory and how appointed, whether the attachment should be to committees, and if so to which committees, or should be to the chambers as wholes but singly, or to joint agencies of House and Senate. (6) But outstanding as practical developments have been steps actually taken to enlarge the facilities and duties of the committees on appropriations. . . .

II

The committee structure of Congress reflects the distinction between authorization and appropriation—between the passage of acts which define purposes, convey power, and authorize approriations, on the one hand, and the year by year provision of money, on the other. The standing committee system had two elements: the legislative committees and the appropriating committees. The separation of authorization and appropriation has the advantage, among others, that it accommodates itself to the technique of planning, for programs may be laid out broadly, to be implemented annually at a tempo suited to conditions. . . .

The appropriations committees of House and Senate work separately. House members, especially, shy away from formalized joint action; experience, they say, shows that it is likely to subordinate them to the Senators. Custom concedes to the House the right to initiate the appropriation bills. The Senate committee is smaller than that in the House; its members serve upon many subcommittees; the staff has less responsibility. In a sense, the Senate Committee on Appropriations sits in an appellate capacity. It circularizes the departments to find out if they have particular items to present in its hearings. Often the agencies choose to take their small cuts at the hands of the House and let well enough alone. But administrators value the opportunity for appeal that the Senate committee affords. The House members, for their part, regard the Senate group as undisciplined and irresponsible. Institutionally, the weight rests heavily on the side of the House. This explains why (despite a few outstanding bits of wartime supervision attempted by the Senate committee) the emphasis in the pages that follow is so generally on the methods of the House Committee on Appropriations.

III

The realities of the appropriations committees are in subcommittees, in the chief clerk, and in the clerks assigned to the subcommittees. The ideal of a concerted consideration of expenditures has not been attained. The committee as a whole sometimes considers what are called questions of policy common to all appropriation bills. . . . But on the appropriation bills themselves, the main committee can hardly be said to act. Bills typically come before the committee an hour or so before they are to be brought on the floor in charge of a subcommittee chairman and his associates. The printed bill and the committee report are ready. Indeed, the report (though still without a number) has been given out bearing the notice that it is "subject to release when consideration of the bill which it accompanies has been completed by the whole committee" and with the request that, before it is released, there be a check "in order to be advised of any changes."

Alterations in the full committee are rare. Nevertheless, in addition to the continuity of its small and well-knit staff, the committee is united by a body of procedures and an atmosphere, by the influence of the chairman, and by the constant direct association of the sub-committee chairmen in the subcommittee on deficiencies. . . .

Since the actualities of the House committee's work lie so largely in its eleven subcommittees, great importance attaches to the assignments of committee members among these groups. The value of the standing committee device is the combination it affords of some specialization in subject matter with a degree of detachment not likely to be found among administrators. But how much emphasis should be placed upon detachment in the choice of the subcommittees that will deal with particular subjects and departments? The selection is made by the chairman of the whole committee, conditioned by the total play of forces in the House. . . .

Whatever the chairman's view, experience shows that the gravitation of special preoccupations can be delayed but hardly resisted. Given time, men will achieve the subcommittee they especially desire and, once on it, they rise by seniority and may thus achieve the chairmanship. Nor is it always necessary to wait long. . . .

It is not Congress, not the House or Senate, not even the appropriations committee as a whole that should be thought of as abstractions, set against administration. The reality is a handful of men from particular states or districts, working with a particular committee clerk on a multitude of details.

The importance of the staff of the appropriations committees can hardly be exaggerated. The modesty of its scale has been truly amazing. . . .

In the case of appropriations, the smallness of the staff has been offset by its continuity and experience. The House committee has had only three clerks since its establishment in 1865 [to 1943] . . .

In the Senate committee continuity of staff has been nearly as marked as in the House. . . . Thus [from 1873 to 1939] the combined service of two clerks covered sixty-six years. . . .

It is the clerk assigned to a subcommittee who takes the proof of the budget (for hearings may begin on some of the bills before its formal presentation) and draws off its material on the wide-margined committee print of the bill, with the supporting material of the estimates run small below each textual item. It is the clerk who prepares many of the questions to be put at the hearings. Sometimes a dependent chairman follows down his list, virtually reading the questions to the departmental representatives. Perhaps the technical question arises whether a given item contains "legislative" matter ordinarily inadmissible in an appropriation bill. "I will ask the clerk to look into that matter." Or, from another chairman: "I am wondering if it is agreeable to postpone the hearing until tomorrow, as Mr. Sheild [Committee Clerk] and I want an opportunity to go over some of these items." It is the subcommittee clerk who works with the chairman in preparing for the crucial process of "marking up the bill" in executive session. He is a consultant in this process; he must keep track of and embody the changes. Then, under very great pressure, he may be almost wholly responsible for writing the report that will accompany the bill—a document with probably growing importance in legislative oversight of administration. . . . The clerk's judgment shapes what goes into the printed hearings. Through all this it is at once the strength and the weakness of the committee aides that they remain "clerks," even "assistant clerks." Some of the staff's relative self-effacement may reflect personal limitations and the protective convenience of routine. Some of it, as will be said again (for the point is crucial), reflects Marcellus Sheild's awareness of the ticklish problem of duplicating leadership under separation of powers. Meanwhile the staff's esprit de corps and cheerful procedural competence has perhaps offset and even delayed the movement for increased staffing around the focus of appropriations. . . .

The really momentous issue is the extent of the staffing under the Committee on Appropriations which would be consistent with good budgetary relations and an integrated responsibility in administration generally. Staffing might easily be pushed to a point where it would bring a legislative budget method into existence in rivalry with the executive budget. An ambiguous responsibility might develop in the departments. There is need for the most careful consideration, not glib endorsement of the idea of staff and more staff.

There is another reason for caution in staffing in addition to the risk of doubling the lines of authority within administration. The peculiar virtue of the lay element in legislative thinking may be sacrificed. The legislator is immediately in touch with his constituents and this gives him an awareness of government from the side of the public. In wielding oversight of administration, it is his duty to bring this practical public sense to bear. How far must this be personal and immediate, not vicarious? In addition, and quite as important, is the criticism which a robust, imaginative lay mind can bring to bear on technical operations. Something of the value of the mingling of special and non-special minds might be lost if the politician-legislator dealt with administration only through an intermediate legislative bureaucracy. . . .

IV

The formal Congressional hearings on the estimates begin, for some of the bills, before the session opens and before the budget has been presented. Hearings on a routine major bill may run for six weeks of nearly daily sessions. Swelled on the one hand by matter prepared in advance (like the justifications) and by information worked up later at the request of committee members during the hearings (usually inserted at the point where the question appears), the printed hearings have become monumental—more than twenty thousand printed pages of material annually. . . .

The limitations of hearings on appropriations as a method of getting at the facts are admitted by Congressmen who participate in the process. . . . Sometimes committee members reveal a kind of defeatism, for they neither fully trust the professional administrator nor know how to challenge him. . . . "I know that there is no use in asking a fellow who is advocating it whether it is sound or not." . . .

The foregoing comments do not deny the expository value of the hearings. Some of the best interchanges are sheerly explanatory. When a subcommittee has recently acquired jurisdiction over an agency, it may consciously go to school in the agency's methods.

Nor do the shortcomings of the method of question and answer deny the galvanizing effect that the mere fear of embarrassing questions may have on the conduct of administration. Inept though it is, and easy though it usually is to parry questions, the annual cross-examination is an ordeal for administrators. On the whole, it is good for them. Some officials at departmental headquarters say that an experience of bureau representatives before a committee teaches more to careless heads of units than lecturing within the department on administrative proprieties. The risk, of course, is that the reflex makes for caution rather than courage. This danger could be lessened by more stress in the hearings on essential results, rather than on methods, provided legislators would make allowance for the extent to which the fruits of governmental action are long-run and indirect. . . .

Consideration of bills in the whole Committee on Appropriations —customarily an affair of an hour or so—is virtually telescoped with the floor debate. A vast majority of the measures—perhaps ninety per cent—are taken up in the House on the same day on which they are considered by the main committee. . . . Certainly the ideal of a broad congressional consideration of major measures—to say nothing of a whole budgetary program—has not been realized. . . .

V

The reports of the committees on appropriations, especially of the House, are prime instruments of legislative control. These reports command increasing notice by administrators, while they raise problems of responsibility that deserve more analysis than they have yet received.

Each bill is accompanied to the floor by a report. This is a pamphlet which, in the case of the regular appropriation bills in the House, runs from twenty-five to fifty pages, including tables. The report is the work of the subcommittee. The full Committee on Appropriations seldom alters a document which, indeed, has already been printed provisionally. More particularly, the report is the handiwork of the subcommittee chairman and of the assistant clerk regularly assigned to the group. Their respective parts in the actual preparation of a report vary with personalities and circumstances. The role of the clerk is necessarily heavy; the writing is apt to fall to him. The product must be appraised in the light of the fact that, in the exigent rhythm of appropriations, an assistant clerk (who often covers two subcommittees, each with jurisdiction over many agencies) has at the most a week of day-and-night work in which to frame the report after the subcommittee has "marked up" the bill in executive session.

In drafting the report, the departmental officers are sometimes consulted. In at least one case in recent years, the departmental budget officer sat through a week-end with the committee clerk in framing many parts of the report. Under these circumstances, naturally, the report is likely to contain remarks that later will provide fulcrums whereby the department can exercise leverage upon its self-assertive parts. Such a nexus of departmental leaders and committee clerks is more than interesting. It is highly significant, for it illustrates two things: first, that the disciplinary strains in government are not a simple alignment of administration as a whole against the legislative body; second, that the pressure of the legislative body may be exerted

in fortifying the central machinery within the administration itself.
. . .

The efficacy of committee reports is the fact that disregard of them
may lead to a cut in appropriations in the following year. A follow-
through is the more likely because, amid the vastness of the governmental operations as presented in the estimates, committees are repetitive; members repeat old questions and pursue old strictures. . . .

Sometimes the strictures in the reports merely put administrators
under notice that certain results are expected and that information on
them must be submitted in the future. There is endless variation, of
course, in the nature of the compulsion applied, the response expected, and the time allowed. Thus notice is often served that, as a
condition to the approval of funds for the year beyond that for which
appropriations are being made, specified information must be presented to the subcommittee. The span of appraisal may be longer than
a year. In the report a few years ago on agricultural appropriations
the committee said of the four regional laboratories set up especially
for the discovery of new outlets for farm products: "At the hearings
the Department representatives were challenged to achieve results
within ten years which will consume sufficient surplus and be of
sufficient commercial advantage to justify the expenditures under this
head and if not to discontinue the laboratories. . . ."

Enough has been said to show the range of intervention in administration through language in reports to the appropriations committee. Much ambiguity attends this method of oversight. Several
factors affect the degree to which an administrator must regard any
particular bit of verbiage as mandatory. How precise is it? Was the
point raised in the hearings and, if so, was it dwelt upon? Did the
administrator himself make any admission or commitment? Did the
legislative body give any especial attention to the item in question?
Especially, was there a vote upon it, as in the rejection of an amendment not desired by the subcommittee? The foregoing are some of
the circumstances which the administrator must consider. His exercise of judgment is apt to be harder because he must reckon with
two chambers.

VI

The discussion thus far has mainly concerned direct relations between subcommittees and administrators when appropriations are
being made. It is appropriate to consider interim contacts during the

year. As a background, it is necessary first to comment on the nature of appropriations in the national government of the United States.

The form and content of appropriating legislation in the national government have received very little analysis, official or academic. It has been the accretion of practice, for the most part stubbornly repetitive, but shaped in the past by countless forgotten situations. The result is highly uneven; there is no standard unit. Within the Department of Agriculture, as Verne Lewis has pointed out, some of the items "were as small as $5,000; other items were as large as $500,000,000."

Once a breakdown of appropriation items has become customary, the tendency is to perpetuate it. Comparison from year to year is aided by repetition, which indeed is encouraged by the law and by the Budget Bureau's instructions. Sometimes, where appropriations have been segregated, efforts at simplification are defeated by outraged subcommittee members who cling to items that have a local habitation and a name. . . .

The prevailing type of breakdown in national appropriations truly evades definition. "Lump sum" is hardly the term for it, apart from some emergency appropriations. But the usual categories are broad. Because of the scope of the ordinary item, the appropriation language itself leaves wide administrative leeway. A crucial question, therefore, is the continuing force of the highly detailed preparatory material: the estimates, the justifications, and remarks made by the administrators in the hearings. . . .

This is a difficult, highly empirical field for practical judgments by administrators on the nature of their obligation. The agencies differ in the degree to which they seek to stick literally to the estimates. Some find it easier than others; much depends on the tempo and the need for adjustment. . . . The attitude of different units varies with their experience. The head of a bureau which has been caught and chastised is jumpy and watchful. Some years ago the estimates meant less than they do now, but recently enough administrators have been in trouble to put all on guard. Sometimes, when consultation seems necessary in the face of a need to disregard the plan of expenditure in the estimates, the Bureau of the Budget is visited. But on occasion it is deemed advisable to clear with a House appropriations subcommittee.

Discipline may follow a departure from the estimates without prior consultation with the subcommittee. . . .

What is impressive, in tendency if not as matured fact, is the extent to which administrators meet with appropriations subcommittees in *ad hoc* sessions during the year. Sometimes the administrators themselves seek the contact as a safeguard; sometimes they are summoned for admonition or worse. The subcommittees vary in the degree to which they engage in such activity. Much depends upon the chairman. But generally speaking, interim supervisory relationships are increasing.

VII

What has been said about continuous control leads directly to the relations of the appropriating groups to the Budget Bureau and generally to the organs of administrative management.

The degree of exactness with which the amounts of the annual appropriations follow the Budget estimates is beside the point of the present inquiry. Negatively, at least, a Budget recommendation is almost an absolute prerequisite of House action. Indeed, members of the Senate appropriations group complain that House conferees frustrate the Senate's initiative by standing in conference against any item that has not been recommended by the Budget. But this does not mean that the subcommittees are unwilling to go behind the Budget figure. Fairly typical was the question put by a subcommittee chairman to the representative of the Civil Aeronautics Authority: "We will start off by asking you how much you asked the Budget for." . . .

. . . The committees (ran the argument) need the complete and first-hand knowledge possessed by the bureau chiefs. Since "under our Budget plan, the function of the Executive is to propose and that of the legislative branch is to dispose, . . . the right to interrogate any and all witnesses on any pending matter of legislation and that of having such witnesses give responsive answers thereto is fundamental and inherent in the legislative branch." All this was put down "to clarify the minds of those in the Department who may have been entertaining unfounded misapprehensions. . . ."

There has been not a little Congressional sniping at the Bureau of the Budget. The subcommittees have at times seemed to be provoking the bureaus to revolt against Budget control. . . .

But collaboration is not absent between the Bureau of the Budget and the appropriations committees. An especially fruitful pattern of cooperation has been followed at times when the whole committee has become aware of a problem common to many of the appropriation bills and has requested the Bureau of the Budget to report on a solution. Thus in 1939 the question of a general policy about administrative promotions was handled in this way. The Bureau's study became the basis of a statute, reflected in turn in subsequent appropriation acts. The Bureau of the Budget has made other inquiries at the instance of the appropriating groups. The act of 1921 provided a broad basis for such requests. . . .

What about closer cooperation in the routine handling of the annual appropriations? Some informal contact already exists between the staffs of the Budget Bureau and the committees on appropriations. But further intimacy, especially if institutionalized, must be developed cautiously. A practicable minimum step would be to have the committee clerks attend the annual hearings before the estimates division of the Budget in the late summer and fall. The clerks, however, should not remain for the executive sessions in the afternoons wherein the Budget examiners discuss and decide tentatively upon revised figures for the units they have had before them in the morning. Even the first-mentioned step would require enlarged permanent staffs for the committees on appropriations. A reasonable minimum would be one experienced assistant clerk for each regular appropriation bill.

No amount of legislative staffing could take the place of executive supervision. Fitful legislative intervention is no substitute for controls within administration. The most valuable contribution of legislative oversight is to galvanize the disciplines of administration itself. It is significant that the reports of the appropriations committees abound in recommendations to administration that it investigate its procedures and organization, sometimes at the bureau or departmental level, sometimes above. The committees frequently disclaim competence for detailed constructive inquiry in these matters. The staff necessary for continuous inquiry could be maintained only at the risk of a harmful division of responsibility, while such a staff would still lack a first-hand sense of operations.

The hazard is that a body like Congress, when it gets into detail, ceases to be itself; it acts through a fraction which may be a faction. This, among other lessons, is a moral to be read in the work of the committees on appropriations.

17   *A Dialogue on Un-American Activities*
ANDREW HACKER

Demea: I am invariably embarrassed when I am called upon to defend the investigation and control of un-American activities. For this means I become associated with the John Birchers, the Minutemen, and other self-appointed crusaders who so raucously ply their brand of patriotism. These overzealous citizens are not people with whom I have much in common, either intellectually or temperamentally. So I hope that despite the fact that my views occasionally parallel theirs you will not charge me with right-wing extremism. The best way to approach the subject, we have agreed, is by focusing on the aims and methods of a single body: the House of Representatives' Committee on Un-American Activities. This is the arm of the United States Congress that has been most vigorous in exposing espionage and subversion. Francis E. Walter, the Committee's chairman in recent years, has pointed out that it summons witnesses to question them about "their activities in and on behalf of the Communist Party, a party universally recognized as a secret criminal conspiracy composed of a small band of revolutionaries."

Philo: I do not see why it should be the job of a Congressional committee to go on a hunt for spies and subversives. Surely that can be done by the Federal Bureau of Investigation, and with more skill and less fanfare.

Demea: My answer to that is not only does the Committee support the FBI, but the FBI thinks no less highly of the Committee. Time and again, J. Edgar Hoover has commended the work of the Committee and its members; never once has he criticized it. So as matters stand the Committee's investigations are welcomed as part of America's internal security program.

Philo: But how does HUAC contribute to the internal security

From Andrew Hacker, *The Yale Review* (Autumn, 1962, Vol. LII, No. 1).

of our country? Its principal activity, you will acknowledge, lies in subpoenaing ordinary American citizens and asking them a whole series of unwarranted questions. They are asked if they are now or have ever been members of the Communist Party. If there is a suspicion that they were members in the past they are asked the names of the people who were in the party with them—even if all that took place fifteen or twenty years ago. Many of the witnesses are willing to talk about themselves, but most do not want to inform on others. Yet HUAC insists on getting names, and it cites witnesses for contempt if they remain silent. It should be clear that those party colleagues of an earlier decade are now respectable citizens. There is no earthly reason for raking up and publicizing their past—and often youthful—indiscretions.

Demea: Your compassion for uncooperative witnesses unfortunately obscures your ability to understand how the Communist conspiracy operates. I will make it clear. Of the 100 million or so adult Americans now living in the United States, about 500,000 have at one time or another belonged to the Communist Party. Almost all these people are of course ex-members, for the current rolls of the party contain no more than 10,000 names. What the Committee is trying to do is to compile a complete record of all 500,000 Americans who were once in the party.

Philo: But why? You admit that 98 percent of them are ex-members. They are now ordinary and perfectly loyal citizens. They sell insurance or teach school. They vote Democratic or even Republican. Most of them are probably in later middle-age with grown-up children. So why spend so much time and energy and money getting the names of people who are no threat to the country's security? It is a purposeless enterprise and it only harms innocent individuals.

Demea: You do not seem to realize that we do not know who, or how many, among that 500,000 have *really* severed their ties with the party. The Committee does know that from time to time the party leadership takes aside carefully-screened members and gives them special instructions. These individuals are ordered to go underground, or, more accurately, aboveground. They are told that they must no longer participate in activities having even a remote party connection; they are instructed to become as nonpolitical and as inconspicuous as possible. Some of these pseudo-ex-Communists, by virtue of their strategic location as scientists or government officials, serve as spies and couriers transmitting documents and information to the Soviets. Judith Coplon and the Rosenbergs are good examples. So is Alger Hiss.

Philo: HUAC didn't discover either Judith Coplon or the Rosenbergs. The FBI did that. The only "spy" HUAC has exposed is Alger Hiss, and that much-overrated exposure took place ten years after he was supposed to have been serving as a Communist agent. If what you call "pseudo-ex-Communists" are so plentifully in positions where they can engage in espionage, why hasn't HUAC—in its 23 years of existence—turned up a single one through its elaborate investigations?

Demea: Most of those who are ordered to "resign" from the party are not engaged in espionage. Their instructions are to go about their regular jobs, subtly infiltrating Communist ideas and policies into whatever stream of life they find themselves. Thus a college professor will cleverly insert portions of the party program into his lectures or a textbook he is writing. A trade union leader will foment strikes in factories working on vital defense contracts. One may even find himself in a policy-making position in the State Department where he can give an imperceptible leftward twist to our Latin American program. While pseudo-ex-Communists such as these are not spies in the strict sense, they are nevertheless engaged in subversion. They are shaping opinions and policies along party lines. The big problem, then, is to discover the seemingly loyal citizens who are actually still under Communist discipline. Let us suppose that of the 500,000 ex-Communists in the country, 450,000 have broken with the party sincerely and in good faith. What is needed is a litmus-test to distinguish these legitimate individuals from the 50,000 who continue under orders from the conspiracy they never really quit. The Committee has devised a test: a truly repentant ex-Communist will, when summoned, answer in full all questions put to him. By the same token, a witness who refuses to help the Committee is, in one way or another, probably still connected with the party.

Philo: But this doesn't answer the question I raised earlier. Suppose that someone was a Communist, say in 1938, and admits this fact to HUAC. Isn't he a "cooperative" witness? Why is he then compelled to name those who were in the party along with him more than twenty years ago? He may know that his ex-comrades are innocent people just like himself, and publicizing their past membership would do them great harm.

Demea: Once again you miss the point because you are unhappy about the Committee's insistence on obtaining names. The real point is that an ex-Communist cannot really know which of his old comrades have legitimately quit the party and which have claimed to but have actually gone underground. By asking each witness for names, by calling those who are named and asking them for still more names, by carrying on this progression in an unrelenting way, the Committee builds up its files. At this very moment there is probably a Communist agent high in government circles, someone who quietly left the party under orders at the time of the Hitler-Stalin Pact or the Czech Coup. Such an infiltrator will only be uncovered if the witnesses who knew him when he was in the party give his name to the Committee.

Philo: There may be logic in your way of putting it; however I must quickly add that there are no facts to support your reasoning. You assume that if you trail the names of everyone who was in a Communist cell at Harvard in 1938 up to the present you will ultimately find a Soviet agent high up in the State Department. My only reply is that neither HUAC nor any of the other investigating committees has found any such agent in the past and it seems unlikely they will do so in the future. . . .

Demea: What about Owen Lattimore? What about Harry Dexter White? Or Lee Pressman? William Remington?

Philo: The people whose names you have just rattled off may or may not have been Communists, but there is no evidence that any of them engaged in acts of subversion while holding government office. I might add that there has been remarkably little espionage despite your preoccupation with the subject. Since the end of the Second World War only fourteen American citizens have been convicted of spying for Communist powers. This means one of two things: either there are very few spies, or there are very many and the FBI has been scandalously remiss in its job. I take the view that there are few, if any, Americans working for the Communists. We have caught and convicted the handful who have been engaged in espionage, and without the aid of HUAC. However the whole logic of HUAC is based on the premise that there *must* be "pseudo-ex-Communists" in high places; and it then proceeds to disrupt the lives of innocent people, often in a tragic way. In fact, I see no reason to assume that someone who refuses to answer HUAC's questions must be connected with the party. There are other reasons, constitutional and moral reasons, why non-Communists will want to remain silent about their own pasts or those of others. Your "litmus-test" doesn't take these reasons into account.

Demea: There is no justification for withholding vital security information from the Committee. The Committee is the best judge of what information is relevant and what is not. Moreover there is no reason why any loyal citizen has to get hurt. The Committee holds its hearings, Chairman Walter has pointed out, "only after painstaking investigation into the identity, background, and activities of witnesses by skilled investigators." The Committee's procedure is to call to a *closed* session someone who has been identified as a one-time party member. Friends, relatives, neighbors, and employers do not know that such an invitation has been issued and there is no reason why they ever have to know. If the ex-Communist gives the names of his former comrades in such a *closed* session, he has made an earnest of good faith and he is treated with courtsey and consideration. He will appear at a subsequent open session only if he himself expresses a willingness to do so. Most go home quietly and no one ever knows that they were interviewed by the Committee.

Philo: You make it sound quite painless. The critical point about HUAC's operations is the way it conducts its *open* sessions, not the closed ones. Those who refuse to answer questions in the closed hearings are then brought to public sessions and are asked the same questions all over again—this time in front of newspaper reporters and even television cameras. However HUAC knows in advance that it isn't going to get any answers from these witnesses. All of your talk about starting a trail of names leading to a Communist agent in the State Department does not explain why HUAC exposes these individuals to public obloquy. Yet HUAC spends hundreds of hours in open hearings every year asking thousands of questions it knows will not be answered.

Demea: These hours are not wasted time. The exposure of uncooperative witnesses to public view alerts the public to the fact that there are still in their midst individuals who refuse to disavow their Communist connections in a thoroughgoing way. The fruitless questioning of such witnesses must be carried on at periodic intervals if popular concern over internal subversion is to be kept alive. The Committee's continuing mandate to operate depends on the public's anxieties over the Communist threat on the home front. This is why the Committee prepared and distributed *Operation*

Abolition. Furthermore, public exposure gives the community, in particular employers and neighbors, the information they need to inflict sanctions on those who defy the Committee.

Philo: I am glad to hear your admission that HUAC aims at alarming the American people. Because of its activities the public has become obsessed with an exaggerated fear of spying and subversion. However HUAC's only tangible accomplishment has been to cause a lot of schoolteachers and social workers to be fired from their jobs. Is that something to be proud of?

Demea: The only people who are fired are those who refuse to help in uncovering conspirators for an enemy power. Putting these people out of their jobs works a great injury on the Communist movement. Suppose that the typical party member or sympathizer earns about $8000 a year and he turns 20 per cent of his income over to the party. If 2000 Communists are fired from their jobs as a result of Committee exposure, then the party will have lost more than $3,000,000 in annual revenues. As more and more members or sympathizers are removed from whatever jobs they have, Communism itself will be pushed further to the edge of bankruptcy. Chairman Walter expressed this concern when he discussed *The Un-Americans*, a book critical of the Committee, on the floor of the House of Representatives. "In calling this mendacious volume to the attention of the House," he said, "I do so with a degree of reluctance, for I have no desire to swell the coffers of the Communist Party by stimulating its sale." What he had in mind was that the author and publisher would donate their royalties and profits to the party treasury.

Philo: Can you actually *believe* that? Your trouble is that you detect diabolical conspiracies all around you. Your aim is to achieve total security for the United States, to forestall even hypothetical dangers no matter what the cost to our liberties. We even part company in the image we have of the witnesses who appear before HUAC. I see a frightened and powerless individual, someone who is being victimized for a past mistake. My compassion and sympathy go out to such a person. I can, in a real sense, identify with him or her. *You* see a clever and cunning enemy of the state, someone who is committing treason and defying the representatives of the people. You have only scorn and contempt for such an individual. And you cheer when HUAC bullies, intimidates, and ultimately imprisons him. The crux of the matter is that HUAC, in asking questions about personal beliefs and associations, refuses to acknowledge that in a free society there are some matters beyond the scope of government investigation. Moreover HUAC infringes on basic liberties despite the fact that the increment to our national security has been nil.

Demea: I am not "opposed" to civil liberties any more than you "favor" Communist subversion. And the Supreme Court of the United States has had dozens of opportunities to declare the Committee's aims in violation of the Constitution, but it never has done so. It has, on occasion, criticized the Committee's techniques of inquiry, however not its mandate or existence. Obviously we part company on many issues and I think our differences revolve principally around what constitutes "subversion" and how many "subversives" there are in America at this time. For my part, I take a broad view of what I regard as subversive activities and I think the Committee is right in casting a wide net. I am, for example, suspicious of anyone who supports Castro's Cuba or who wants to see Red China in the United Nations. I am wary of people who seek the ending of nuclear testing by the United States, and frankly I am mistrustful of the motives of many of those who wish to abolish the Committee on Un-American Activities. All of these are Communist-supported causes and those who promote them are, knowingly or not, acting under Communist discipline. "One meaning of subversion," Professor Willmoore Kendall has written in *The Committee and Its Critics*," is the undermining of a people's allegiance or faith in its institutions." And what about immoderate attacks on the institution of free enterprise? Or criticism of customary patterns of racial separation? While I acknowledge that reforms are needed in many areas of American life I think that too many college professors, schoolteachers, journalists, entertainers, public officials—people in positions where they can influence the thinking of others—are serving to weaken national morale and self-confidence. I would say that activities that undermine our will to survive as a nation are Un-American activities.

Philo: You tell me that there are all sorts of people with subversive, or Un-American, ideas and you are saying in effect that these people should be silenced. This is nothing less than abridging free speech and controlling independent thought. In my judgment our Republic is robust enough to tolerate heretics and dissenters; and it can put up with such people even if they happen to support causes that the Communists also support. I believe that Americans are a sturdy, skeptical breed; that they can be exposed to radical ideas and will evaluate them with good sense. It seems to me that you regard *yourself* as having a superior intelligence and a character of extraordinary strength. *You* are not corrupted by "subversive" ideas because you are able to distinguish truth from error. However your attitude toward the rest of your fellow citizens is censorious and patronizing. You look on *them* as weak, ignorant creatures who cannot be trusted to listen to certain utterances. Instead of smearing certain people and ideas as "Un-American," why don't you just come out and tell the public that *you* know best what they should be allowed to hear.

Demea: There is a difference between heresy and conspiracy. A free society can put up with dissent but it cannot tolerate agents of an enemy power. Do you think that Communist conspirators are entitled to the protections of the First Amendment?

Philo: Let's get back to HUAC and its practices. Appearing as a witness can be a devastating experience, one that can destroy a career or even a life. HUAC follows none of the canons of fair legal procedure. I know that a witness can have counsel present. But that lawyer can only whisper advice; he cannot object to questions or make statements on behalf of his client. Nor can counsel cross-examine a witness after HUAC has made its accusations. At a Seattle hearing a witness was asked such questions as "Have you been trained in garrotting?" and "How many people have you murdered?" What good is having counsel present if he cannot cross-examine his client after these insinuations so as to put the record straight? In other words it is impossible for a witness to present his side of the story. Moreover, witnesses are not allowed to confront their accusers; they cannot question or even know the identity of the informers who "named" them and who accused them of being Communists. All of these practices violate civil liberties. They infringe on the constitutional rights of citizens.

Demea: The so-called "rights" you are talking about apply to proceedings in a court of law. They apply there because a court has the power to punish a person: it can fine him or send him to jail or even take his life. When he was tried for perjury, Alger Hiss and his lawyers had all the rights you mention. But the Committee belongs to the legislative, not the judicial branch of our governmental system.

Philo: HUAC can and does send people to jail. Witnesses who choose not to cooperate are cited for contempt and are sent to Federal prison.

Demea: Professor Carl Beck, in writing his book *Contempt of Congress*, followed up all the contempt citations and convictions growing out of the Committee's hearings in the twelve-year period from 1945 to 1957. During that time countless people refused to cooperate with the Committee. But only 135 were cited for contempt. And you should note that these citations were only *recommended* by the Committee. The actual contempt charges were voted by the entire House of Representatives. So if you want to fix blame, put it on the members of the popularly-elected chamber of the Congress. And that is not all that Professor Beck found. Of the 135 who were cited, each one had the opportunity to take his case to court—where all his constitutional rights would be respected. What happened in the courts? Only 37 cases ended in conviction and imprisonment. Of the rest, 12 cases never came to trial, 73 witnesses won acquittals in the courts, and 13 were pending at the time the research was concluded. A grand total of 37 people being sent to jail in a twelve-year period is hardly the reign of terror you make it out to be.

Philo: In my judgment 37 convictions is 37 too many. But imprisonment is not the only harm that befalls a witness. HUAC is notorious for the verbal maulings that take place at its hearings.

Demea: Politics is a serious business and those who take controversial positions must not be surprised if some harsh criticism is leveled at them. It is not just Communists who are given a rough afternoon on the witness stand. The same thing happened to the network and drug company executives when Senator Kefauver conducted his investigations into their industries. And don't forget the ridicule that was vented on the bankers and utilities men during the Black and Nye probes of the 'thirties. These are the chances that must be taken by anyone whose activities arouse the suspicions of Congress. Being the target for some discourteous remarks is not the end of the world. Do you approve of questioning businessmen but disapprove when it comes to subversives?

Philo: There is a difference in the two cases. The real harm done to HUAC witnesses is not at the hearings, but afterwards. Professor Daniel Pollitt, writing in the *University of North Carolina Law Review*, followed up what happened to 64 witnesses who pleaded the Fifth Amendment during 1953 and 1954. Fifty out of the 64 lost their jobs. When the businessmen who had been investigated by Kefauver and the others went back to their communities they found not a discharge notice in their pay envelopes but a sympathetic drink at the club and perhaps even a testimonial dinner from the leading figures of their industry. There are no official figures on what has happened to all the witnesses who have refused to cooperate with HUAC, but there is good reason to believe that most of them were fired soon after they were investigated. Here are some of the employers that discharged people just because they stood on their constitutional rights. It is worth citing more than just one or two: General Electric, Westinghouse, RCA, U. S. Steel, Pittsburgh Symphony Orchestra, American Federation of Musicians, Combined Jewish Appeal of Chicago, Station KCBS in San Francisco, Bethlehem Steel, Office Employees International Union, Seattle Fire Department, Jennings Memorial Hospital in Detroit, University of Colorado, Detroit *Times*, Universal International Pictures, Wayne State University, International Association of Machinists, George Washington University, Detroit *News*, Philadelphia Board of Education, Detroit Symphony Orchestra, University of Miami in Florida. Of 110 California teachers who were named in connection with a San Francisco hearing, 72 were out of their jobs within several months.

Demea: If these companies and unions and universities and symphony orchestras don't want to employ such people that is their decision. But then you should direct your criticism at General Electric and the Seattle Fire Department, for they did the firing. The Committee cannot compel an employer to discharge a witness.

Philo: But HUAC creates the pressures that cause employers to act as they do. And who are the people who get fired? HUAC has a sadistic tendency to pick on the little fellow, on the person who is easily victimized. Those who are summoned to hearings seem inevitably to be schoolteachers, social workers, laboratory technicians, union employees, municipal civil servants, reporters, or musicians. These are a far cry from the Morgans and DuPonts who were investigated in the 'thirties.

Demea: You have shifted your ground from civil liberties to economic security. And your main worry seems to be that people have lost their jobs. That is not a civil liberties question: no one has a constitutional right to a job with Bethlehem Steel or the

Detroit *News.* I imagine that if everyone who defied the Committee were wealthy like Cyrus Eaton or Corliss Lamont then you would not be complaining. However America is now largely a nation of employees and this makes people dependent on the good will of those for whom they work. There was a time, I suppose, when self-employed or otherwise independent citizens could take controversial positions without worrying about economic reprisals. You are really criticizing the conditions of dependency, and hence the insecurity, that so many people work under. And you are also criticizing employers who, out of caution and fear of adverse publicity, fire uncooperative witnesses. The Committee should not be your chief target.

Philo: I am worried about the general conditions you have described. That is why civil liberties need a stronger defense than ever before. One of the purposes of constitutional guarantees is to protect citizens from economic victimization.

Demea: A while back I pointed out that the Committee's contempt recommendations have been accepted by the House of Representatives, usually unanimously. And the Committee's composition has been a fair reflection of the character of its parent chamber. In its 23 years of existence a total of 45 Congressmen have served on the Committee. Fourteen states, nine Southern and four Midwestern, have provided more than half the members. In addition, over two-thirds of the 45 Committee members came from rural areas or towns with less than 50,000 population. And over half of them lived in localities that are losing population, either absolutely or relative to the rate of national growth. There is reason to believe that the Committee's activities are part of a more general "provincial revolt" against what might be termed a growing "metropolitan" America. The provinces are aware that they have been losing power and status over the past several decades. They have also been losing population, especially among their younger and more productive people. Hence there are deep suspicions and resentments arising in communities that feel left out of the mainstream of American life. And their concern goes even deeper because they sense that the traditional values of our nation have ceased to command respect in those parts of the country that are growing the fastest. Metropolitan America is too tolerant, too pragmatic in its moral values and too experimental in its political practices. The Committee, in focusing on subversive tendencies in the United States, is in part responding to the deep-seated discontents of the provinces. Nor should you underestimate the size of provincial America. Over 90 million of our fellow-countrymen live in rural areas or small towns.

Philo: These grievances may exist, although I think the people you are speaking about have some obligation to adjust to the twentieth century. I agree that Communism is a threat, but it is a distortion of the facts to say that the problem will be solved by hunting for subversives inside the country. If the provincial America to which you refer wants a scapegoat onto which it can pin the blame for all its ills, I can only say that we ought not to condone such irrationalism. Nor ought we to encourage such a gross simplification of a complex international problem.

Demea: You accused me of not trusting the American people to think for themselves. Are you willing to abide by the judgment of the men and women they have elected to office? In 1961, when the House of Representatives was weighing a $331,000 appropriation for the Committee, 412 Congressmen voted in favor and only six were opposed. This is an impressive margin, and those supporting the continuation of the Committee included liberal Democrats as well as conservative Republicans. If you believe in majority rule through the agency of a representative legislature then you should acknowledge that the American people support the Committee and its works.

Philo: I am not denying that HUAC can be construed as an instance of American democracy in operation. But it is certainly not an example of majority rule functioning at its best. What concerns me is that HUAC, through its investigations and accusations, precipitates emotions that ought best to be controlled. It brings out the impulse to be a Junior G-Man, to show that we can be "tough" if we want to. In a society where women dominate the family and work is increasingly sedentary, there is a tendency to try to prove one's masculinity by showing how hard-headed we can be on issues like internal subversion. And there is another side to this popular urge to investigate our neighbors. George Kennan, in a speech reprinted in the *Princeton Alumni Weekly*, commented on "the people who sublimate their own sex urge in the peculiarly nasty and sadistic practice of snooping on others." I am not saying that HUAC is the basic cause of such behavior. But I am saying that it has served to bring out the suspicions, the hostilities, and the prejudices that are latent in our society. In a way HUAC is a narcotic, and just because people like it —or think they do—it does not mean it is good for them. Finally, because of HUAC, people are afraid to make controversial statements or to join organizations because some day a Congressional inquiry might summon them to account. HUAC has helped to spread this fear so that it affects not only the majority who are already dissenters but also the conformist majority. For the mind of the majority has been cramped by the prevailing atmosphere and the tragic thing is that these people do not even realize what has happened to them. This constriction of thought and action is the real threat to American freedom. And HUAC is not fighting this threat. It is fomenting it.

THE MEANING OF THE MODERN
ASSEMBLY

18   *Congress: The Middle Level of Power*
C. Wright Mills

More and more of the fundamental issues never come to any
point of decision before the Congress, or before its most powerful
committees, much less before the electorate in campaigns. The en-
trance of the United States into World War II, for example, in so far
as it involved American decision, by-passed the Congress quite completely. It was never a clearly debated issue clearly focused for a public decision. Under the executive's emergency power, the President, in
a virtually dictatorial way, can make the decision for war, which is
then presented to the Congress as a fact accomplished. "Executive
agreements" have the force of treaties but need not be ratified by the
Senate: the destroyer deal with Great Britain and the commitment of
troops to Europe under NATO, which Senator Taft fought so bit-
terly, are clear examples of that fact. And in the case of the Formosa
decisions of the spring of 1955, the Congress simply abdicated all
debate concerning events and decisions bordering on war to the executive.

When fundamental issues do come up for Congressional debate,
they are likely to be so structured as to limit consideration, and even
to be stalemated rather than resolved. For with no responsible, centralized parties, it is difficult to form a majority in Congress; and—
with the seniority system, the rules committee, the possibility of filibuster, and the lack of information and expertise—the Congress is all
too likely to become a legislative labyrinth. It is no wonder that firm

From *The Power Elite*, by C. Wright Mills (pp. 225-267). © 1956 by Oxford
University Press, Inc., and reprinted by permission.

Presidential initiative is often desired by Congress on non-local issues, and that, in what are defined as emergencies, powers are rather readily handed over to the executive, in order to break the semi-organized deadlock. Indeed, some observers believe that "congressional abdication and obstruction, not presidential usurpation, has been the main cause of the shift of power to the Executive."

Among the professional politicians there are, of course, common denominators of mood and interests, anchored in their quite homogeneous origins, careers, and associations; and there is, of course, a common rhetoric in which their minds are often trapped. In pursuing their several parochial interests, accordingly, the Congressmen often coincide in ways that are of national relevance. Such interests seldom become explicit issues. But the many little issues decided by local interest, and by bargain, by check and balance, have national results that are often unanticipated by any one of the locally rooted agents involved. Laws are thus sometimes made, as the stalemate is broken, behind the backs of the lawmakers involved. For Congress is the prime seat of the middle levels of power, and it is on these middle levels that checks and balances do often prevail. . . .

. . . As a political actor, the Congressman is part of the compromised balances of local societies, as well as one or the other of the nationally irresponsible parties. As a result, he is caught in the semi-organized stalemate of the middle levels of national power.

Political power has become enlarged and made decisive, but not the power of the professional politician in the Congress. The considerable powers that do remain in the hands of key Congressmen are now shared with other types of political actors: There is the control of legislation, centered in the committee heads, but increasingly subject to decisive modification by the administrator. There is the power to investigate, as a positive and a negative weapon, but it increasingly involves intelligence agencies, both public and private, and it increasingly becomes involved with what can only be called various degrees of blackmail and counterblackmail. . . .

There is another way of gaining and of exercising power, one which involves the professional politician in the actions of cliques within and between the bureaucratic-like agencies of the administration. Increasingly, the professional politician teams up with the administrator who heads an agency, a commission, or a department in order to exert power with him against other administrators and politicians, often in a cut-and-thrust manner. The traditional distinction between "legislation" as the making of policy and "administration" as its realization has broken down from both sides.

In so far as the politician enters into the continuous policymaking of the modern political state, he does so less by voting for or against a bill than by entering into a clique that is in a position to exert influence upon and through the command posts of the executive administration, or by not investigating areas sensitive to certain clique interests. It is as a member of quite complicated cliques that the professional politician, representing a variety of interests, sometimes becomes quite relevant in decisions of national consequence.

If governmental policy is the result of an interplay of group interests, we must ask: what interests outside the government are important and what agencies inside it serve them? If there are *many* such interests and if they conflict with one another, then clearly each loses power and the agency involved either gains a certain autonomy or is stalemated. In the legislative branch, many and competing interests, especially local ones, come to focus, often in a stalemate. Other interests, on the level of national corporate power, never come to a focus but the Congressman, by virtue of what he is as a political and social creature, realizes them. But in the executive agency a number of small and coherent interests are often the only ones at play, and often they are able to install themselves within the agency or effectively nullify its action against themselves. Thus regulatory agencies, as John Kenneth Galbraith has remarked, "become, with some exceptions, either an arm of the industry they are regulating or servile." The executive ascendancy, moreover, has either relegated legislative action—and inaction—to a subordinate role in the making of policy or bends it to the executive will. For enforcement now clearly involves the making of policy, and even legislation itself is often written by members of the executive branch.

In the course of American history, there have been several oscillations between Presidential and Congressional leadership. Congressional supremacy, for example, was quite plain during the last third of the nineteenth century. But in the middle of the twentieth century, with which we are concerned, the power of the Executive, and the increased means of power at its disposal, is far greater than at any previous period, and there are no signs of its power diminishing. The executive supremacy means the relegation of the legislature to the middle levels of political power; it means the decline of the professional politician, for the major locale of the party politicians is the legislature. It is also a prime indicator of the decline of the old balancing society. For—in so far as the old balance was not entirely automatic—it was the politician, as a specialist in balance and a broker of contending pressures, who adjusted the balances, reached compromises and maintained the grand equilibrium. That politician who best satisfied or held off a variety of interests could best gain power and hold it. But now the professional politician of the old balancing society has been relegated to a position "among those also present," often noisy, or troublesome, or helpful to the ascendant outsiders, but not holding the keys to decision. For the old balancing society in which he flourished no longer prevails. . . .

In the old liberal society, a set of balances and compromises prevailed among Congressional leaders, the executive branch of the government, and various pressure groups. The image of power and of decision is the image of a balancing society in which no unit of power is powerful enough to do more than edge forward a bit at a time, in compromised countervailance with other such forces, and in which, accordingly, there is no unity, much less coordination, among the higher circles. Some such image, combined with the doctrine of public opinion, is still the official view of the formal democratic system of power, the standard theory of most academic social scientists, and the underlying assumption of most literate citizens who are neither political spokesmen nor political analysts.

But as historical conditions change, so do the meanings and political consequences of the mechanics of power. There is nothing magical or eternal about checks and balances. In time of revolution, checks and balances may be significant as a restraint upon unorganized and organized masses. In time of rigid dictatorship, they may be significant as a technique of divide and rule. Only under a state which is already quite well balanced, and which has under it a balanced social structure, do checks and balances mean a restraint upon the rulers.

The eighteenth-century political theorists had in mind as the unit of power the individual citizen, and the classic economists had in mind the small firm operated by an individual. Since their time, the units of power, the relations between the units, and hence the meaning of the checks and balances, have changed. In so far as there is now a great scatter of relatively equal balancing units, it is on the middle levels of power, seated in the sovereign localities and intermittent pressure groups, and coming to its high point within the

Congress. We must thus revise and relocate the received conception of an enormous scatter of varied interests, for, when we look closer and for longer periods of time, we find that most of these middle-level interests are concerned merely with their particular cut, with their particular area of vested interest, and often these are of no decisive political importance, although many are of enormous detrimental value to welfare. Above this plurality of interests, the units of power—economic, political, and military—that count in any balance are few in number and weighty beyond comparison with the dispersed groups on the middle and lower levels of the power structure.

Those who still hold that the power system reflects the balancing society often confuse the present era with earlier times of American history, and confuse the top and the bottom levels of the present system with its middle levels. When it is generalized into a master model of the power system, the theory of balance becomes historically unspecific; whereas in fact, as a model, it should be specified as applicable only to certain phases of United States development—notably the Jacksonian period and, under quite differing circumstances, the early and middle New Deal.

The idea that the power system is a balancing society also assumes that the units in balance are independent of one another, for if business and labor or business and government, for example, are not independent of one another, they cannot be seen as elements of a free and open balance. But as we have seen, the major vested interests often compete less with one another in their effort to promote their several interests than they coincide on many points of interest and, indeed, come together under the umbrella of government. The units of economic and political power not only become larger and more centralized; they come to coincide in interest and to make explicit as well as tacit alliances.

The American government today is not merely a framework within which contending pressures jockey for position and make politics. Although there is of course some of that, this government now has such interests vested within its own hierarchical structure, and some of these are higher and more ascendant than others. There is no effective countervailing power against the coalition of the big businessmen—who, as political outsiders, now occupy the command posts —and the ascendant military men—who with such grave voices now speak so frequently in the higher councils. Those having real power in the American state today are not merely brokers of power, resolv-

ers of conflict, or compromisers of varied and clashing interests—
they represent and indeed embody quite specific national interests
and policies.

While the professional party politicians may still, at times, be
brokers of power, compromisers of interests, negotiators of issues,
they are no longer at the top of the state, or at the top of the power
system as a whole.

The idea that the power system is a balancing society leads us to
assume that the state is a visible mask for autonomous powers, but in
fact, the powers of decision are now firmly vested within the state.
The old lobby, visible or invisible, is now the visible government.
This "governmentalization of the lobby" has proceeded in both the
legislative and the executive domains, as well as between them. The
executive bureaucracy becomes not only the center of power but also
the arena within which and in terms of which all conflicts of power
are resolved or denied resolution. Administration replaces electoral
politics; the maneuvering of cliques replaces the clash of parties.

19   *The Devitalization of Executive Power*
WALTER LIPPMANN

1. THE ELECTED EXECUTIVE

Our inquiry has shown, I believe, that we cannot take popular
government for granted, as if its principles were settled and beyond
discussion. We are compelled to agree with Sir Henry Maine who
wrote, some seventy years ago, that "the actual history of popular
government since it was introduced, in its modern shape, into the civilized world," does "little to support the assumption that popular
government has an indefinitely long future before it. Experience

From *The Public Philosophy,* by Walter Lippmann (pp. 40-50), by permission of Little, Brown and Company-Atlantic Monthly Press. Copyright 1955,
by Walter Lippmann.

rather tends to show that it is characterized by great fragility and that since its appearance, all forms of government have become more insecure than they were before."

We have been dwelling upon the devitalization of the executive power as the cause of the fragility that Maine speaks of. It is, I have been saying, the disorder which results from a functional derangement in the relationship between the executive power on the one hand, the representative assemblies and the mass electorates on the other hand.

Democratic states are susceptible to this derangement because congenitally the executive, when dependent on election, is weaker than the elected representatives. The normal drainage of power in a democratic state is away from the governing center and down into the constituencies. And the normal tendency of elections is to reduce elected officers to the role of agents or organized pluralities. Modern democratic governments are, to be sure, big governments, in their personnel, in the range and variety of their projects, the ubiquitousness of their interventions. But to be big is not necessarily to be strong. They are, in fact, swollen rather than strong, being too weak to resist the pressure of special interests and of the departmental bureaucracies.

As a rule competition in the electoral market works like Gresham's law: the soft money drives the hard money out of circulation. The competitive odds are heavily against the candidate who, like Burke with the electors of Bristol, promises to be true to his own best reason and judgement. The odds are all in favor of the candidate who offers himself as the agent, the delegate, the spokesman, the errand boy, of blocs of voters.

In a modern democratic state, the chief executive office must be elective. But as heredity, prescription, consecration, rank and hierarchy are dissolved by the acids of modernity, the executives become totally dependent on election. They have no status and no tenure which reinforce their consciences, which invest them with power to withstand the tides of popular opinion and to defend the public interest.

They hold their offices for a short time, and to do this they must maneuver and manipulate combinations among the factions and the pressure groups. Their policies must be selected and shaped so as to attract and hold together these combinations. There are moments, the "finest hours," when communities are lifted above their habitual selves in unity and fellowship. But these moments are rare. They are not the stuff of daily life in a democracy, and they are remembered like a miracle in a dream. In the daily routine of democratic politics, elected executives can never for long take their eyes from the mirror of the constituencies. They must not look too much out of the window at the realities beyond.

2. THE PROTECTION OF THE EXECUTIVE

During the nineteenth century good democrats were primarily concerned with insuring representation in the assemblies and with extending the control of the assemblies over the executive power. It is true that the problem of the inadequate executive, overridden and dominated by the assembly, was very much in the minds of the Founding Fathers at the Philadelphia convention, and it has been a continuing concern of the critics and opponents of democracy. But until the twentieth century the problem was not sharply and urgently posed. That there was such a problem was well known. But it was not the immediate problem.

For some generations before 1914, the West enjoyed fine political weather. Moreover, the full force of the coming enfranchisement, emancipation, and secularization of the whole population had not yet worked its consequences. Governments still had authority and power, which were independent of the assemblies and the electorates. They still drew upon the traditional sources of authority—upon prescription, hereditary prerogative, and consecration.

Yet the need to protect the executive and judicial powers from the representative assemblies and from mass opinion has long been understood. Many expedients have been devised to soften, to neutralize, to check and to balance the pressure of parties, factions, lobbies, sects. The expedients have taken, says Bryce, two general forms, the one being to put constitutional restrictions upon the assembly and the other, "by a division of the whole power of the people," to weaken it. This has been done by electing the legislature and the executive separately, or by having the legislative bodies elected by the differing constituencies and at different times.

The constitutional mechanisms have never themselves been sufficient to protect the executive. And much invention and reforming energy have been applied to finding other ways to insulate the judicial, the executive and the administrative functions from the heavy pressures of "politics" and "politicians." The object has been to separate them from the electoral process. The judiciary must be independent of fear and favor. There must be no connection between the judgment of the courts and the election returns. The civil service, the military services, the foreign service, the scientific and technical services, the quasi-judicial administrative tribunals, the investigating commissions, the public schools and institutions of learning, should be substantially independent of the elections. These reforms were inspired by the dire effects of the spoils system, and they were pushed as practical remedies for obvious evils.

Yet implicit in them there is a principle which, if it can be applied deeply enough, gets at the root of the disorder of modern democracy. It is that though public officials are elected by the voters, or are appointed by men who are elected, they owe their primary allegiance not to the opinions of the voters but to the law, to the criteria of their professions, to the integrity of the arts and sciences in which they work, to their own conscientious and responsible convictions of their duty within the rules and the frame of reference they have sworn to respect.

3. The Voters and the Executive

The implied principle may be defined in other terms by saying that while the electors choose the ruler, they do not own any shares in him and they have no right to command him. His duty is to the office and not to his electors. Their duty is to fill the office and not to direct the officeholder. I realize that, as I have stated it, the principle runs counter to the popular view that in a democracy public men are the servants (that is, the agents) of the people (that is, of the voters). As the game of politics is played, what I am saying must seem at first like a counsel of perfection.

There are, however, reasons for thinking that it is not an abstract and empty bit of theorizing. One is that until comparatively recent times, it has been the principle on which the election of rulers—lay and spiritual—has usually been carried out.

In the early church, says Acts VI, the twelve apostles called the multitude of the disciples to them and said, "Look ye out among you seven men of honest report, full of the Holy Ghost and wisdom, whom we may appoint over this business." When these men had been chosen, and had prayed, "the apostles . . . laid their hands upon them." Having been ordained, they were not the servants of the multitude who had elected them, but of God.

This principle applied to the election of Popes. As Suarez says, "The Pope is elected by cardinals, yet he receives his powers from God immediately." The same principle applied to elected kings. After the electors had chosen the king, he was crowned and anointed. Then his duty was to his own vows and not to the electors. The act of election did not bind the ruler to the electors. Both parties to the transaction were bound only to the office; the electors to designate a king worthy of the office, the king to fill the office worthily.

If we look closely at the matter, we find, I believe, this must be the principle of election when the electors are choosing, not someone to represent them to the government, but the governors themselves. Though it is not too well recognized, there is a radical difference between the election of an executive and the election of a representative. For while the executive is in honor bound not to consider himself as the agent of his electors, the representative is expected to be, within the limits of reason and the general public interest, their agent.

This distinction has deep roots in the political experience of Western society, and, though unrecognized in principle, it is implicit in our moral judgments. Everyone who has a case in court is entitled, we believe, to be represented by a lawyer who, within the law and the code of professional practice, is expected to be the partisan and advocate of his client. But this presupposes not only that his opponent will be effectively represented too, but that the case will go to a court where the judge is not an advocate and has no clients. The judge is bound by his judicial vows. The same ethical standards are recognized, though they are applied less rigorously, in the executive branch of the government. No President or head of a department could afford to admit that he was using his office to further the interests of a client or of a pressure group, or even his party. His acts must be presented as taken in obedience to his oath of office, which means taken disinterestedly and rationally. He must never in so many words admit that in order to gain votes he sacrificed the public good, that he played "politics." Often enough he does just that. But fealty to the public interest is his virtue. And he must, at the very least, pay it the homage of hypocrisy.

When we move over to the representative assembly, the image is different, and the ethical rule is applied, if at all, loosely and lightly. The representative is in some very considerable degree an agent, and the image of his virtue is rather like that of the lawyer than of the judge. There are, of course, occasions when he is in fact the holder of one of the great offices of state—as when he must speak and vote on a declaration of war and the ratification of a treaty. But in the general run of the mundane business which comes before the assembly, he is entitled, indeed he is in duty bound, to keep close to the interests and sentiments of his constituents, and, within reasonable limits, to do what he can to support them. For it is indispensable to the freedom and the order of a civilized state that the voters should be effectively represented. But representation must not be confused with governing.

4. The Enfeebled Executive

In the effort to understand the malady of democratic government I have dwelt upon the underlying duality of functions: *governing*, that is, the administration of the laws and the initiative in legislating, and *representing* the living persons who are governed, who must pay, who must work, who must fight and, it may be, die for the acts of government. I attribute the democratic disaster of the twentieth century to a derangement of these primary functions.

The power of the executive has become enfeebled, often to the verge of impotence, by the pressures of the representative assembly and of mass opinions. This derangement of the governing power has forced the democratic states to commit disastrous and, it could be, fatal mistakes. It has also transformed the assemblies in most, perhaps not in all, democratic states from the defenders of local and personal rights into boss-ridden oligarchies, threatening the security, the solvency, and the liberties of the state.

In the traditions of Western society, civilized government is founded on the assumption that the two powers exercising the two functions will be in balance—that they will check, restrain, compensate, complement, inform and vitalize each one the other.

In this century, the balance of the two powers has been seriously upset. Two great streams of evolution have converged upon the modern democracies to devitalize, to enfeeble, and to eviscerate the executive powers. One is the enormous expansion of public expenditure, chiefly for war and reconstruction; this has augmented the power of the assemblies which vote the appropriations on which the executive depands. The other development which has acted to enfeeble the executive power is the growing incapacity of the large majority of the democratic peoples to believe in intangible realities. This has stripped the government of that imponderable authority which is derived from tradition, immemorial usage, consecration, veneration, prescription, prestige, heredity, hierarchy.

At the beginning of our constitutional development the King, when he had mastered the great barons, was the proprietor of the greatest wealth in the realm. The crown was also the point from which radiated the imponderable powers to bind and to command. As the King needed money and men for his wars, he summoned representatives of the counties and the boroughs, who had the money and the men he needed. But the imponderable powers, together with very considerable power in land and in men, were still in the King's own hands. Gradually, over the centuries, the power of the Parliament over the supplies of the government grew larger. They had to appropriate a larger proportion of a much greater total. At the same time, in the white light of the enlightenment and the secularization of men's minds, the imponderable powers of the crown diminished.

Under the stress and the strain of the great wars of the twentieth century, the executive power has become elaborately dependent upon the assemblies for its enormous expenditures of men and of money. The executive has, at the same time, been deprived of very nearly all of his imponderable power: fearing the action of the representative assembly, he is under great temptation to outwit it or by-pass it, as did Franklin D. Roosevelt in the period of the Second World War. It is significant, I think, certainly it is at least suggestive, that while nearly all the Western governments have been in deep trouble since the First World War, the constitutional monarchies of Scandinavia, the Low Countries, and the United Kingdom have shown greater capacity to endure, to preserve order with freedom, than the republics of France, Germany, Spain and Italy. In some measure that may be because in a republic the governing power, being wholly secularized, loses much of its prestige; it is stripped, if one prefers, of all the illusions of intrinsic majesty.

The evaporation of the imponderable powers, a total dependence upon the assemblies and the mass electorates, has upset the balance of powers between the two functions of the state. The executive has lost both its material and its ethereal powers. The assemblies and the class electorates have acquired the monopoly of effective powers.

This is the internal revolution which has deranged the constitutional system of the liberal democratic states.